A
RACE
FOR
THE
FUTURE

A RACE FOR THE FUTURE

How Conservatives Can Break the
Liberal Monopoly on Hispanic Americans

MIKE GONZALEZ

CROWN
FORUM
NEW YORK

Published in the United States by Crown Forum, an imprint of
the Crown Publishing Group, a division of Random House LLC,
a Penguin Random House Company, New York.
www.crownpublishing.com

CROWN FORUM with colophon is a registered trademark of
Random House LLC.

Library of Congress Cataloging-in-Publication Data is available upon request.

ISBN 978-0-8041-3765-2
eBook ISBN 978-0-8041-3766-9

Printed in the United States of America

Book design by Lauren Dong
Jacket design by Andrew S. Janik

10   9   8   7   6   5   4   3   2   1

First Edition

To Siobhan

CONTENTS

PREFACE

B Y THE TIME THIS BOOK IS PRINTED, HISPANICS MAY HAVE BE-
come the largest population group in California. When that
line is crossed, surely by the 2016 presidential election, Hispanics will have a plurality in the Golden State, followed by non-
Hispanic whites, with Asians coming in third at roughly twice the
number of African-Americans, who will be a distant fourth. No
one group will account for more than 40 percent of the population. Every group enumerated as a distinct ethnic identity by the
US Census will be a minority in California.

California, in so many ways emblematic of America, symbolizes
the profound demographic change the nation has undergone in the
last few decades.

Hispanics have been the majority in Los Angeles County for
several years. With 9 million residents, LA County has a population greater than that of Michigan or forty other states. But unlike
Michigan, which brings up Rust Belt images of failed industries
and decrepit cities, LA County is the home of the beautiful people. Beverly Hills, Pacific Palisades, and Rodeo Drive are the perfect sun-soaked backdrops. Los Angeles houses the one industry in
which we are indisputably the leader: Hollywood, the Dream Fac-
tory. The people who tell our tales and present our image back to
ourselves and to the world live in LA County.

California: the land that for many in my generation symbolized the American Dream: the Beach Boys, the Brady Bunch, Disneyland, Annette Funicello. It is now more the Mexican-American Dream and, to a lesser extent, the Salvadoran-American Dream and the Guatemalan-American dream.

By 2013, Hispanics accounted for 38 percent of the population, and non-Hispanic whites for 39 percent. The population statistics for those two groups have been going in the opposite direction of each other for years. Not only are Hispanic birthrates going up, but whites are also having fewer babies. Whites also are fleeing California in the thousands every year for Nevada, Utah, Colorado, Arizona, and Texas. From 2000 to 2010, California lost 1.5 million more people to other states than it gained from them, reversing an inflow trend that had held for decades during the heyday of California Dreamin'.

For the vast majority of non-Hispanic white Californians, the purpose of the flight isn't to escape minority status. It's to leave behind the crushing taxes and the asphyxiating regulation that is making all these Atlases shrug and refuse to keep carrying the burden.

When they escape to Texas, refugees from California's welfare state find a low-tax, low-regulation booming economy in which Hispanics, again mostly of Mexican origin, are also fast approaching the tipping point of parity with non-Hispanic whites. They now constitute 38 percent of the state's population, compared with 45 percent for whites, and are growing at a much faster rate. According to the 2010 Census, the Hispanic population rose by a staggering 42 percent in the first decade of this century, accounting for two-thirds of the state's population growth.

Texas's mostly Mexican-American Hispanics have a lower unemployment rate than California's, are more entrepreneurial, own their own homes at a higher rate, go to church more often, have stronger family units, and have children who perform better academically. They also vote Republican at a higher rate than California's Mexican-American Hispanics. Unsurprisingly, the Democratic Party and the Obama administration would like to make Texas's

Hispanics more like California's. They are concentrating resources in the Lone Star State for a big voter push and have set as their target the state's Mexican-Americans. If the Democratic Party succeeds at turning Texas blue, it could win every presidential election as far as the eye can see.

The nationwide demographic change also has been eye-popping. Some 50.5 million US residents checked the box for "Hispanic" or "Latino" in the 2010 Census, accounting for 16.3 percent of a total population of 308.7 million and making the United States the second largest Hispanic country in the world after Mexico. Only ten years earlier, the Hispanic population of the United States had stood at a mere 35.3 million. In fact, our Hispanic-origin population is 20 percent larger than Spain's. Hispanics are now the second largest group in the United States, easily edging out African-Americans, who currently account for 12.6 percent of the nation's population.

Hispanics lopsidedly voted 71–29 for Barack Obama in 2012 and played a pivotal role in such battleground states as Colorado, Nevada, New Mexico, and Florida. After November 2012, the conservative movement to which I belong finally began to pay attention to the demographic question in earnest. Did this result mean that Hispanics had gone permanently to the liberal side? A debate quickly ensued among conservatives about what to do as liberals rubbed their hands at the prospect of having a lock on the Hispanic vote. "Demography is destiny" became their battle cry.

But is any of that true? More important, how did America get here? How did demography, so important in a democracy, change so massively and so rapidly? What does a future in which one-third of America is Hispanic hold?

HOW WE GOT HERE

This book will try to shine a light on facets of the Hispanic presence in this country that receive little attention elsewhere. It is a book about who Hispanics are, how they got here, and what's happened to them since their arrival. It also will focus on what America's profound changes in the last half century—the War on

Poverty programs, the civil rights era, and the sexual revolution, among them—have meant for them. It is an in-depth look at how liberals have achieved dominance over Hispanic voters and offers proposals for how conservatives can turn things around over the long term. Finally, I care about Hispanics having the opportunities they need to better themselves, to become upwardly mobile and make this land even better than it was when they arrived—in other words, to take up the path every other immigrant group has followed. The choices Hispanics make politically will affect how successful they are.

Hispanics, of course, have been a permanent presence in this land since Admiral Pedro Menendez de Aviles landed in Florida and claimed it for Spain in 1565. Most Americans don't know this history, but they ought to. Three decades after Menendez, his compatriot Don Juan de Oñate arrived in the Rio Grande Valley, and the two poles of Hispanicism in North America—Florida and the Great Southwest—were established. It all happened decades before Jamestown and Plymouth Rock.

The great population bulge that is having such a deep impact on our demography and our democracy has little to do, however, with Menendez and Oñate, as important as they may be.

The rapid rise in Hispanic numbers in the last half century was not the result of the natural growth of the Hispanic population that was in this country by the mid-twentieth century but mostly the consequence of government fiat. It was Congress that altered America's demography by taking sweeping, consequential actions while blithely ignoring underlying economic forces. Congressional legislation also created a problem we now regularly tear ourselves apart trying to solve and one indelibly associated with Hispanics in the public mind: illegal immigration.

It was Congress that decided in 1964 to end the successful "bracero" temporary guest worker program, which had been around for two decades, balancing our labor demand with Mexico's surplus labor supply. It was also Congress that in 1965 passed the Immigration and Nationality Act. After our leaders acted, the demographic numbers looked very different.

In 1960, there were fewer than 7 million Hispanics in a country of 150 million, mostly Mexican-Americans and accounting for less than 4 percent of the overall US population. If their numbers had grown at the same pace as the rest of the country, Hispanics today would number around 15 million, not 50 million.

Illegal immigration was negligible or nonexistent in 1960, but after Congress did the unions' bidding and ended the bracero program, illegal immigrants rushed the border to fill jobs left vacant by the disappeared migrant workers. They were welcomed by willing US companies. Illegal immigration wasn't a problem at all, let alone one tearing the country apart, until Congress created it.

Soon after that, federal regulators decided to create Hispanics. That's right: Hispanics, the subjects of this book, do not exist as such before the 1970s. The term is a bureaucratic contrivance invented by the federal agencies to co-opt growing numbers of Mexicans, Cubans, Puerto Ricans, Central Americans, and others into the Great Society affirmative action programs created by the Johnson administration.

How America absorbed the post-1965 immigrant wave will be the subject of much of this book. Since 1965, millions of people have come to this country from Latin America and the Caribbean—including my family and me—seeking freedom and the chance to make a better life. A series of social changes, groundbreaking legislation, and policies that changed the course of history—and, many argue, may in time change America's character—have conspired, however, to constrain the very mobility Hispanics come here seeking.

The fact that this potent combination of related upheavals coincided with the start of one of the biggest demographic changes America has ever experienced—the Hispanic upsurge—means that we can properly speak of trends set on a collision course. They include the following:

- The establishment of a massive welfare state that, whatever its intentions, has been very destructive to the human and social capital necessary for mobility

- The breakdown of the American culture of marriage and the sense of community, particularly in working-class areas in which Hispanics are overrepresented

- The bureaucratic creation of an artificial Hispanic ethnicity that was put in place to give this new group protected status

- The introduction of an alien "minorities" discourse that emphasizes group differences and seeks to maintain them in place under the banner of "multiculturalism," something new and divisive in American culture

- The end of the schoolhouse's function as the primary institution that taught the values needed to maintain a republic and the shared knowledge necessary to grasp complex concepts rich with cultural references

These changes accentuated and exacerbated, but did not wholly create, cultural traits the Hispanic immigrants brought with them, including these:

- An initial unfamiliarity with a unique volunteer culture that has built American civil society

- An expansive concept of the family that puts sending money to extended family members overseas ahead of saving for needs here in the United States such as emergencies and college tuition

- A process of continuous immigration, mostly in the case of Mexican-Americans, that produced a series of "first generations" from the 1840s to the present and thus sharpened ethnic differences

These challenges have often combined to keep too many Hispanics separate from mainstream America and may consign them to an underclass status indefinitely unless we act. It is immaterial whether these results are the very opposite of what most of the architects of these changes intended; the outcomes are the same. The impact that government has had on the mobility of Hispanics, whether newly arrived or here for generations, has often been nefarious yet often goes unexplored.

More often than not, Hispanics come to this country with a strong work ethic, intact families, and alert children ready to learn. The harsh reality is that for a not insignificant number many of these advantages disappear over time because the social fabric of the neighborhoods where they live has been eroded by the changes that started in the 1960s.

This is why social scientists use the term *downward assimilation*. This means that contrary to popular belief, Hispanics *are* assimilating; the problem is that too many are assimilating downward into pathologies that have been created among working-class communities in the America of the twenty-first century. This book is being published as we mark fifty years since President Johnson's War on Poverty speech. Hispanics are in many ways the casualties of this war.

It isn't surprising that many social indicators are much worse for Hispanics than they are for people in this country on average. The Hispanic illegitimacy rate, the most troubling of all because it stands upstream from most other dysfunctions, is 53 percent, much higher than the non-Hispanic white rate of 29 percent. As with everything else, there are distinctions—the rate is worse for some nationality groups than for others—but the overall trend *for all Hispanic groups* is not good.

All this probably helps explain why generational progress seems to be stalling for many Hispanics, not just compared with non-Hispanic white Americans but also in contrast to previous generations of immigrants. This is not what we want to see with such a large and young demographic. Hispanics can succeed in America today, and many, many do, but the overall trends should concern us.

The national debate since the 2012 election has not been about how to improve the economic advancement that has eluded many of the 45 million Hispanics who are here legally. Instead, the country spent a good part of 2013 and the start of 2014 arguing over whether to legalize 11 million people who are in the United States illegally, of whom an estimated 8 million are Hispanic. As this book went to print, it was still unclear whether the White House and Congress would agree on a bill. Either way, it is far more vital to address the deeper cultural issues. The fight over illegal immigration can best be seen as a proxy war for feelings and attitudes that lie beneath the surface and that are linked to an evident lack of mobility among many Hispanics. In fact, if all politicians do is alter the legal status of illegal immigrants and do nothing about the issues addressed in this book, it is unlikely that the standard of living of the Hispanic population will improve or that the voting patterns of Hispanics will change.

Therefore, we will leave the debate over what to do with the illegal population to the politicians and in this book concentrate instead on America's radically changing demography, how we may have hampered Hispanics' upward progress through social programs and cultural transformations, and what we can do differently in the future.

Even though we are dealing with some harsh realities, we can broach these subjects by hitting the optimistic notes that were struck by Jack Kemp and Ronald Reagan. If we remove the obstacles we have put in the way of their success, there's no reason why the immigrants who came here from Latin America won't react the same way as did those who came here from other parts of the world, succeeding and becoming a part of America's mainstream, not a minority apart from it.

HISPANICS?

Before we discuss Hispanics, however, we need to know who they really are. In this book I will use the term *Hispanic* when I have no other choice in referring to people of very different backgrounds (and even *Latino*, which, as I will explain, is a very silly idea), but it is important to understand up front that *Hispanic* is a term fabricated by bureaucrats. It does not correspond to the realities of the different national groups that it includes, and in Part I we will go through who the different groups are. The use of the Spanish language by all these groups has created for outsiders the illusion that a monolithic group exists. But Hispanics don't much think of themselves as such but rather as Cubans, Mexicans, Puerto Ricans, and so forth. It's important for the reader, therefore, to understand the differences in backgrounds and the way they inform each group's experience in America.

Mexicans and Dominicans are more different from each other than Polish-Americans are from German-Americans. Even people as racially and geographically close as Cuban-Americans and Puerto Ricans can be as distinct from each other as Boston Irish are from South Carolina Scots-Irish. As anyone who knows anything sociologically about those two groups can tell you, you don't relate to them the same way.

Consider Cubans, who are generally more conservative politically and have more years of education than the other Latino groups in this country. Cubans mostly came here for political reasons, escaping from Fidel Castro's communist dystopia, unlike Puerto Ricans, who are here for economic reasons and are American citizens who easily go back and forth between their island and what they call "the mainland."

Puerto Ricans can have different outlooks depending on where they live in the United States. Those in New York—the so-called Nuyoricans—tend to be at the lower end of the income scale and vote liberal. Those in Florida, a growing cohort, more often have managerial jobs and occasionally pull the lever for Republicans, though they refused to do it for Romney.

And there are more: Central Americans escaping first civil wars and now drug violence, Dominicans vying to establish an identity in the Northeast that is neither Puerto Rican nor African-American. And Mexicans, by far the largest nationality group numerically, the most important culturally, and the ones who have been in the United States the longest.

Collectively labeling these disparate people as Hispanic ignored their distinct realities. The reaction of our political leaders and regulators to the sudden inflow of Mexicans, Puerto Ricans, Salvadorans, Cubans, and the rest was basically to say: "We can't deal with this; we need to neatly fit all of you into a neat round hole."

The creation of the term *Hispanic* was also an attempt to fit the recent immigrants into a new racial paradigm emerging in the 1960s and 1970s. Nobody bothered to ask the subjects at hand what they thought of such an experiment. If they were going to be homogenized, many might have opted for attempting to join the community of all Americans rather than being classified as members of an official minority. Given an opportunity, they would have wanted to emulate the American values of constant self-improvement, thrift, strong families, and religious observance that had produced, after all, the prosperity and freedom that beckoned them here in the first place. It was these characteristics, which they knew as American from watching old movies in their home countries (I say "old" because Hollywood no longer portrays America in such virtuous lights), that in their heart of hearts they wanted to adopt. No one immigrates here to be balkanized into a minority and to slide into urban dysfunctions.

In other words, the rule makers blithely ignored the potential consequences of their actions.

THE PERFECT STORM

In Part II we'll deal with the perfect storm that took place when this large immigrant influx suddenly washed up on a country that was itself going through a vast social tornado that was tearing up norms that had been in place for two centuries.

The new immigrants—Puerto Ricans in the '50s, Cubans in the '60s, and Mexicans throughout but especially after the end of the bracero program—came as America was going through the civil rights struggle, the sexual revolution, the emergence of what Tom Wolfe has aptly termed the Me Generation, the creation of a massive welfare state, and profound changes in the classroom.

The civil rights movement informed the way the bureaucrats

would deal with Hispanics. The regulators took their cues from the changes taking place—the decision to grant special privileges to African-Americans to make up for past wrongs—and reacted to the incoming immigrants by creating a new minority that they could park alongside African-Americans—Hispanics—even though for the millions coming in there were no past wrongs to remedy. Hispanics soon appeared in the list of "protected minorities" under several federal laws, and the Equal Opportunity Commission started demanding that private employers report employment information on them. Hispanics subsequently found a place as a group on the US Census form.

Up to this point Americans hadn't divided their world between minorities and whites or thought in terms of a "people of color" ideology. Immigrants had streamed into America since before it became a republic. Sometimes, as in the case of Jews and Italians, they hadn't been thought of as white at first but then were transferred over to whiteness through a process of racialization, the term sociologists use to describe the creation of a racial identity where one did not exist before.

By forcing the new Latin American immigrants into a minority straitjacket, the policy makers created roadblocks to assimilation into values that created a society worthy of leaving everything behind to join. The public sphere, where all Americans were supposed to come together as one culture to the benefit of one another and the commonweal, became atomized to the detriment of the newcomers and their children. Barriers, which always exist when immigrants come to a country, were reinforced by bureaucratic labeling.

The impact such unprecedented cataloging had on the Hispanic immigrant population is rivaled only by the effects the sexual revolution and the new welfare state had on them. The Age of Aquarius and the Great Society continue to affect the whole country, but the consequences they had on immigrants were magnified because immigrants constitute such vulnerable groups—they come not just bereft of goods but also bereft of memories of what the country used to be like.

The sexual revolution, nicknamed "the unmarriage revolution" by Manhattan Institute scholar Kay Hymowitz, transformed a country where marriage and stable families were the norm into one in which today more marriages fail than succeed and 41 percent of births take place out of wedlock. The consequences of such turmoil are sweeping and foretell much societal instability to come.

The growing national consensus of the Left and the Right—in a country where consensus doesn't happen anymore—is that children growing up without the benefit of a mom and a dad severely under-perform those who grow up with them. This is not finger wagging or puritanism but common sense and social science. Brookings and the Heritage Foundation don't agree on much, but we agree on this: children from broken homes will have greater cognitive difficulties, drop out of college at a higher rate, and end up incarcerated more often.

The welfare entitlements created by President Lyndon Johnson and enlarged by every president since, Democrat or Republican, have played a part in breaking up families or stopping people from marrying in the first place. They penalize couples, as a mother may see her income drop substantially if she agrees to live with her children's father.

In addition, the welfare state encourages irresponsibility by its very nature. If a man knows that he does not need to act responsibly because the government will step in, what is it that will keep him at home? Social conventions? Those are gone. As Charles Murray pointed out back in 1984 in *Losing Ground*, controlled government experiments carried out in the late 1960s and 1970s on the impact that the negative income tax, or welfare payments, would have on marriage formation were conclusive: "Does welfare undermine the family? As far as we know from the NIT experiment, it does, and the effect is large." Murray wrote of changes in the law in 1970 that made it hard or impossible for the imaginary welfare recipient couple Harold and Phyllis to marry and keep their benefits:

> From an economic point of view marriage is dumb. From a non-economic point of view, it involves him in a legal relationship that has no payoff for him. If he thinks he may sometime tire

of Phyllis and fatherhood, the 1970 rules thus provide a further incentive to keep the relationship off the books.

Kay Hymowitz noted that the same thing happened from a woman's perspective: "Enabled by welfare, the women let the men know they could manage without them."

The Great Society thus created vast pockets of welfare dependency. Government inevitably tears up social and human capital in those communities where it intrudes, as it crowds out churches and other volunteer organizations in which people came together for mutual aid. Once a government agency starts to provide a benefit to a community, it obviates the need for civil society to act. One of the big problems is that it was those volunteer organizations that greased social and economic mobility.

All these ills hit many of the new Hispanic immigrants where they lived—literally. One of the unprecedented parts of the social transformation of the last three decades in America is that not all communities have been hit the same way. The dislocations of the last few decades have been dramatically felt at the lower income levels, in which order is collapsing, whereas in the upper-level communities the social fabric has held more or less intact.

To put it another way, one of the results of the '60s is that in America today we have increasingly a multiethnic upper-income class and a multiethnic lower-income class. They live in different neighborhoods, go to different schools, and have throughout their lives very little interaction with each other. Mobility between the classes, once one of the hallmarks of this country, has been reduced for those with damaged social infrastructure.

Many Hispanics have thrived, earn high incomes, and are rewarded by living in leafy neighborhoods with good schools. As new immigrants or the descendants of recent immigrants, Hispanics, however, are unsurprisingly overrepresented in the lowest income quintiles, not in the stable neighborhoods with good schools.

Those Hispanics in the lowest income quintiles will be increasingly trapped there, along with poor African-Americans and non-Hispanic whites. What compounds the problem for Hispanics, however, are the artificial barriers to integration that our institutions have thrown in their way.

It isn't as if the schoolhouse will level the playing field for Hispanics. Strategically used since the Founding Fathers to teach American and immigrant children civic values such as the volunteerism and hard work that are needed for successful adult lives and a successful republic, schools gave up that role at midcentury. Gone are the texts that once taught all Americans, native or immigrant, how to be an upstanding citizen with the civic knowledge needed to help the republic survive.

As they taught civics to all, the schools had also taught knowledge that would be tacitly shared by all members of society. Schools in all parts of the country instilled in all Americans the same cultural code, derived from sources as varied as the Bible and the McGuffey Readers. Without this shared knowledge, we can't comprehend statements that are permeated with cultural references. An oft-cited example is a news report on a cricket match. Unless you are versed in the terminology of the sport, chances are that you won't understand anything even though you would know every word. Likewise, democratic debate breaks down if we don't all understand what is meant by "community," "the franchise," and "liberal values."

When schools stopped teaching the same content to all Americans, the nation's reading comprehension levels began to fall off the table. This hit Hispanics particularly hard. Because so many are new to the country, the sudden halt in instruction in a unifying culture created informational lacunae that are harming the society at large.

These were all policies put in place if not by progressives, at least by people in both the Republican and Democratic parties who favored big government solutions and by policy makers and bureaucrats who get paid to always think of government involvement. But conservatives have not been very helpful either.

Traditionally conditioned to be wary of the alien and not having been taught to recognize the value of the Hispanic culture in the forging of the American spirit, conservatives all too often have failed to pull up the welcome wagon. What has happened as a result is that progressives have had a monopoly on explaining to Hispanics their vision of America. Allowing liberals free access to the hearts and minds of such a great number of people makes no sense, especially when one considers that many of the Hispanics who do not vote (and Hispanics have the lowest voting participation of all the groups recognized by the US Census) tell pollsters that they are largely conservative. Nobody has courted their vote!

The liberal indoctrination has been conducted through subtle and not so subtle means. Schools and social institutions controlled by the Left send out their messages mostly subliminally. Not so the US Department of Agriculture, which with a heavy hand has even crafted radio soap operas in Spanish to persuade Hispanics to drop their natural resistance to being a public burden and accept food stamps.

What this has created is a self-fulfilling prophecy. By letting liberals be the ones to integrate Latinos, conservatives in many cases have gotten exactly the immigrant alien they feared.

SO WHAT TO DO?

The question now is how to proceed. To address these problems and craft a long-term strategy for conservatives it is best to appeal to the social sciences and think in terms of the three different types of capital that are essential to success in America.

The first is financial; it's the stuff in your pockets and in your bank account as well as all the other material assets you own. Hispanic immigrants, like all immigrants, come here with precious little of it. That does not have to be insurmountable because in America the next two forms of capital, though not material, are still important for success.

One is human capital: education and other acquired skills, as well as the traits that used to be known as "character"—the habits of persistence, honesty, work ethic, punctuality, thrift, and the like. These character traits we carry with ourselves across borders, and no dictator can ever take them away. Once these traits have been transmitted to us, we are in charge of them and only we can allow them to deteriorate. Hispanic immigrants like all before them have tended not to come with long lists of college degrees but have made up for that with perseverance, thrift, and a strong work ethic. They self-selected—the ones here are the ones who had the get-up-and-go spirit that is a requisite for emigration.

The third might be the most important: social capital. This last form of capital consists of the social networks people create in their interactions with others: families, church associations, the Boy Scouts, bowling leagues, the PTA, neighborhood sports teams, and the like. Immigrants to America were always good at building these networks, from neighborhood clubs to the Knights of Columbus to the Ancient Order of Hibernians. Social capital is the way social scientists refer to the voluntary institutions that make America exceptional.

Success in this country, more than in other advanced societies, depends on the interaction of all these forms of capital. Hispanic communities have some deficiencies in all three that must be addressed. To be sure, whites and blacks in the lower income classes also lack these forms of capital, but because immigrants come here without money and find themselves without an extended family network, a settled tradition, or real estate they can call their own, they must busily re-create human and social capital. The difference today, as opposed to centuries past when the Irish, Czechs, and East European Jews were streaming in, is that our current political and economic systems actually discourage the virtues that lead to the creation of the types of nonfinancial capital and in their place instill the vices that produce entropy.

"The interactions among these kinds of capital are complicated, which is one reason government programs tend to be ineffective at promoting mobility," wrote the Heritage Foundation's Stuart Butler in a seminal *National Affairs* article in 2013. "Distant, unwieldy government bureaucracies are not capable of identifying precisely which cultural influences need to be changed, or of changing them in ways that address local circumstances and guarantee improved outcomes for the poor."

Obviously, our political leaders must persist in the hard work of reforming our welfare system, starting by putting back in place the mandatory work requirements that President Obama in 2012 sought to waive in the welfare reform law signed by President Clinton in 1996. Requiring work in exchange for benefits reduces the attraction of depending on government. Capping the growth of the eighty-plus means-tested welfare programs is also a must.

But we need more, because fifty years of growing perverse incentives and dependence on government have devastated entire neighborhoods and the families in them. As the author Peter Wehner once put it to me, "What do you do, withdraw the knife and let the wound heal by itself?" In other words, we need to study and support institutions that work to transform neighborhoods where the social foundation is gone into communities that are thriving once again.

The questions for Part III, then, will be about building capital: How do we help Hispanics caught in the welfare trap break free of it so that they can repair their human, social, and financial capital? A strategy of rebuilding the three different types of capital may be the only way to mend the damage caused by the War on Poverty, the sexual revolution, the minority rights revolution, and so forth.

What we need are ideas and policies that will help Americans of Latin American origin succeed as previous waves of immigrants have. To achieve this we need to include all aspects of conservative civil society (donors, social welfare groups, foundations, churches) as well as the involvement of any Americans across the political spectrum who really are serious about alleviating poverty. Without education, intact families, a savings habit, safe neighborhoods with thriving volunteer institutions, and a generally healthy civil society, the only way immigrants and natives can get ahead is all too often through crime. The gang has a strong pull because it is an aberrant form of social capital; it gives individuals that which we all need: something greater than ourselves.

Those of us who get the importance of keeping the Hispanic family together and reversing the rise of illegitimacy must promote these values actively to all Hispanic groups, especially Mexican-

Americans, who often come in with strong nuclear families but watch that asset dissolve over time.

Turning to education, the struggle to give all American children the instruction they need to face twenty-first-century challenges is happily on the verge of no longer being entrapped by the Left-Right disputes that plague so many other issues in America. The abject failure of so many of our public schools, especially in the inner city, is so clear that even Hollywood is starting to make documentaries about it.

And Hispanics are indeed huge fans of school choice and charter schools, anything that will give parents the opportunity to hang on to their children and not lose them to drugs and gangs.

Saving gets little attention, but it is one of the most important predictors we have of whether someone will be able to make it out of the lower income quintiles and into the higher ones. The research shows, incidentally, that it is not a matter of how much one saves but the fact that one has a habit of saving. Saving is also important for home ownership and as a source of start-up capital for small businesses.

But civil society can't repair the three types of capital on its own. The majority-producing machine that liberals have erected the last fifty years is nearly in place. The only way to reverse the process is for political leaders to rise up and make the case to Americans—to Hispanic Americans—in the political arena. Whoever becomes the Republican Party's presidential candidate must be able to speak this language. The political vision must be compelling: the case must be made that there is a way out, that communities can heal.

Conservatives should see sending Hispanics a mobility message as a grand project, something only *they* can do. Allowing liberals to have a monopoly over Hispanic outreach has certainly not worked out for Hispanics. As George Will wrote in 2013, "America's limited government project is at risk because the nation's foundational faith in individualism cannot survive unless upward mobility is a fact."

Conservatives who care about the survival of this project should understand that Hispanics are the trophy in the philosophical contest being waged between progressives who see a large role for government and conservatives who prefer a much more limited one. One state, in fact, epitomizes this conflict: Texas. There a battle is brewing pitting economic mobility against dependence on government, or what I call the Texas model versus the California one. I devote a whole chapter to it because it is so important politically for the rest of the country.

Will speaking in these tones persuade Hispanics to vote for Republicans? There are no silver bullets, but let's put it this way: harsh tones and talk of self-deportation by a man who, however decent he was, seemed out of touch with "people like us" produced a 29 percent level of support. A message that lets Hispanics know that conservatives understand their contributions to the making of America, specifically those made by Mexican-Americans, and recognize the struggles of their schools, their communities, and their families and have alternatives to offer will get political leaders a foot in the door and will over time bear fruit.

A welcoming message is an assimilationist message; therefore, it's best to state up front why assimilation is desirable, why it is a goal we should not blithely consign to the dustbin of history. America, quite simply, is unique not just in the present world but historically. It is, as Lincoln called it, "the last, best hope of earth" because it is humanity's first experiment in the proposition that men and women are able to gather voluntarily in communities large and small to solve a great variety of issues without government interference. Government here is, in fact, strictly limited to powers enumerated in the Constitution, and it is set up *only* to safeguard rights that men and women received from their Creator, not from a legislator or a bureaucrat. America, being "of earth," cannot expect to have heavenly perfection, and America hasn't been perfect always. But the experiment has proved successful enough, attaining the greatest freedom and prosperity for the greatest number. This is why America attracts to its shores immigrants from all corners and lately a lot of people like me from former Iberian colonies. This is why political leaders from Winthrop to Kennedy to Reagan have not shied from using the "Shining City upon a Hill" imagery that Jesus employed in the Sermon on the Mount.

But this experiment depends on those who come to refresh this promise, making their own contribution without altering the basic formula that produced these blessings. The Founding Fathers recognized early on that this was a nation of immigrants, but they always (and rightly) warned about reproducing here the dysfunctions of other lands (which so many progressives so often seem so enamored of). Assimilation does not mean, to be sure, the abandonment of traditional cultural values, and some research suggests that immigrant communities integrate into American life more easily when their members retain ethnic pride. Previous generations of immigrants have gotten the balance right, but multiculturalists are getting in the way of Hispanics' ability to replicate this success.

This brings us to one of the last points I will make in this book. Many worry that the jury is still out on whether the great demographic change we have seen in this country in the past half century will help the United States continue to have the freedom and prosperity that incited people to come here in the first place or whether it has changed everything radically.

This usually is discussed in hushed tones but sometimes is aired nationally, even politely. It was in fact laid out beautifully in 2010 on National Public Radio's *Tell Me More* in an interview dealing with Hispanic underperformance in school. Host Allison Keys was interviewing NPR education correspondent Claudio Sanchez, who said at one point:

> There is a lingering fear that this is a community, a population, that is not ready to contribute enough and it went to this nation's well-being, to its quality of life. And so there's this lingering fear that, you know, there's this population that's going to put the United States in a hole, economically and otherwise and culturally. And I am not just talking about xenophobia, I'm talking about folks who are legitimately concerned about where this population is going.

This is an important debate that can no longer be swept under the nation's rug. Ignoring the roots of these questions has not helped Hispanics, even if the intent to conceal it might have been laudable, such as celebrating immigration or protecting Hispanics from bigotry.

Some critics have claimed that Hispanics are "unassimilable." This was said about the Jews, the Italians, the Poles, and many others before them, and so it should always set our radar buzzing. Hispanics are eminently assimilable. They are just looking, in the words of Leo Grebler, for "assimilative opportunities." The problem is that our government and cultural institutions are busy throwing up barriers to integration.

It will help if all of us stop thinking of Hispanics (or Latinos) as a homogeneous, uniform group. The term has outlived its usefulness and creates more confusion than clarity. Salvadorans came here for very different reasons than did Puerto Ricans, behave differently, and even look different.

Continuing to ignore these issues may put at risk America's unique construct. The blueprint under which America operated for its first two hundred years saw the nation as a liberal democracy in which individual rights were safeguarded and everyone enjoyed equal protection under the law. In this model—let's call it the Founding Fathers' Model—the country had a common civic culture in the public sphere, where individuals voluntarily formed little platoons to solve mutual problems. Immigrants from all corners of the planet were not immediately welcomed into these social and civic organic groupings, but soon they or their children cracked the code and were accepted.

Fans of a multicultural model see the Hispanic demographic bulge as the force that will finally tip the country into their model. This would be their vindication after having lost the debate between assimilation and multiculturalism to the assimilationists in the 1910s.

One reason the assimilationists won the debate back then, and can again, is that it is their model that holds the most attraction for immigrants. They arrive on these shores looking for liberty and economic success, yes, but there's more. The American Dream encompasses something larger than a house in the suburbs with a two-car garage, as it is often synthesized, or minimized, by the media. The American Dream that shines through is the whole package, the goodness of a family-oriented, civic-minded citizenry encapsulated in the direct democracy of New England town meetings or barn raisings across the Midwest; immigrants know that whatever their supposed betters in Hollywood and academia tell them, there really is a "Norman Rockwell, Frank Capra" America out there, as Senator Mike Lee put it at an antipoverty conference in 2013—a nation of "plain ordinary kindness, and a little looking out for the other fellow, too." If given a choice, Hispanic immigrants and their descendants would elect to fit into this America. That's why they—we—come.

This vision, properly called a dream because it is the epitome of every working person's aspiration but one that is attainable too, has many, many advantages over the liberal alternative, which at bottom can be described as nihilist, the dictionary definition of which is "the belief that traditional morals, ideas, beliefs, etc., have no worth or value."

The question is, then, what are conservatives prepared to do? Since the Democratic Party as it is currently constituted is the agent of the welfare state, it will fall mostly to Republican policy makers to create and promote the alternative. Abdicating any responsibility for helping Hispanics assimilate is no longer an option. The result of this neglect has been to allow the Left to have something close to a self-serving monopoly on the Hispanic heart and mind. Voices on the right warning conservative politicians that they're wasting their time with Hispanics because they are a lost cause, that we must just reform the welfare state and everything will fall into place, thus preach a dangerous counsel. Harvard's Robert Putnam hit the nail on the head when he admonished us that it would be ahistorical for conservatives—who see themselves as the keepers of the national flame—to walk away from the challenge to social solidarity posed by Latin American immigration. Conservatives must break the closed, self-reinforcing loop (liberal policies—family breakup—

weaker communities—votes for politicians who promise even more government support) not only because it would benefit the Republican Party or even because it would benefit Hispanics but because it would benefit the country—something conservatives care about.

As they reach out, however, conservatives should make sure they haven't bought into the uncaring caricature of themselves that the media have held up and thus heed the warnings of Yuval Levin at the Ethics and Public Policy Center. Conservatives, he writes, "often make a mistake when we talk about the welfare state. We talk in terms of it creating 'dependency.' In fact, dependence is the human condition. Everybody is utterly dependent on others. The question is: are you dependent on people near you who are also dependent on you, and who therefore can help you develop certain kinds of habits of responsibility, or are you dependent on a distant provider of material benefits that asks nothing of you in return? The latter is not so much dependence as a kind of false independence."

At the very heart of conservatism, in fact, are community and the interdependence on one another it brings. The man said to be the founder of modern conservatism in the late eighteenth century, the Anglo-Irish political philosopher Edmund Burke, famously said that "to love the little platoon we belong to in society, is the first principle (the germ as it were) of public affections. It is the first link in the series by which we proceed toward a love to our country, and to mankind." This is a philosophy so much at the center of the conservative American view of the good life that Heritage's president, Jim DeMint, devoted an entire book to it in 2014. The little platoon is only a better term for social capital, the most important of the three types of capital.

The welfare state will be changed only when politicians join community institutions to make the case for reform to all, including Hispanics. "You have to push on both fronts," politics and civil society, Yuval Levin told me. What we have at hand is a race for the future; the side that wins it will see its vision implemented. The side that wins, wins America.

But before they can convince Hispanics that the full promise of America is available to them, conservatives must convince themselves of that fact. For this they must learn to look beyond the picture of Hispanic failure that the Left has depicted and in some ways even helped produce and envision the alternative: the Mexican-American family celebrating Thanksgiving on the cover of an imaginary *Saturday Evening Post*.

Chicago's United Neighborhood Organization (UNO) is one of the nation's largest grassroots groups dedicated to Hispanics. It operates thirteen charter schools in that city, provides immigration services, runs a literacy campaign, and helps with health care services. UNO is serious about the challenges the Hispanic community both faces and poses to the country. Its mission statement reads:

> Hispanic immigration also carries a set of serious challenges that will test our community's ability to prosper. The nation's largest drop-out rate, gang violence, and teenage pregnancy, among other problems, have for decades stifled this group's potential and accomplishment.
>
> Even so, practical solutions to these problems are scarce, as pragmatism often takes a back seat to agendas that portray Hispanics as a victimized community. This depiction of Hispanics as "victims" is enormously inaccurate. Hispanics must be challenged to take full advantage of American possibilities through deep investments in family, civic involvement and, especially, in the education of its next generation.

This book will attempt to figure out how to overcome challenges and help Hispanics thrive and contribute to the vision of America's Founding Fathers.

PART I

VARIED PEOPLE, VARIED ISSUES

Chapter 1

THE MEXICANS

Culture consists of connections, not of separations.

—CARLOS FUENTES

I N 1970, UCLA SOCIAL SCIENTISTS LEO GREBLER, JOAN MOORE, and Ralph Guzman published the groundbreaking *The Mexican-American People: The Nation's Second Largest Minority*, a comprehensive study of Mexican-Americans' social, economic, and cultural problems. Based on 1,550 interviews, the study, the first of its kind, was an in-depth look at economic mobility in that community. The use of the term *minority* in the title was self-referential. Until then, Mexican-Americans weren't talked about in this way—only black Americans were. The authors' stated goals were to "redefine Mexican-Americans in terms of race" and gain for them the affirmative action benefits that President Johnson's War on Poverty was starting to bestow on black Americans. Moore patted herself on the back for this years later:

> It may have been something of a miracle, then, that Mexican-Americans came to be defined as a minority. Our effort to redefine the population was a small part of a broad trend, dominated by the efforts of Chicanos themselves—advocacy organizations, movement groups, elected representatives, and outspoken scholars. There were consequences that would make most of us feel good: Mexican Americans became beneficiaries

of affirmative action, and their barrios became targets in the war on poverty.

A generation after *The Mexican-American People* was published, professors Edward Telles and Vilma Ortiz, also of UCLA, discovered the interview files "gathering dust" at the university and decided to reinterview as many of the original subjects as possible. Eventually they were able to locate and interview 684 of the nearly 1,200 respondents who had been younger than age fifty and 758 of their children. What resulted is one of the best longitudinal studies of Mexican-Americans ever conducted, published in 2008 as *Generations of Exclusion: Mexican-Americans, Assimilation and Race.*

What Telles and Ortiz found does not make easy reading for those of us who believe immigration and the melting pot are existential attributes of our country. Across the board in education and income, Mexican-Americans had regressed from one generation to the next. Immigrants and their children actually had performed better because they had been able to retain some aspects of the strong family structure they had brought from Mexico. But, write Telles and Ortiz, "the third and fourth generation do worst of all, suggesting downward assimilation in education." Prospects for the fifth generation were poor, too.

"American public schools have failed most Mexican-Americans, contrary to what they did for European Americans," the authors concluded.

Throughout their book, Telles and Ortiz make clear that in their view this outcome is mostly the result of discrimination, though as social scientists they must stick to the facts in their research, and thus they report that skin color had little impact on educational attainment and that the children of families who attended church services regularly had more years of schooling. What does not seem to have dawned on them, or on Moore, is that this generational regression may not be *despite* their success at redefining Mexicans as a racial minority and making the barrios targets of government help but *because* of it. Ready and able to join the

American mainstream, Mexican-Americans had the plug pulled on the success escalator.

The realization of Mexican-Americans' American Dream is of supreme importance not just to themselves or to Hispanics but to the fate of this country. At 33 million strong, they don't just over-shadow the two other main Hispanic groups, the Puerto Ricans and the Cubans, who combined account for less than 7 million; at their present rate of growth Mexican-Americans by themselves will soon outnumber African-Americans. Figuring out how to stimulate their upward mobility therefore should not be left to the political calculus of the Democratic and Republican parties; it is a question of national importance. If those who, like me, contend that govern-ment assistance and minority status have hindered their progress are right, we need to turn our policies around.

Mexicans have been here longer than any other Hispanics and have left an unrivaled cultural legacy. At the same time, they have made up the lion's share of the immigrant groundswell since 1965. This creates an important dichotomy. Mexican-Americans are the oldest Hispanic culture in our country, and at the same time they are also the newest. The post-1965 demographic bulge was mostly Mexican, and immigration in the twenty-first century has been mostly Mexican.

The Obama machine—always sharply attuned to cultural crosscurrents—understands the political importance of Mexican-Americans. During the 2012 election the Obama campaign named as its cochair Eva Longoria, who's a celebrity, a woman, and, more important, a Mexican-American. Barack Obama himself used to appear regularly on *Piolín por La Mañana*, the number one radio show in Los Angeles for listeners age twenty-five to fifty-four *in any language* until it was canceled.

Because they are concentrated in a handful of key battleground western states, Mexican-Americans can provide the margin of vic-tory in tight electoral college races. A relatively small swing in one direction or the other will change election results in Colorado, Ne-vada, New Mexico, or Arizona.

The cultural and political impact of Mexicans is likely to grow. By 2050—not too long from now—every fourth face you see will belong to a person of Mexican ancestry. Already today Mexican-Americans constitute, all by themselves, more than 10 percent of all Americans—more if one counts the many white or black Americans with some Mexican ancestry. As a group they must now be considered right up there with such other statistically significant ethnic groups as the Germans, the Irish, and the Scots-Irish.

In fact, only Americans who claim to be of German origin, at 15.2 percent of the population, outrank Mexican-Americans. Mexicans outrank Irish-Americans (10.8 percent), Italians (5.6 percent), and Americans of English origin, who clock in at just 8.7 percent in this former British colony.

Almost three-quarters of the growth in the Hispanic population in the first decade of this century (11.2 million out of 15.2 million) was accounted for by the increase in US residents who self-identify as being of Mexican origin. Most US residents of Mexican ancestry live in two states, California and Texas, which with 11.4 million and 8 million residents of Mexican origin, respectively, account for 61 percent of all people of Mexican origin in the United States. But the Mexican phenomenon is hardly relegated to those two states; according to the Census Bureau, Mexican residents represented the majority of the Hispanic population *in forty states*. The Hispanic boom you hear so much about has been a Mexican boom.

This growth has been rapid, too. Though the Census Bureau did not start taking reliable statistics on Hispanics till around 1980, one can extrapolate from questions that were asked in the decennial censuses starting in 1930, such as "Spanish surname" or "Spanish origin," to form a relatively clear picture of their rise.

Pew Research and other institutions have estimated that in 1960 the entire Hispanic population accounted for less than 4 percent of the country's inhabitants and was only slightly higher at 4.7 percent a decade later. The overwhelming majority of those Hispanics in 1960 would have been of Mexican origin, given that Puerto Ricans didn't really start moving to the mainland in high numbers till the late 1940s and that Cuban immigration was negligible till the

Cuban Revolution in 1959. Hispanics from other countries were even rarer.

Today, the 12.7 million immigrants born in Mexico make up the largest group of immigrants in the United States and amount to one-third of the entire US immigrant population all by themselves. This is a seventeen-fold increase since 1970, according to Pew Research. The second largest immigrant group, Filipinos, account for only 5 percent of immigrants living in the United States.

More than half of US residents who were born in Mexico, or 55 percent, are here illegally. Looked at another way, six of ten illegal immigrants in the United States were born in Mexico; this shows how the illegal immigrant issue is largely a Mexican issue.

This is a situation that has hardly improved the image of Mexican-Americans. Even though only 7 million out of 33 million people of Mexican ancestry (born here or in Mexico) who live in the United States are here illegally, suspicion of illegality sometimes carries over to the entire group.

That is of course misleading. As we have seen, the 80 percent of US residents of Mexican origin who are here legally includes Americans of the oldest pedigree. Mexican-Americans have been part of the national fabric since well before the Civil War. The only thing that's new is the immensity of the numbers.

PART OF OUR HISTORY

Culturally, Mexican-Americans have left an impression on our country that may be second only to Britain's. Culture west of the Mississippi and south of the Rockies is the result of the explosive fusion of two great civilizations: the Anglo-Saxon and the Spanish, the American and the Mexican.

This culture also encompasses northern Mexico, whose folkways and customs have more in common with those of South Texas and New Mexico than with that of the Mexican state of Chiapas on the tropical border with Guatemala. Frontier ranching life had a leveling effect that made northern Mexico much more egalitarian than that country's south.

"South Texas is part of a cultural region the stretches as far south as Monterrey, Mexico, and extends through large parts of the southwestern United States, a culture of cowboys and rugged individualism," said Aaron Peña, a former Texas state representative from Hidalgo County, right in the Rio Grande Valley. "Our history taught us to survive on our own. These people on the *frontera*, on the other side of it, could not depend on Mexico City, which was far away and remote. So our cultural region prized the individual. We depended on one another, on family, on community."

America's culture and character are greatly affected by these values. The cowboy, that most enduring of American icons, cannot be understood outside this context, without his lasso, his bronco, or his rodeo—or his basic simplicity, stoicism, and honor, all qualities associated with Mexican men. No less tough an hombre than John Wayne was a great admirer of Hispanic culture because of these attributes. Lest we forget, all three of the Duke's wives were Hispanic. Without its Mexican influence, the Southwest would just be a scorching version of the Midwest, and the Midwest, for all its allure, simply lacks the storied and legendary character of the Wild West.

This cultural importance is not taught sufficiently in schools, as there are elements on both the right and the left who are uncomfortable with it. Conservatives might think, wrongly, that such a stress may be the equivalent of such empty gestures as Hispanic Heritage Month. Progressives, for their part, prefer to lionize such radical figures as farm union leader Cesar Chavez.

Much of what gets taught about Mexican-Americans in our public schools—especially to Mexican-Americans—emphasizes discrimination. Some official segregation did take place, though it was never on the same level as that suffered by African-Americans. Liberals blame the problems recounted in the preface—high rates of out-of-wedlock births, high school dropout, achievement gap, incarceration, and so on—on this history, not on the end of the marriage culture and bureaucratic barriers to assimilation. Thus, it is important to review the record.

America inherited a large Mexican population when Texas

joined the Union in 1845 and the United States won the Mexican War in 1848, gaining as a result the lands that are now the states of New Mexico, Nevada, Utah, and California; most of Arizona and Colorado; and parts of Oklahoma, Kansas, and Wyoming. All told, this was about half of Mexico with some 100,000 Mexicans in those lands, unevenly distributed.

THREE MAIN GROUPS

Mexicans are very varied, so varied in fact that it might be useful to think of them as being members of three different groups.

The first are those who have been here for many generations, whose ancestors were here already in the 1700s or before—the descendants of the preexisting Hispanic population. This is the group that can claim to have partly forged the West.

The second important group is made up of the descendants of those who started crossing the border during the unstable two decades that followed the outbreak of the Mexican Revolution in 1910. This group also includes those who came after the end of the bracero guest worker program and the passage of the Immigration and Nationality Act in 1964 and 1965 (the ending of the former and the passage of the latter are important turning points in the history of immigration that we will look at later in this book). The third, fourth, and fifth generations that social scientists are looking at now are included in this group.

The third group is made up of current immigrants: people born in Mexico and their US-born young children. This group obviously includes all the estimated 7 million or so illegal immigrants who are here from Mexico. Legal or illegal, they show optimism, have a strong work ethic, and have stronger family units that do many Mexican-Americans born here, but these advantages are all too often quickly frittered away.

These are fluid distinctions: constant immigration means that these three groups are hardly cohesive, and there have been first-generation Mexican-Americans from 1845 to the present. Many Americans of Mexican origin today will have a link to the 1700s on one side and an immigrant parent on the other. But looking at the phenomenon of Mexican-Americans through this generational lens helps clarify some issues.

OUR MEXICAN FOUNDING FATHERS

Many "Mexicans" in western states such as New Mexico, Colorado, and Texas have ancestral roots in those territories dating back to the 1700s or earlier. Two prominent examples are Manuel Lujan, a former member of the US House of Representatives from New Mexico, and Ken Salazar, a former Colorado senator, both of whom went on to become secretaries of the interior, the former for George H. W. Bush and the latter for Barack Obama.

These men, who served in different decades and belonged to different parties, share the fact that they descended from Spaniards who arrived in the US Southwest in the 1500s. Whether one can call people like Lujan and Salazar Mexican at all is, of course, a question worth pondering. Their music, their cuisine, and their family structures—in a word, their culture—do have much to do with Mexico. But the fact that they are Americans of ancient lineage cannot be denied.

In terms of numbers, Mexican-Americans who can boast of such long pedigrees are few. They are symbolically important, however, especially in New Mexico and Colorado and to a lesser extent in Texas. Their problems and concerns are very different from those of Mexican-Americans from other areas as well.

Land issues, for example, are more important than immigration in New Mexico, where 55 percent of the land belongs to the federal government, the state, or the Indian reservations. It shouldn't be a surprise that much of the deep poverty in this state is found in public lands.

Sit with New Mexicans for a lunch of carne asada and green chilies and you're much more likely to get an earful about land grants dating back to the 1700s or earlier, which the locals insist were taken away by the federal government, than you are to hear a word about immigration.

Talk, for example, to Jesse Anzures, a New Mexican I met in Albuquerque in 2011, whose family has been there for seventeen generations or so. He chewed my ear off about land deeds, conquistadores, and permanence.

"I'm a New Mexican. I was never a Mexican," he said to me in 2012, referring to the fact that Nuevo Mexico was the name used by Oñate in the 1500s and that the area was separate from Mexico until its independence from Spain, though even then it was a Mexican territory, not a state. "We were never a part of Mexico. We were a different colony."

How does he feel about immigration? "We've gotten inundated from Mexico because of this driver's license thing. I gotta tell you, I'm not very happy about it," he said about the decision by the legislature in Santa Fe to give illegal immigrants driver's licenses.

Reminiscing about his family, the sixty-six-year-old Anzures says, "On my dad's side you have to go back to the 1600s to find someone from Mexico. On my mom's side it's different: her mother was Mescalero Apache, while my maternal grandfather—who was Spanish, French, and Yaqui—was a refugee from Pancho Villa," he said, referring to the many Mexicans who crossed the border to escape the destabilization created by the Mexican bandit in the early 1900s.

"We were designated as Mexicans only after 1848, never before that," gripes Anzures, referring to the year New Mexico became a US territory. What he really cares about is forcing the federal government to return the land that the Spanish Crown granted to his ancestors and those of many other New Mexicans in the sixteenth, seventeenth, and eighteenth centuries. Many of the descendants feel that their land was stolen by the federal government, which owns an astonishing 42 percent of the state of New Mexico. "Some of my ancestors came here with Oñate in 1598, and from there they went kind of west. One, Pedro Duran Chavez, was given land grants of forty thousand acres by the king of Spain sometime around 1692. Another, Francisco Duran Chavez, was given forty-three thousand acres," says Anzures, who epitomizes southern novelist William Faulkner's observation that "the past is not dead. It's not even past."

THE IN-BETWEEN GENERATIONS

Next comes the group in between, whose ancestors probably arrived here sometime in the twentieth century, escaping either the violence that accompanied the Mexican Revolution or the poverty produced by the economic regime put in place by the revolution's victors. These in-between generations live in all fifty states but especially in California, Arizona, Nevada, Texas, and other western states.

These second-, third-, and fourth-plus-generation Americans constitute the largest cohort of the 32 million Mexican-Americans and have needs and profiles different from those of Mexican-Americans who have been established here for centuries or who have themselves immigrated. They deserve the most attention, and not just because they are numerically superior to the other two groups.

The data show that despite being here for two, three, or more generations, this group of Mexican-Americans has had difficulty catching up with the progress made by similar generations of white and Asian immigrants.

It's not just Telles and Ortiz who are raising the alarm. Jeffrey Grogger and Stephen Trejo, economists at the University of Texas who have looked into this generational bulge, argue in a 2002 paper for the Public Policy Institute of California that these second- and third-generation Mexicans bear a special burden. "Intergenerational progress for Mexican Americans appears to stall after the second generation, with only modest improvement in educational attainment *and no wage growth observed between the second and third generations*" [my italics]—a stunning indictment indeed.

This group, Dr. Trejo told me, represents "a real challenge. If they are still going to maintain lower educational standards going forward, they are not going to reach their full potential."

Others, such as Alejandro Portes and Ruben Rumbaut, agree. Telles and Ortiz speak of "specially high dropout rates and substandard school performance for Mexican-American youth" after many generations in this country.

It is this comparatively poor performance of second- and third-plus-generation Mexican-Americans that causes the biggest backlash against immigration. As Grogger and Trejo put it, "If intergenerational improvement in education, jobs and earnings does not occur at a predictably high rate, the political pressure to more carefully monitor immigration will surely intensify."

In other words, whether we articulate it to ourselves or not, evidence confronts us daily that many second- and third-generation Mexican-Americans are not ramping up as rapidly as other immigrants who came before them, and this causes some people to harbor anti-immigrant feelings.

This was the conclusion of one of the most wide-reaching research studies undertaken on the issue of generational comparisons. Demographer Donald J. Hernandez looked across a number of markers and found that for Mexican-Americans especially, "along a number of important dimensions, children and adolescents in immigrant families appear to experience better health and adjustment than do children in native-born families."

It is for this reason that so many wonder if the melting pot, that great pressure cooker of upward mobility, no longer is cooking up success. The breakup of the family and the high incidence of illegitimate births, which get worse in the second generation, surely aren't helping. Children of immigrants must rely on strong families to negotiate such issues as cultural duality, but if there's no family safety net to catch you, you will drop faster through the cracks.

Sure enough, according to the American Community Survey, this is one of several areas that get worse the longer Hispanics are here. For example, 72 percent of the children of immigrants live in a house headed by a married couple, a rate that falls precipitously to 52 percent for the Hispanic children of US-born parents.

DOWN IN THE BARRIO

When I was doing research for this book, I headed out west to California. I wanted to spend time in East Los Angeles and asked one of the taxi drivers at the Beverly Hills Hotel on Sunset Boulevard if he would take me for a long tour there. He looked at me uncertainly. "You're staying in all this beauty," he said plaintively, spreading his hands as if to embrace our surroundings. "Why do you want to go to that horrible place?" I thought about the juxtaposition and then asked him as we both got in the car: "Just curious. Where are you from?" "Somalia," he answered with a wide smile. As he drove us away somewhat dejectedly, our car wending its way among all those jogging daughters and wives of the successful Iranian-Americans who predominate in that area, I thought to myself: Imagine that—a man from the country that defines the term *failed state* does not like to drive in East LA.

In Spanish, *barrio* is a neutral term that simply means "neighbor-hood." In this country, however, it is freighted with negative con-notations, and there is a reason why. East Los Angeles is a poster city for the types of problems Americans see. There the population is about 97 percent Hispanic, mostly Mexican-American, and about half of those people are second generation or more. A sprawling ghetto, East LA is known as the place for Mexican-Americans born here, as opposed to the immigrant hub of Pico-Union. It is not a success story; violent crime and property crime are about twice the national average.

The same thing can happen throughout California.

"In California right now you can't just say I'm not in a gang anymore. You join or they will just come after you," says Luis Her-nandez, a former gang member who spent years in eight different California county jails but righted his life after his daughter was born and is now using his experiences in his work as a youth coun-selor.

The way Luis and others tell it, the environment in much of California's Mexican world has become one where breaking out of vicious circles is difficult at best. "It's almost impossible to succeed. You are growing up without good influences. Gang members tell you, 'You're going to wear red or we're going to kick your ass.' So you learn to like wearing red. Then they change and say, 'No, now it's blue.' You give up. You just learn to follow whatever is next. It's all peer pressure."

The question of why kids are brought up by peers rather than by parents has a multitude of answers. In some cases it is because the fathers just check out or were never a presence in the home to start with. In other cases, the parents themselves are on drugs.

In Luis's case it happened for a reason that is part of the immigrant story: his parents stayed together, but they both worked two jobs.

"My father worked the night shift. He played in a band at night. All he did was work and sleep," said Luis, remembering what it was like growing up where he was born, Hayward, in the San Francisco Bay Area. The result is that Luis dropped out of school in the ninth grade. But even when he was in school, the environment wasn't great: "We racially profiled ourselves: black kids hung out in one hall, Mexicans in another." His school had Filipinos and Asians, too, but few whites.

His neighborhood also offered no escape: "We had to play outside because we lived in a one-room house. Other parents in the neighborhood weren't around either. They either had too many kids or were on drugs."

His mother, realizing that he needed good influences, got Luis into the Boy Scouts and even bought him uniforms. "But they bought used uniforms that had all these names like Bobby and Steve, and we were embarrassed because people knew they did not belong to us."

The rest of his relatives were no help. One uncle who had gone to prison "used to tell me all the time, 'The gangs will give you respect; don't ever be a snitch.' That was just embedded into our brains early on: street law."

Luis is working with kids now because "if you get them while they're young and their brains are still growing, you can still teach them about right and wrong. If a kid sees the ugly side of gang life, he won't go there. But you have to get them early, not when they're sixteen or seventeen years old. You have to get them when they're still in elementary school."

Not all Mexican-Americans from a gang-infested barrio have to end up in prison before they can turn their lives around. Some of them graduate from high school and end up in Georgetown. Meet Jonathan Espinoza.

"My kindergarten teacher put this sign up at the front of her class that said, 'Class of 2016.' I went up and told her that she had it wrong, that we were the class of 2012, but she said, 'Wrong. I want you all to go to college,'" Jonathan, a freshman studying government and philosophy at Georgetown when I spoke with him early in 2013, told me, describing the first time he had heard about the possibility of a college education. Not all teachers were that encouraging. Jonathan had a third-grade teacher who once said to the entire class: "All you little Hispanic kids, you're all going to end up on the corner, working at the burger shop, or on welfare."

With regard to Jonathan, she was wrong, and kindergarten's Ms. Kanol was right. Jonathan experienced real poverty growing up in Santa Ana, California. "We lived in an attic. There were times my mother didn't eat so that we could. She always refused to go on welfare, though." But Jonathan did forge ahead.

The grandson of Mexican immigrants who worked making parts for Boeing, "sticking aluminum pieces in a press all day," Jonathan found an inventive way to elude the gang violence that has been the downfall of so many kids like him. In middle school he cut a deal with a gang leader in which Jonathan would tutor him and his friends in exchange for protection in the schoolyard.

"In middle school the quad was separated into different gangs, and if you stepped into the wrong territory, they kicked your butt. The kids brought knives to school and smoked pot there," Jonathan said, adding that "a lot of people from my neighborhood and people I went to middle school with ended up in gangs. Already in elementary school I was given a terrible time because I am light-skinned, so they called me *güero* [the Mexican word for blond] and teased me."

But Jonathan had an advantage. "I had a reputation as a good student. So one of the gang leaders came up to me very early on and said, 'If you help me do the bare minimum and put a good word in for me with the teachers, I will make sure no one touches you.'"

The fact that someone like Jonathan was able to make it out of a dysfunctional system and is using one of the best paths out of the cycle of poverty—education—proves that one can indeed make it in America with effort and the right encouragement. The trick is creating the conditions for both, enabling the formation of the human and social capital without which financial capital comes only through illicit activity.

What we must realize is that it is in the milieu of Santa Ana and Hayward that, with the best of hopes to make it in the land of opportunity, many Mexican immigrants settle to live. This is our last group, the actual immigrants, those 12 million US residents who were born in Mexico.

THE IMMIGRANTS AND THEIR CHILDREN

They can be US citizens or not. They can reside in this country legally or illegally. As mentioned before, they bring with them concepts that are important for success: strong families, respect for adults, and above all industriousness.

In fact, a 2010 study by the American Psychological Association found that children of Mexican immigrants, benefiting from a tough-love upbringing and strong family bonds, entered kindergarten with social skills and levels of cooperation on a par with those of white kids despite their families' poverty. Those advantages, however, soon were eroded by poor teaching and negative peer pressure in the neighborhoods where immigrants live.

On the negative side of the ledger, they come here with few years of education—not what you want in a knowledge economy and welfare state in which the average family with high school dropout parents ends up costing society a net $1.2 million.

The average Mexican immigrant today comes in with a middle-school education on average (around 8.6 years of education, according to Grogger and Trejo), and the stats don't show much improvement among youths. Only 28 percent of Mexicans who immigrate between the ages of fifteen and twenty-one graduate from high school, compared with around 87 percent of US-born white youths and 78 percent of African-Americans. The number rises slightly to a 40 percent graduation rate for Mexicans who come here between the ages of five and fifteen.

Mexican immigrants are well represented not just in California but back east, in the South, and in the Midwest. In cities such as New York and Boston, where the only Hispanics until a couple of decades ago were likely to be Puerto Ricans, Dominicans, or the odd wandering Cuban, Mexican residents are a new phenomenon. They began showing up in the 1980s, assiduously taking up menial jobs such as restaurant work. Their industriousness soon was noticed, and they became sought-after employees.

It is the same in the South, where the only Mexicans one saw only a few decades ago were nomadic migrant workers who looked after harvests and lived unseen and not very nice lives in trailer camps, apart from urban or suburban populations. Today, the influx of Mexicans in the South who are nonnomadic is so large that it has begun to affect electoral races in unexpected places such as North Carolina and Georgia.

This large population transfer has taken place rather quickly. As recently as 1970, five years after the passage of the Immigration and Nationality Act, only 760,000 people born in Mexico were living in the United States, accounting for just 1.4 percent of Mexico's population. Ten years earlier, people born in Mexico were just the seventh largest group of immigrants, behind such traditional sources of immigration as Germany, Italy, and the United Kingdom.

These categories are all gross generalities, of course. Mexican-Americans of all generations live in all fifty states. Mexican-Americans can also have one parent born in Puebla and the other with roots going back to Oñate, as we saw with Jesse Anzures. But these divisions along generational lines can be useful in understanding the multifaceted experience of those we call Mexican or Mexican-American.

HOW THEY VOTE

The biggest difference, to be sure, will always be between Mexican-Americans and other groups rather than between

Mexican-Americans from different immigration waves. As a whole, Mexican-Americans vote for Democrats, though Mexican-Americans as a whole are not necessarily liberal. It's hard to pinpoint exactly what the Mexican-American vote is, as the exit polls do not break down the Hispanic vote by national origin.

We can, however, approximate what it was in 2012 because Resurgent Republic and the Hispanic Leadership Network conducted a very good poll, the Survey of Hispanic 2012 Voters in Florida, Colorado, New Mexico, and Nevada, which was carried out by phone between November 28 and December 7, 2012.

The survey respondents were overwhelmingly Mexican-American in Colorado (69 percent), New Mexico (67 percent), and Nevada (68 percent), but those numbers actually understated the Mexican-American presence among those respondents, especially in Colorado and New Mexico. In addition to Mexican, the respondents were offered the choice of Cuban, Puerto Rican, Central American, South American, and "Other." No other group scored higher than 5 percent in Colorado or New Mexico, and in Nevada only Central Americans scored as high as 9 percent. "Other," however, was chosen by 21 percent in Colorado and 27 percent in New Mexico (and 11 percent in Nevada).

The presence of "Other" in these high numbers must mean that the majority of these people were the Mexican-Americans of ancient lineage who were discussed earlier in this chapter, given that many of them like Jesse Anzures reject the label Mexican and that New Mexico is not crawling with Argentine or Paraguayan émigrés. If we make this assumption, the respondents in the Resurgent Republic and the Hispanic Leadership Network survey were close to 90 percent Mexican-American in Colorado, well over that in New Mexico, and just under 80 percent in Nevada.

With that in mind, the results support the view that Mexican-Americans align mostly with the Democratic Party. A close reading of the questions and answers makes clear, however, that Mexican-Americans' main gripe with the GOP is that the party doesn't even make an effort to understand their needs. Only one-fifth of the respondents said the Republican Party cared about the middle class, and even fewer, around 12 percent, said that Republicans understand the needs and concerns of Hispanic voters. Even fewer than that, 11 percent, said that Republicans "make an effort to win Hispanic voters."

On many of the policy questions, however, these Mexican-American respondents aligned with conservative values and policy proposals in the range of 30 percent to 50 percent, numbers that if translated into electoral results could have given a Republican presidential candidate the victory.

Another question in which the Republican Party performed abysmally provides food for thought, however, and reveals rays of hope for conservatives. To the question "Which party shares my values on social issues like gay marriage and abortion?" only 21 percent in Colorado, 24 percent in New Mexico, and 15 percent in Nevada said the Republican Party. That view is contradicted by other responses, however. Only 44 percent of Mexican-Americans in Colorado support gay marriage, and the bottom falls out in Nevada and New Mexico, where only 41 percent and 33 percent, respectively, back gay marriage. As for abortion, fully 38 percent in Colorado and Nevada are pro-life, a number that rises to 48 percent in New Mexico. The numbers clearly belie the claim that the Republican Party does not have the same social values as Hispanics.

And the numbers get better when it comes to merit pay, or tying teachers' compensation to the performance of their students, a position long associated with the Republican Party and rejected by a Democratic Party in hock to the teachers' unions. Fully 48 percent of respondents in Colorado, 52 percent in New Mexico, and as many as 54 percent in the union stronghold of Nevada favor merit pay.

As for government spending, around 40 percent of the respondents believed that the best way to improve the economy and increase job opportunities was to cut spending and lower taxes. And strong majorities, in the range of 60 percent in all three states, agreed with this statement: "Small businesses are struggling from taxes that are too high and regulations that are too burdensome."

What gives? These answers make many of the problems that Republicans experience with Mexican-Americans crystal clear.

Mexican-Americans largely hold conservative social views and agree with the GOP on saving the students, not the teachers' unions. But they don't know that Republican candidates agree with them because the party has done a woeful job of reaching out to Mexican-Americans. Even worse, the Republican Party has allowed the Democrats to associate the Republican brand with the offensive views of a Tom Tancredo rather than with the inclusive ones of Jack Kemp and Ronald Reagan.

Democrats make the effort and reach out to Mexican-Americans, not just presenting their policy positions in as appealing a light as possible but also painting the GOP in the worst possible light. Close to 80 percent of the respondents said they were contacted by the Obama campaign at least once in the battleground states of Colorado and Nevada, and 50 percent said they were contacted more than five times by the Obama campaign. Just 60 percent said they were contacted only once by the Romney campaign, and the number who were contacted more than five times hovered around 30 percent.

Mexican-Americans have not been well served by being beholden to one side only, and the fault mainly lies not with them but with Republicans, who have been less than eager to reach out to them. It is up to the GOP to make the next move.

Chapter 2

PUERTO RICANS

*We are at last waking up to the fact that a long term plan must be
made for this island and it is at present being worked out, including
all the government departments concerned.*

—ELEANOR ROOSEVELT ON PUERTO RICO

W HAT THE SOUTHWEST IS TO MEXICAN-AMERICANS, THE
Northeast has historically been to Puerto Ricans. The
windswept cement jungle of New York and the urban blight
of postindustrial New England cities somehow became the unlikely
backdrop for an island people from the Caribbean.

But before you start hearing the Jets and the Sharks whistling in
West Side Story, here's a bulletin: all this is changing. The word you
will keep hearing when you try to understand what is happening to
Puerto Ricans is *dispersion*, though a better word might be *reconfig-
uration*. Everything you thought you knew about Puerto Ricans is
changing.

Dispersion refers to the fact that stateside Puerto Ricans are in
the middle of a historic geographic redistribution.

New York's five boroughs, where nearly 90 percent of US-based
Puerto Ricans lived in the '50s, are now home to only 25 percent of
the Puerto Ricans who live in the United States. The largest gainer
of Puerto Ricans has been Florida, where only 1 percent of Puerto
Ricans lived six decades ago; that state now boasts one-fifth of the
total stateside Puerto Rican population. A great trek has been taking place right under our noses, but only a few people have noticed.

The trek is gaining speed as Puerto Ricans leave the island in
droves to escape an economic free fall that has taken place since

2006. According to the *Washington Post*, during the seven-year recession, "the population has shrunk by more than 138,000 to 3.7 million, with the vast majority of the outflow headed to the mainland." Of some 60,000 who left Puerto Rico in 2012, most came to the Sunshine State, said the *Post*.

As 2013 drew to a close, the open question was: Would Puerto Rico be the next Detroit and have to file for bankruptcy? One fear among US taxpayers is that Puerto Rico may be tempted to ask the federal government in Washington for a bailout. The recession has left the island with $70 billion in debt and $37 billion in unfunded pension obligations. Only 41 percent of Puerto Rico's adult population was working or looking for work in 2013. The recession has also driven dependence on government assistance to new levels. Around 37 percent of the people in Puerto Rico are on food stamps, compared with 15 percent in the rest of the United States. According to the *Post*, Puerto Ricans on the island were twice as likely as the rest of the US population to be receiving Social Security disability benefits in 2013.

It's not all bad news economically for Puerto Ricans stateside. Their geographic shift is combined with an economic revolution that has been massive and little noticed. Puerto Ricans, previously associated with high levels of poverty and urban hardship, are gaining ground in education and are earning higher wages, especially those in Florida.

At the same time, paradoxically, they remain the most poverty-stricken group among all Hispanics and have by far the worst cultural indicators. As we will explore in later chapters, their illegitimacy rate is over 60 percent, a rate that is second only to that of African-Americans. The Puerto Rican unemployment rate is consistently higher than that of other groups. In 2012, the most recent figures we have, the unemployment rate of US-based Puerto Ricans was 12.4 percent, 40 percent higher than that of the rest of the country. Close to 30 percent of US Puerto Ricans live below the poverty line. In Puerto Rico itself, the unemployment rate in 2013 was more than double what it was in the rest of the United States, hovering around 15 percent.

Stratification is the word here. The Puerto Rican community is reflecting what is happening throughout the country. Although some people are getting wealthier, some people are being left behind.

For those trapped in the cycle of poverty, the dependence on government assistance they learned in Puerto Rico is brought over to the mainland. Writer and commentator Linda Chavez observed in 1991, "Many Puerto Ricans, unlike other Latinos, come to this country already well-versed in the ways of the welfare state. About 70 percent of persons living in Puerto Rico receive some form of government assistance," a figure that roughly holds true today.

Chavez is not alone in noticing this issue. Columnist Jay Fonseca wrote in July 2013 in the Puerto Rican newspaper *Primera Hora*, in a column titled "Are We Lazy?" that it is worth much more to be on welfare in Puerto Rico than to hold a job that pays the minimum wage of $8.13 an hour.

"The Boricua (the native Taíno Indian name by which Puerto Ricans also go) community had always been hardworking until something changed: in November 1974 food stamps arrived," Fonseca concludes. His point that it was governments both in San Juan and in Washington that slowly got Puerto Ricans on the island hooked on government help is important. "Little by little they kept introducing this 'help' and the typical Boricua family was left with a very basic question, 'Is it worth it to work?'"

The dependency culture is much stronger for Puerto Ricans in New York than for those in Florida, however. Almost a third of Puerto Ricans in New York live in poverty compared with 22 percent nationwide, according to the American Community Survey. Angelo Falcón, senior policy executive of the liberal Puerto Rican Legal Defense and Education Fund, estimates that some 60 percent of New York welfare recipients are Puerto Rican.

Whether rich or poor, Puerto Ricans cannot be ignored politically. In 2008, Puerto Ricans crossed an important threshold: for the first time there were more Puerto Ricans living in the fifty states (4.2 million) than on the island of Puerto Rico itself (3.9 million). The ones who live here outnumber the ones back home: that's not true for any other Latino group.

The majority of Puerto Ricans here are now born here. Whereas the island over the past decade has been experiencing a population decline, here on what Puerto Ricans call "the mainland" the number of Puerto Ricans has ballooned, making Puerto Ricans 9 percent of the overall Hispanic population and 1.5 percent of the entire US population.

This all makes Puerto Ricans the second largest Hispanic group living in the United States after Mexicans and the second oldest large group living here after Mexicans.

Yet Puerto Ricans are unlike Mexican-Americans in almost every way. They were not here in the 1850s but started arriving in large numbers a century later. Their growth also had nothing to do with the post-'65 immigrant influx. In fact, Puerto Ricans are not affected by immigration law at all. Puerto Ricans are American citizens even though Puerto Rico is not a state; they can come and go as they please. Ending the bracero program did not affect them in 1964; passage of the Immigration and Nationality Act of 1965 meant nothing to them.

All these trends have significant political and social repercussions. Politicians are beginning to wake up to this. The heavily Democratic turnout of Puerto Ricans in Florida played a significant role in giving that state to Barack Obama in 2012. But Florida Puerto Ricans can be characterized as swing votes more than their Northeastern brethren can. They voted for Jeb Bush in large numbers, for example. Any program that conservatives devise to reach out to Hispanics should encompass Puerto Ricans.

But politicians (or marketers, for that matter) must appeal to Puerto Ricans on their own terms. Not a single Puerto Rican is here illegally; they're not even immigrants. They are full US citizens, and they have their own issues. Mexican-Americans in New Mexico care about land rights issues, and Cubans care about Castro; Puerto Rican activists care most about statehood for their island.

To fully understand what moves Puerto Rican voters today it is necessary to have some acquaintance with their history. What has happened on the island over the last 115 years goes a long way toward explaining the Puerto Rican experience both stateside and on the island and why Puerto Ricans vote the way they do

The first thing to understand is that Puerto Ricans are true circular migrants, though not in the same way as the Mexican guest workers who were here during the bracero program. Many Puerto Ricans regularly move back and forth between the island and the US mainland, settling here for a few years and then returning home for a few more. The Spanish expression for this is *el vaivén*, "the coming and going." The Puerto Rican anthropologist Jorge Duany has called Puerto Ricans "a nation on the move."

We cannot therefore look at Puerto Ricans on the US mainland in isolation. We must look at a whole society in constant churning. What happens politically and socially on the island has repercussions on mainland politics.

There is really no good analogy for this. It is unlike the experience of someone like me, who left Cuba in 1972 never to return. It also has nothing to do with the experience of a Mexican-American who has been here for four generations. The closest analogy is to a migrant American who moves from Indiana or Oregon to New York because of work except that when this Hoosier or Oregonian moves back and forth between her home state and Manhattan, she does not transit between languages and cultures; someone moving back and forth between New York and Bayamón does.

AMERICANS WITH AN ASTERISK

Puerto Rico is a US territory, but Puerto Ricans cannot vote for president as long as they reside in Puerto Rico. Once they cross over to the mainland, however, they can vote in every election, and they usually pull the lever for the person with a *D* at the end of his name.

All this is the result of the 1898 Spanish-American War, which pitted the United States against Spain in two theaters of war: the Caribbean and the Far East. It was a quick conflict, one of the last of the nineteenth century. In ten short weeks the United States shattered the last remnants of the four-centuries-old Spanish Empire, gaining Cuba and Puerto Rico in the Western Hemisphere and the Philippines and Guam in Asia, all of which had been Spanish possessions.

Puerto Rico was an afterthought. It was Spanish cruelties during Cuba's war of independence—a bloody conflict that had been fought on and off since 1868—that caught America's attention. The New York press, especially the Hearst newspapers, publicized the plight of the Cubans, and in the end the United States was drawn in.

In Puerto Rico there had been comparatively little clamor for independence from Spain, but after the United States entered a war with Spain, Puerto Rico was caught in the conflict and also was liberated. A much smaller island than Cuba, Puerto Rico saw some action, but to a much lesser degree. Only eight Americans died in the taking of Puerto Rico from Spain. After it was all over, the United States promised independence to Cuba and the Philippines, which they got, respectively, in 1902 and 1946.

Not Puerto Rico. It had been Spanish for nearly four hundred years—from the time it was conquered by Juan Ponce de León in 1509 until 1898, when the United States took possession at the Treaty of Paris that officially ended the Spanish-American War. Since then, Puerto Rico has been under US sovereignty. It is one of the few political entities in the world today that has never experienced independent sovereignty (one has to discount the Taíno Indian presence that existed on the island before Columbus, as that was not Puerto Rico). This permanent colonial existence has produced a mind-set that, as we shall see later in this chapter, accounts for some of the problems Puerto Ricans encounter here and on their home island.

In 1952, with the adoption of a territorial constitution, the island's territorial government acquired the name it still goes by today, the "Commonwealth" of Puerto Rico. What is a commonwealth? is a good question. The state governments of Virginia, Massachusetts, Kentucky, and Pennsylvania are also commonwealths, but that's not what we mean here. Like those four states, Puerto Rico has jurisdiction over a host of local matters such as education, health, and housing, and as with those states, the US federal government decides on issues such as immigration, defense, and the currency.

Unlike Virginia, Massachusetts, Kentucky, and Pennsylvania, Puerto Rico remained a territory when it adopted the term *commonwealth* under the Territory Clause of the US Constitution. Like residents of the nation's other territories, a Puerto Rican living in Puerto Rico is a US citizen, but paradoxically he cannot vote for president. The minute he moves to say, Kansas, he can vote all he wants.

For decades, territorial commonwealth status seemed to suit the majority of Puerto Ricans just fine. In 1952 they approved the island's constitution, which confirmed the territorial status, with an 82 percent majority and until 1993 supported it in every referendum. Puerto Ricans liked having the advantage of being able to move to the mainland as they pleased, having access to US markets, and having their money supply dictated by the Federal Reserve (whatever one may think of the likes of Alan Greenspan and Ben Bernanke, it is an immutable fact that having the greenback is preferable to the hyperinflation that has plagued many Latin American countries).

At the same time, Puerto Ricans clearly like having their own distinctive culture. A significant number of Puerto Ricans think of themselves as a nation unto themselves, and in fact, Puerto Rico has all the attributes of a nation: a separate language, culture, music, and history.

What Puerto Ricans have essentially done, then, is split the atom of the nation-state, the political blueprint that has been in existence since the 1600s. Puerto Ricans, those on the mainland and those on the island, belong to a nation, which is Puerto Rico; they at the same time belong to a state, which is the United States.

Along with political dependence has come economic dependence. Puerto Rico in fact has never been independent. Alone in all of Latin America, it never waged a bloody war of independence, and it doesn't want independence from the United States now. It should surprise no one that such a background lent itself to the perpetuation of a culture of dependency.

FROM SPANISH ABSOLUTISM TO NEW DEAL CENTRAL PLANNING

The United States must assume its fair share of responsibility for the continuation of this unhealthy culture of dependency. It was, if anything, deepened by progressive policies imposed from Washington. Starting in 1932 and for several decades to come, Puerto Rico became a workshop for the woolliest New Deal policies ever produced by the central planners who surrounded President Franklin Delano Roosevelt.

Prominent among Roosevelt's self-styled Brain Trust was one Rexford Guy Tugwell, and it was Puerto Rico's misfortune that early on in the Roosevelt administration the island caught the eye of this good-looking, most radical member of Roosevelt's inner circle. Roosevelt eventually appointed Tugwell governor of Puerto Rico in 1941, the last Anglo politician sent by Washington to run the executive branch of the island's government. As early as 1934 Tugwell had advised Puerto Rico on the antimarket "500 acre law."

Tugwell became best known for his involvement in the creation of the New Deal's infamous Resettlement Administration (RA), which he headed and which envisioned creating planned communes outside American cities. Having the government set up greenbelt concentration camps and tearing down parts of living cities ended up being too much for the US Supreme Court, which declared the RA unconstitutional and shut it down. Tugwell and his social planning ideas were denounced by many as communistic.

But when the president appointed him governor of Puerto Rico, Tugwell was given a free hand to experiment with a whole island. To a central planner this was the equivalent of a seven-year-old waking up on Christmas morning to find a train circling the tree, smoke spewing from the locomotive. The result, says Jorge Bonilla, a Puerto Rican conservative firebrand who sought the Republican nomination in Florida's 9th District in 2014, was that "Puerto Rico became a laboratory for every New Deal policy imaginable. And it is these liberal policies that put in place all sorts of dysfunctions, causing a breakdown of the family in Puerto Rico."

Many of these policies came to be known later under the label Operation Bootstrap. They were in essence attempts at social and economic engineering, with a touch of eugenics (it isn't a coincidence that these things often travel together). The goal was to transform the island's economy overnight from agriculture to manufacturing. The plan was to pick a handful of champion industries, such as tuna packing and pharmaceuticals, and entice companies to the island with tax breaks.

The problem with the government picking champion industries is that it always ends in tears. As Mitt Romney said to President Obama during one of the debates, in one of the few highlights of his snakebitten campaign, "You don't pick winners and losers, you just pick losers." That is what nearly always happens when some bureaucrat is left to decide what industry the economy needs rather than leaving that decision to consumer demand.

In its original form in 1952, the constitution of Puerto Rico recognized "the right of every person to obtain work" and "the right of every person to a standard of living adequate for the health and well-being of himself and of his family, and especially to food, clothing, housing and medical care and necessary social services."

Another passage of the constitution would warm the hearts of today's central planners in the Obama administration:

> In the light of their duty to achieve the full liberty of the citizen, the people and the government of Puerto Rico shall do everything in their power to promote the greatest possible expansion of the system of production, to assure the fairest distribution of economic output, and to obtain the maximum understanding between individual initiative and collective cooperation.

Bear in mind that these ideas were not fathered by the Soviet Politburo but by Washington's best and brightest, working under the Caribbean sun. How did Bootstrap and the commonwealth constitution work out?

Employment decreased during the 1950s. At the start of the decade it had stood at 596,000 jobs, but that went down to 542,000 in

1960. Unemployment rose from 12.9 percent in 1950 to 13.3 percent in 1960, a more negligible change but one that shows that the programs failed.

The economic and social policies took a toll on the philosophical outlook of the people as well. The promotion of policies such as Operation Bootstrap and the New Deal–inspired constitution ensured that most Puerto Ricans were ideologically reared on a steady diet of government knows best—something they had been used to all their history, first with Madrid and now with Washington. It may at least partly explain why Puerto Ricans of all socioeconomic backgrounds, races, or geographic distribution are the most faithful supporters of liberal causes in America among Latinos.

"Puerto Rico has had this colonial mind-set from the start. It began when Spain was there. There was always a king to provide for you, a Spanish captain general. Then when the United States came in, a US governor," says Bonilla.

Throw in New Deal central planning and the result is that "there's no ingrained notion of self-reliance, of enduring freedoms." The result today, he says, is, "There's always been this notion that federal dollars are going to bail us out. Take progressive policies and Latin American propensity for graft and what you have is Puerto Rico. Who is going to be the one who is going to give us more food stamps?"

The constitution of 1952 failed in other ways. By breaking the link that exists for most people between citizenship and nationality, the island's anomalous status essentially frustrated a healthier, fuller notion of national identity or at least introduced contradictions that are still to be worked through. It has caused quintessential Puerto Rican patriotism to be pushed out in often perverse ways and sometimes amusing ways.

"On the one hand, you have a population that has overwhelmingly demonstrated the greatest loyalty that citizens could possibly have to the United States, in the distinguished service and sacrifice of hundreds of thousands of Puerto Ricans in the armed forces," says Ken Oliver-Méndez, a veteran aide to three former Puerto

Rican governors. "At the same time, the lack of full integration into the American political family has also, no doubt, had the effect of perpetuating the notion that Puerto Ricans aren't real Americans."

A small minority seeking independence has helped propagate this notion. In 1950 a group came very close to assassinating President Truman, killing White House policeman Leslie Coffelt. Four years later four Puerto Rican terrorists managed to get into the visitors' gallery of the US House of Representatives and started shooting semiautomatic pistols at members debating a bill below, wounding five but miraculously killing none. Twenty years later, Puerto Rican terrorists were suspected of involvement in a bomb attack at New York's LaGuardia Airport in 1975. The attack killed eleven people and plunged my family into consternation, as my sister and one of my cousins worked at an airport shop at the time. We didn't hear from them for hours in that pre–cell phone era.

As is always the case, these fanatics resorted to terrorist means because the people were not with them.

But the terrorist acts that took place are a reminder that the halfway house of "unincorporated" territorial status (not of the United States, not out of it) and the economic policies that were being implemented as a result created strains. In the end, the biggest proof that the reforms fell short of the mark is that during those midcentury decades, hundreds of thousands of Puerto Ricans were leaving their island in the Caribbean to toil in freezing and forbidding New York.

THE GREAT MIGRATION

While radical nationalists were trying unsuccessfully to rally their compatriots to the cause of independence and Puerto Ricans were voting overwhelmingly in favor of maintaining the island's ties to the United States, a much more important trend was taking place. Nearly half a million people, more than 21 percent of the island's population at the time and fully a quarter of the labor force, left Puerto Rico and moved to the United States during the 1950s.

Ninety percent of them wound up in New York's five boroughs of Staten Island, Queens, Brooklyn, Manhattan, and the Bronx, especially the latter two.

Why so many Puerto Ricans suddenly went on the move is a subject of much interest. Agriculture, the island's mainstay, lost its luster at midcentury, starved by Operation Bootstrap. In 1948, agriculture had accounted for over 17 percent of Puerto Rico's economy; by 1960, that figure had dropped to less than 10 percent.

Passage of the referendum on the territorial constitution in 1952 is seen by some as a factor that contributed to the Great Migration of Puerto Ricans to New York. With it, Puerto Rico's status within the American family had been reaffirmed, and people could travel back and forth without visas or other border problems.

Vast improvements in Puerto Rico's life expectancy and infant mortality also may have contributed to a surplus of people. According to the Center for Puerto Rican studies at Hunter College, between 1954 and 1964 "life expectancy rose by ten years, and the birthrate declined by five percent. Per capita income doubled as the labor force shifted from an agrarian-based economy to an industrial one. School enrollments also increased." Immigration to New York may have acted as a needed safety valve.

But the labor force was surplus because something was not working economically. Governor Luis Muñoz-Marín actively encouraged emigration, a tacit acceptance that whatever he was doing could not keep his people fully employed.

Whatever the reasons that caused the Great Migration to New York, we know some things about the Puerto Ricans who suddenly up and moved. A people principally issued from Puerto Rico's mixture of the Spaniard, the African, and, to a lesser degree, native Indians and above all mostly rural suddenly transported itself to New York in the hundreds of thousands and there tried to make its way in an intimidating, almost feral inner city.

There's no doubt that these immigrants came from the countryside. In 1940, almost 70 percent of Puerto Rico's population was rural and not very well off, with a per capita income of $125. Many did not go straight from the fields to Harlem but stopped over in Puerto Rican cities.

As the author Julio Morales put it, "the family was uprooted twice. First there was a movement from Puerto Rican rural towns to the slums in Puerto Rican cities. Unable to secure employment, Puerto Ricans moved out of the slums to New York."

It was these Puerto Ricans, then, who found themselves in the hundreds of thousands in New York. A rural people used to the semitropical sun beating down on their straw hats were suddenly trying to make their way in a freezing northern city.

Many of them were visibly part black in a country where Jackie Robinson had only just recently broken the color line in sports; few spoke English or knew how to negotiate the simplest challenges. They had never seen a subway, an escalator, or a toaster. Then there were the actions of a handful of fanatics in Washington, which had an additional negative impact on the image of Puerto Ricans among the rest of the American population.

We cannot say, thus, that the planets were exactly aligned for a welcoming reception to a city that is unforgiving under the best of circumstances.

"We came here in '52 and moved to 84th Street, between Amsterdam and Columbus, a neighborhood where the Irish were predominant," seventy-eight-year-old Adolfo Carrión, father of the former Bronx borough president and mayoral candidate who bears the same name, said in an interview. "I'll never forget what my brothers told me when I got here: 'Never go out alone. If you go out alone, the Irish will beat you up.' We always had to go out in a group."

For the eighteen-year-old islander from Gurabo, the culture shock was immense: "The buildings were too big and all looked the same. They had small windows, and you couldn't ever see the sun. Everything was always dark. I missed the warm weather and also human warmth, which frankly I didn't find here." Snow was shocking. "This white thing kept falling," he said.

Within a week he was ready to go back to Gurabo, near San

Juan. "My brothers convinced me to stay. I told my brothers, 'No way. This is not for me.' They told me that I would get used to the cold weather."

But it was the constant battling with the Irish of the Upper West Side that seems to be etched in Mr. Carrión's mind. "The Irish wanted to push us out; the Puerto Rican had to dig in. Even Puerto Rican women were harassed when they went outside. I remember well what a friend told me back then: 'It's the Irish who are going to have to leave. Not us. We will stay.'"

Things got better because the Irish did leave, not all and not right away, but enough so that a rough new balance of power was established.

With African-Americans, too, there was friction, mostly over opportunities. "The Puerto Rican was a sandwich people, sandwiched between other people."

There was one New York group Mr. Carrión remembers the Puerto Ricans getting along with: Jews. "We rented from them. I remember very well my Jewish landlord saying to me, 'Don't feel bad about being harassed. Don't take it personally. This happened to us all when we came here. All immigrants have been harassed. It's got nothing to do with you.'"

This was the time, let's not forget, when Puerto Ricans were identified as one of the poorest groups in the United States, with poverty rates the same as or higher than those of African-Americans. It was also the time when Puerto Ricans began to be associated with gang activity. It was the period when Leonard Bernstein decided to give the Romeo and Juliet story a West Side setting. The music to *West Side Story* is splendid and will always be part of my youth, I must admit, but I also can see my uncle Ramón fulminating in our house in Queens in the early 1970s about how this leftist composer, "this Bernstein," had romanticized gangs and thus was contributing to a growing perception problem. Ramón, as usual, was right.

Puerto Ricans became a fixture of New York, as much a part of it as the Jews, the Irish, the Italians, the Episcopalians ensconced in the Upper East Side, and the African-Americans up in Harlem.

But once again, Puerto Ricans had an asterisk. After arriving in New York, few Irish and Italians ever went back to the Emerald Isle or Sicily more than one or two lucky times in their lives. No Jews went back to Poland or Lithuania, ever, with good reason.

All this amounted to a "cultural guillotine" that was often a cause of sadness for the individual but helped the group overall by almost compelling some degree of assimilation, of acceptance that this was your new country to which you slowly transferred allegiance and affection. Puerto Ricans, however, circulated back and forth, and that has an impact. *El vaivén.*

In the 1970s, the number of Puerto Ricans moving back to the island began to exceed the number leaving for the continental United States. Though the net number of immigrants has changed over the decades, this coming and going is an important pattern. More important, many move back and forth several times and maintain residences in both places.

As Puerto Ricans began their circular migration between the island and Manhattan (some refer to both as "the Puerto Rican islands"), they also started to look for other places to live on the mainland. Philadelphia has seen a notable increase over the years, and the reason for that must be that it is only two hours from New York City but much more affordable. Others went to Chicago, where there has been a well-established Puerto Rican community for decades.

Economically, New York started to change in the 1970s; soon the manufacturing base that had employed thousands of Puerto Ricans (and Italians and Jews before them) would be gone. The city's economic base was to be replaced by service sector jobs, and Puerto Ricans faced new competition in the form of Dominicans and Mexicans, who began streaming into New York in the 1980s and of whom there are now close to 600,000 and 305,000, respectively, there. In 1993, Rudy Giuliani may have driven one of the last nails in the coffin by replacing as mayor the hapless David Dinkins, making New York, especially Manhattan, safer and a better place to live, which of course meant much more expensive.

The movement out of New York began in the 1970s, only two

decades after the Great Migration had filled New York's inner city with Puerto Ricans. It is important to note, too, that the Puerto Rican population of New York State has continued to grow, as documented by each decennial census; it's just that it hasn't kept up with the birthrate. Between 2000 and 2010, for example, it grew by only 21,000, from 1.06 million to 1.08 million. As a percentage of the entire Puerto Rican population living on the US mainland, New York State's share plunged from 30 percent to 25 percent during that decade.

As far as the New York metropolitan area is concerned—the five boroughs and northeastern New Jersey—the Puerto Rican population has fallen in terms of actual numbers, from 848,902 in 2000 to 839,405 in 2008, and as a percentage of the Puerto Rican population in the United States from 24 percent to 20 percent.

MICKEY RICANS

Of all the states in the Union, it has been Florida—the land discovered for European eyes five hundred years ago by none other than Puerto Rico's first governor, Juan Ponce de León—that has beckoned the most. Unlike New York, it is not freezing half the time. Its countryside, with its royal palms and lime trees, resembles Puerto Rico's a whole lot more than do the inner-city high-rises of the Northeast.

There was one problem with Florida: for decades its main Hispanic presence has been Cubans, who haven't always seen eye to eye, politically or otherwise, with Puerto Ricans. The biggest Cuban footprint, however, has been in south Florida and, to a lesser extent, in Tampa. Central Florida was more virgin territory in which to establish an identity.

Puerto Ricans thus began to wedge themselves into central Florida, in the towns along Interstate 4, which runs from Tampa, through Orlando, to Daytona Beach. The so-called I-4 corridor is now something every political practitioner knows about, since it has the power to determine statewide electoral outcomes. Sometime in 2012, I started to hear worried voices inside the Romney camp saying that "the I-4 corridor isn't budging." They were right to be concerned. It went for Obama 80–20 on election night.

The size of Florida's Puerto Rican population—what some journalists have started referring to as the Mickey Ricans to draw a contrast with the Nuyoricans and because so many of them were attracted by the opportunities offered by Disney World—is nothing to sneeze at. Back in 1970 only 300 Puerto Ricans were found by the census to be living in Orlando. By 2012, that number had grown a thousandfold to 300,000. South Florida was next, with close to 208,000 Puerto Ricans recorded in 2010, and not far behind was Tampa, the other end of the I-4 corridor, with almost 144,000. In both Orlando and Tampa, Puerto Ricans are now the largest Latino group, and they are second in south Florida, with only the Cubans ahead of them.

The Mickey Ricans are very different in outlook from the Nuyoricans, though as we saw on election night, politically they still tack left more than any other Hispanic group.

To start with, they largely live in suburbs or in the suburban subdivisions for which Florida is so well known. Even if we are not talking about Beverly Hills, they are no longer living on top of each other in New York's inner city.

Many of Florida's Puerto Ricans also come directly from professional and managerial ranks in Puerto Rico, where journalists have begun to take increasing note of the brain drain taking place as the professional exodus to Florida increases. Still, many do work in blue-collar jobs and in the service sector, for example, in Disney World.

Puerto Rican household income in Florida in 2010 was over $41,000, close to the state average of $47,661, compared with $33,400 in New York (a bigger difference when one takes into account that the cost of everything is much lower in Florida). More Puerto Ricans in Florida also identified themselves in the American Community Survey of 2006–2010 as being white, 73.7 percent, than in the rest of the country, where that number is only 53.1 percent. A higher percentage of Florida Puerto Ricans are Protestant, often evangelical.

All this—a higher educational and income status than Puerto Ricans up north and a higher percentage of self-identification as white—would lead one to believe that the Mickey Ricans would vote in higher percentages for the GOP, unlike their New York brethren, who supported Clinton's 1996 reelection at a 93 percent clip, second only to African-Americans.

Only something's gone wrong. Although Jeb Bush was able to capture the state's Puerto Rican vote during both of his gubernatorial races and his brother George W. Bush was competitive in 2000 and 2004, Florida's Puerto Rican vote swung decisively toward the Democrats in 2008 and 2012. In the 2012 election they are estimated to have voted for Obama at an astonishing 80–20 rate.

Puerto Ricans turned out for Obama in such high numbers because of a combination of factors. Florida's Puerto Ricans may indeed be more affluent and educated, but the history recounted in this chapter may very well have made many of them just as leftward-inclined as their blue-collar compatriots.

Puerto Rican stars such as Ricky Martin and Marc Anthony, who headlined fund-raisers for Obama, certainly had an impact, as did Jennifer Lopez, who has made rude comments about Sarah Palin. "We were clobbered in terms of star power," said Oliver-Méndez, who staffed Romney's Hispanic media operation at the Republican National Convention. "Even John McCain did better on that score, and with only a fraction of the budget, when he nabbed Daddy Yankee's endorsement," continued Oliver-Méndez, referring to the Puerto Rican reggaeton star Ramón Luis Ayala Rodríguez.

The Obama campaign was also extremely savvy in microtargeting the Puerto Rican vote in Florida, running highly effective videos praising the president for appointing Puerto Rican Sonia Sotomayor to the US Supreme Court. One ad, featuring a Puerto Rican lawyer named Nydia, said in Spanish of Romney, "He offended me when he stated he would have voted against her nomination . . . and now he wants our vote for president? Mr. Romney, the time has come to pay the bill!"

There was also José La Luz, the man the AFL-CIO tasked with voter mobilization in Florida. La Luz is straight out of central casting: a union leader with heavy leftist sympathies. He began his political career as a member of the Puerto Rican Socialist Party, which was close to Castro's Cuba.

Of course, it says a lot about the labor movement and the Obama campaign that this is the man they brought to work the Puerto Rican vote in Florida, but he was very effective. His modus operandi was to tie Romney to companies that supposedly exploit Puerto Rican labor. In other words, this old socialist pursued the same strategy as the national Obama campaign, just in Spanish and with a Puerto Rican accent.

None of this would have worked, of course, if Puerto Ricans weren't already overly susceptible to grievance mongering. But it is axiomatic of the colonial mind-set that everything gets blamed on the metropolis.

"Puerto Ricans are very open to grievances; it's part of the frustrated national identity," Jorge Bonilla told me. "The president appealed directly to grievance culture in his microtargeting campaign."

But the GOP should bear in mind that Puerto Ricans have shown themselves to have a deep love for this country that reveals itself in military service. Hundreds of thousands of Puerto Ricans have served patriotically in the US Armed Forces, to whom we all owe a debt of gratitude. This level of civic participation in our military institutions doesn't come out of nowhere. We run into these people and their children in all walks of life and everywhere. Douglas MacArthur spoke movingly about them during the Korean War:

> The Puerto Ricans forming the ranks of the gallant 65th Infantry on the battlefields of Korea . . . are writing a brilliant record of achievement in battle and I am proud indeed to have them in this command. I wish that we might have many more like them.

We must also count Representative Raúl Labrador and former Puerto Rico Governor Luis Fortuño, rock-ribbed commonsense conservatives. But Labrador is elected by the people of Idaho, where there are precious few Puerto Ricans, and Fortuño lost his

2012 reelection bid because he had the effrontery to fire 13,000 government workers. We must ask, Why does the Puerto Rican electorate in New York and Chicago elect the likes of Representatives Serrano, Velázquez, and Gutiérrez?

Perhaps the lessons imparted by Professor Tugwell and by Spanish colonial governors before him were learned all too well. But history is not destiny. Straight talk about the real options for moving Puerto Rico out of its territorial halfway house, the likelihood of which is low, at least for the moment, and the perils of welfare dependence to the community that falls prey to it would be beneficial both to Puerto Ricans and to the country they call the mainland.

Chapter 3

THE CUBANS

*We even boast of our afflictions, knowing that affliction produces
endurance, and endurance, proven character, and proven
character, hope.*

—SAINT PAUL'S LETTER TO THE ROMANS

WHEN JOSÉ CALLEJA CAME TO THIS COUNTRY FROM CUBA IN
1960 at the age of twenty-two, he had no money, no job, and
no degree. He had been in his fourth year of medical school
in Havana, but that summer communists took over the University
of Havana and purged professors they didn't like. José was expelled
because he belonged to a Catholic association. With no future in
what was soon to become a totalitarian state under Fidel Castro,
José decided to leave his native land. He went to New York, where
he had family.

"I had no economic means whatsoever," he told me in an interview, "but soon I got lucky and found a job as an orderly at St. Francis Hospital." St. Francis belonged to the Franciscan Sisters of the
Poor, who had opened another hospital, St. Joseph, to treat patients
with tuberculosis across the street on East 109th Street. That was
another stroke of luck.

"After several weeks working the night shift at St. Francis I got
someone to give me a second job at St. Joseph's. So I worked at St.
Joseph's from seven to three, then crossed the street and punched
the clock at St. Francis and worked there from three to eleven," says
José.

His jobs were not very glamorous, to say the least. "At St. Joseph's I collected the sputum of tubercular patients. I would put it

in a metal box and take it to the technicians so they could analyze the level of bacteria. At St. Francis my job was to clean up elderly patients."

José says he didn't mind. "I was obsessive about finishing my career and getting my medical degree." After a couple of years of cleaning up excretion and collecting spit, José was able to put together enough money to go to Spain and finish his fifth year of medical school at the University of Madrid. He returned to the United States and did a medical internship at a psychiatric hospital in Columbus, Georgia, and a residency at the Menninger School of Psychiatry in Topeka, Kansas. In 1970 he opened a private practice in psychiatry in Fort Lauderdale.

Today José, seventy-seven, is retired. "Last year I celebrated our fiftieth anniversary of graduation with all my friends who started medical school with me in Havana in the '50s," he told me on the phone after a workout at the gym he has in his home in Miami. All his children are now adults with careers of their own.

"My daughter did her undergraduate work at Georgetown and got her law degree at GW, my oldest son did undergraduate at Boston College and got his graduate degree at the University of Miami, and my youngest son did his undergraduate at the University of Florida at Gainesville and graduate studies at FIU. My grandchildren—well, they're still in school," José recounts proudly.

THE FOUNDING MYTH

I am telling this story not because it is true, which it is, but because stories like it were once the stock in trade of the Cuban experience in the United States. José's story is like thousands I heard growing up Cuban-American in New York and Florida.

The scene was the same; the elders sat on the sofa and yakked and yakked and yakked some more, recalling the lawyer friend or relative who had to work as a janitor at the courthouse when he first came to Miami and then studied at night to pass the Florida bar exam, or the doctor who had to take a job as a male nurse at Miami Memorial, or the architect who sharpened pencils, and so on. The words wafted over to the younger generation at the other end of the room as they talked with their cousins or watched football or whatever else was on TV. These were stories they'd heard a million times.

For many, the message stuck. Whether life ended up imitating legend or the legend was real, this is a strong component of the Cuban Miami founding myth. The Pilgrims struggled in the Massachusetts wilderness till they had a good harvest; the pioneers struck out for the prairies, braving the elements and the Indians; Cuban-Americans arrived with no money but with professional degrees or just a few years of college, like José, and did whatever they had to do to get back on their feet. Their dignity was not lost by mopping floors (or much worse) but reaffirmed. Their travails and sacrifices were no mark of shame to be hushed but were worn on the sleeves of the guayabera, the white linen rancher shirt Cuban men wear no matter what their social status, especially as they get older.

"I always tell people, when you want something, focus and make all the sacrifices you need to make to accomplish your goals," José told me. "You have to stop doing many things that are easier and more pleasurable. When people tell me, 'I can't pursue my dream; it's too hard,' I tell them, yes you can." It's what I heard over and over: be the first in the office in the morning and the one who turns out the lights.

Has this celebration of work and education helped Cubans succeed in America? You'd have to say that although it didn't apply to all (there are many lazy and uneducated Cuban-Americans even if my mother would deny it in her most unreasonable moments), this general attitude has been a strong component of success. But it was tied to other ingredients.

For starters, unlike any other Hispanics, Cubans who reach US soil are allowed to stay legally, a decision made by the Kennedy administration and codified by Johnson in 1966 under the Cuban Adjustment Act.

But there were many other elements at work. The Cubans who arrived here in the '60s and '70s were largely from the professional classes and more affluent families. They had lost all their financial capital because Castro did not let them take a dime out of Cuba, but Castro could not take away their human capital. Their background helped many do something that has eluded some other Hispanics: build up their human capital and re-create social capital in their communities. Financial capital always follows.

Cuban-Americans' fervent anticommunism made them fervently capitalist, and Castro's ardent anti-Americanism made them ardently pro-American. They were practically cut off from their home island and couldn't send money back to their relatives, but they could use that money to invest here or save for their children's college education. The sharp political differences between Washington and Havana also meant that Cubans experienced the same kind of cultural guillotine that had been the lot of European immigrants before them and that encouraged a level of commitment to this country that Mexicans, Salvadorans, and others simply are not compelled to make.

Making a clean break from their homeland spelled incredible personal hardship for exiles who never saw or hugged family members again. Paradoxically, it also made for a virtuous cycle that helped many of the Cubans who arrived here in the first two decades after Castro achieve a measure of success.

The Cuban community in the United States is changing, however, and like the Puerto Rican migration to Florida, this is a development taking place under the surface but with significant political and social implications. A series of decisions taken by the Clinton and Obama administrations have eroded many of these differences, with negative consequences for Cuban-Americans and the country at large.

In 1994 President Clinton agreed with the Castro government that Cubans on makeshift rafts or boats caught at sea no longer would be allowed into the United States. At the same time, the administration agreed that at least twenty thousand immigrants would be permitted to come from Cuba in an orderly process. It is important to note that advising President Clinton were some pro-rapprochement Cuban-American businessmen who wanted to do business with Cuba. These decisions took the choice on who would come to this country away from the Cuban people and gave it to the Castro government, which would help select who was allowed to leave the island and said it would employ "persuasive methods" to discourage people from leaving by sea.

In fact, the US Interest Section in Havana has outsourced the vetting process for who is to come here to Castro regime officials. "The first level of interviews are done by the Castro employment agency, lowering the political threshold," the Cuban-American activist Mauricio Claver-Carone told me. Cubans coming in through the "orderly" process, regardless of their political views, get to enjoy a system set up for political exiles.

The numbers coming to the United States under this orderly process have risen, creating a continuous migration effect in a community that hadn't experienced emigration in large numbers in years. The Department of Homeland Security reported in September 2008 that in the previous twelve months it had given residency permits to 41,000 Cuban citizens. In 2013 the Cuban government said some 46,000 Cubans had left legally, most coming here. This was the largest exodus out of the island since the 1960s.

Looking at these numbers, the Obama administration saw an opportunity. In 2011, it relaxed restrictions on traveling and remittances to the island, making it easier for the new immigrants with fresh ties to the island to travel back and forth and send money to relatives.

These changes have encouraged the view that Cubans are economic migrants, no different from other Hispanics. This new Cuban migrant (not a political exile) is no longer so axiomatically anticommunist or procapitalist. His remittances mean that less hard-earned cash is invested here but goes to enrich the bank reserves of the Castro regime. The traveling has meant that the cultural guillotine that was in place for my generation has been lifted. The whole evolution also calls into question the preferences conferred by the 1966 Cuban Adjustment Act, which allows Cubans, as refugees from communism, to have legal residency in the United

States. The upshot is that the new Cuban-Americans are less likely to vote Republican, a point we will touch on again later in this chapter.

A SUCCESSFUL GROUP

Until these changes were made, the Cuban-American success formula had produced results. Miami is flush with Cuban businesses; there were more than 120,000 Cuban-American firms with paid employees in 2007, according to the Miami-Dade County Department of Planning and Zoning. There were also well-known national business giants. One is Carlos Gutierrez, CEO of Kellogg's before joining the cabinet of George W. Bush. Even more prominent was Coca-Cola's late CEO Roberto Goizueta, legendary for the thirty-six-fold increase in shareholder value during his tenure at the helm of Coke.

In politics Cuban-Americans are also well represented—too well, according to critics. Though they are now numerically the fourth largest Hispanic group in the country after Mexican-Americans, Puerto Ricans, and Salvadoran-Americans; they account for only 1.78 million people; and they total just 3.5 percent of all Hispanic Americans and a tiny 0.05 percent of the US population, there are three Cuban-Americans in the US Senate, a chamber of only a hundred people. The three Cuban-American senators—Marco Rubio, Republican of Florida; Ted Cruz, Republican of Texas; and Bob Menendez, Democrat of New Jersey—are moreover the only Hispanic members of the US Senate.

Cuban-Americans also had better cultural indicators than most of the other Hispanic groups. The following data come largely from the Pew Hispanic Center, which does wonderful work on data collection.

Cuban-Americans have a higher educational attainment than do the other groups. One of four Cuban-Americans has at least a four-year college degree, double the rate for Hispanics in general (a figure already inflated because it includes Cubans) and only 5 percentage points lower than the rate for non-Hispanic whites. But among Cuban-Americans born in the United States, the figure goes all the way up to 39 percent, higher than the 33 percent of non-Hispanic whites.

The median household income is $38,000, just above that of Hispanics and well below that of non-Hispanic whites, which is $48,000. But again, native-born Cuban-Americans top that, with a median household income of $50,000. The poverty rate is also half that of Hispanics in general: 13 percent of Cuban-Americans fall under what the government considers to be the poverty line compared with 27 percent of Hispanics and 10 percent of non-Hispanic whites.

According to one of the most wide-ranging studies comparing generations, conducted in the 1990s by the demographer Donald Hernandez, "Cuban children in native-born families are actually less likely than white children in native-born families to receive AFDC, other welfare, housing assistance, heating assistance, and WIC benefits."

Cuban-Americans are far more politically conservative than the other Hispanic groups and are very politically engaged. The 2006 National Survey of Latinos found that 28 percent of Cubans considered themselves Republican, compared with 15 percent for Mexican-Americans and 11 percent for Puerto Ricans. Only one-fourth of Cuban-Americans told the survey that they were Democrats compared with 29 percent and 50 percent for Mexican-Americans and Puerto Ricans, respectively.

Much was made of reports that Barack Obama had edged out Mitt Romney in 2012 for the Cuban vote, 49 percent to 47 percent. That 47 percent for the GOP standard-bearer would of course be much higher than the 29 percent support Hispanics in general gave Romney, but even these results may have been skewed.

Those numbers came from the Democratic pollster Bendixen & Amandi International. A separate scientific analysis of Cuban-American votes in Florida's Dade County, the home of Little Havana, conducted by Dario Moreno and Kevin Hill for the Cuba

Democracy Public Advocacy Corp., found that Romney won 58 percent of the Cuban-American vote to Obama's 42 percent, or about the same as the 59 percent of the non-Cuban white vote Romney received around the country.

Racially, Cuban-Americans consider themselves another white European group to a much higher degree than do other Hispanics. More than 85 percent of Cuban-Americans ticked the box for white in the 2010 Census, compared with 53 percent of both Puerto Ricans and Mexican-Americans. The numbers were even lower for Central Americans.

Anthropologists interpret these self-identifications as a good proxy for feelings of inclusiveness and belonging. The more you feel yourself to be a part of this country, the more likely you are to see yourself as white. Cubans have a very high level of marriage with non-Hispanic whites at 50 percent in the second generation, whereas only 32 percent marry other Cubans.

In 2006, the Pew Hispanic Center's National Survey of Latinos asked Hispanics whether they considered the United States, as opposed to their countries of origin, their real country. A total of 52 percent of Cuban-Americans said yes, compared with 36 percent of Mexican-Americans, 35 percent of Central Americans, and 33 percent of Puerto Ricans. This is ironic, for as Pew pointed out, Puerto Ricans are "U.S. citizens by birth." Cubans also become US citizens at a higher rate: 60 percent versus the Latino average of 26 percent and 56 percent for white immigrants from Europe.

A smaller percentage of Cubans than of other Hispanics also told Pew that they saw discrimination as a major problem in this country. For Cuban-Americans the rate was only 45 percent compared with 58 percent for Mexican-Americans and 59 percent for Puerto Ricans.

On foreign policy, Cubans offer another stark contrast to other Hispanics. The anticommunism of the older wave has meant many Cuban-Americans are more supportive of the United States playing a strong, activist role overseas compared with other Hispanic groups; Cuban-Americans unabashedly see the United States as a force for good in the world, a theme often repeated by Cuban-

American politicians such as Senator Marco Rubio and Representative Ileana Ros-Lehtinen.

There are paradoxes. Cuban-Americans, for example, buck the conventional wisdom that using English breeds success and is a sign of patriotism. A whopping 69 percent of Cuban-Americans under age eighteen said in the Pew survey that they speak Spanish at home, slightly higher than the rate for other Hispanic groups, which averaged 67 percent. When it comes to the over-eighteen population, however, 89 percent speak Spanish at home, considerably higher than the Hispanic average of 80 percent. Even native-born Cuban-Americans speak Spanish at home at a relatively high rate of 64 percent.

Perhaps my own experience as a boy in Jackson Heights, Queens, can shed some light. We children—my three cousins, my sister, and I—were not allowed to speak English inside the home. We were also corrected when we made grammatical errors, admonitions that grew in severity if the mistake was to use Spanglish. In a sea of English outside, our elders explained, our ability to speak proper Spanish would deteriorate unless we took these measures.

We may have been the only family in Jackson Heights, perhaps in all of New York City, that regularly listened to country and western music in the early 1970s. My uncle Ramon also constantly extolled the virtues of wearing cowboy boots. Toward the end of his life he couldn't stop telling me how proud he was that I was working for the Heritage Foundation, of which he had been a member for years.

All this Ramon did in Spanish. I don't recall ever having a conversation with him in English when others weren't present. To tell the truth, I never saw a contradiction.

Religion offers another paradox: Cubans may be more politically conservative than other Hispanics, but a smaller percentage, 58 percent, say that religion is very important in their lives, compared with 68 percent of Mexican-Americans and 65 percent of Puerto Ricans. The latter two groups back up their religious avocation by regularly attending church once a week at a 45 percent rate for Mexicans and 42 percent for Puerto Ricans, compared with 39 percent for Cuban-Americans. (Self-reported weekly church partic-ipation for Americans is 41 percent, compared with 15 percent in France and 11 percent in the United Kingdom, so all Americans, Hispanic or not, go to church far more often than do our cousins across the Pond.)

On social issues, Cubans oppose gay marriage at a higher rate than do other Hispanics, with 63 percent being against it, com-pared with 56 percent and 48 percent, respectively, for Mexican-Americans and Puerto Ricans. When it comes to abortion, however, Cubans are far more liberal—only 45 percent think it should be illegal, compared with 58 percent and 50 percent for Mexican-Americans and Puerto Ricans, respectively.

On some economic issues, Cuban-Americans are closer to His-panics' views than to those of the country in general. Over half of the respondents, 54 percent, told Pew that they would prefer to pay higher taxes to get more government services, compared with 58 percent of Puerto Ricans and 65 percent of Mexican-Americans.

Lastly, Cuban-Americans are far more geographically concen-trated than both Mexicans and Puerto Ricans. They like to ghet-toize, even if their southern Florida suburban ghettos are nicer than the South Bronx or East LA.

The picture that emerges, then, is of an ethnic group that fifty-plus years after it began arriving here has met with a measure of success, votes conservative, and is on its way to assimilation. This relative success also may have been a function of familiarity with the American system, which was bred by proximity and history, in this case intertwined. Anything that smacks of intrusive govern-ment or the indoctrination of children raises the hair on their backs and will send them to the voting booth in droves.

A CHANGING COMMUNITY?

But there might be bad news for conservatives on the horizon, as I alluded to earlier: the Cuban-American community may indeed be changing. Pundits who write about such an evolution usually attribute it to generational change, with younger Cuban-Americans becoming more liberal. The indications are that what is really happening is a result of the less anticommunist Cubans who are immigrating.

Cubans, like the other groups we've looked at, are best understood by examining the different waves that have come and the different geographic locations where they live. Cuban-Americans who live in New Jersey or Tampa, the two areas of highest concentration after Miami, have always been slightly more liberal than the Miami Cubans, for example.

With regard to immigration waves, there have been roughly three main ones.

The first immigrants were the people who left in the first two decades after Castro's takeover. They initially included people in the upper echelons of society and business, some of whom had worked for the dictator Fulgencio Batista (not the same thing, as the many, many people of working-class background who were supporters of Batista), the professional and managerial classes, and members of all classes, including farmers, who disagreed with communism.

The second wave included some 125,000 whom the government let escape in a chaotic seven-month boat lift from the western Cuba port of Mariel in 1980. Castro used the occasion to empty his prisons and mental health hospitals to poison the streets of Miami. The mayhem, along with the Iranian hostage crisis, drove home to American voters that Jimmy Carter had lost control of foreign policy. President Reagan sent the criminals and mental patients back to Cuba, but a stigma remained attached to the honest majority of exiles who escaped in the boat lift, the so-called Marielitos. This was very unfair; many children of Marielitos are now in Ivy League schools.

The third wave consists of those who have come since 1994 through the "orderly process" described above. It is these last Cubans who are moving the Cuban-American vote somewhat leftward. They support lifting the US embargo on Cuba at a much faster rate than the previous waves, see themselves as Americans at a much lower rate—only 18 percent are US citizens compared with 90 percent of those who came to the United States before 1980—and travel back and forth to Cuba at a much higher rate.

These new Cubans chafe under the ascendancy of the old Miami guard, whom they no longer recognize as even Cuban. After half a century of communism, they look at the work ethic of the preceding generation of exiles as something alien.

Most important, the new Cubans travel back and forth to the island constantly, making use of the changes put in by President Obama and flouting the old exile convention that—barring once-in-a-lifetime exceptions to say good-bye to a dying parent—one could go back to a nonfree Cuba only with a gun in one's hand.

"The people today don't come out of principles but only for economic reasons," scoffs José Calleja. "As soon as they put some money together, they go back to visit. Their attitude here is different, too. They don't come here to win."

Barack Obama noticed this. People thought he was touching the third rail of Florida politics when he eased restrictions on travel and remittances, but President Obama was as usual taking a long-term view of things. He realized that if you move the Cuban-American community to the left, you get Florida for keeps.

Someone else who has noticed is Florida Senator Marco Rubio, who is sounding the alarm. In March 2013, Rubio told a crowd in Miami that he believes the Cuban government is intentionally picking immigrants with no ideological animus toward the Castro regime or perhaps even sympathy for it, Cubans who will go back and forth and spend the money they earn here in Cuba. "This is designed to work this way," Rubio told the Cuba Democracy PAC. "They are deliberately allowing certain people to leave because they know they will come back with that money, because they know they will send money back. This is a policy aim of the Castro regime. This is not by accident, this is by design."

Rubio then zeroed in on the main problem with this new outlook. "I also know that there are people who come here and six months after they arrive, a year and a half after they arrive, they're going back to Cuba eighteen times a year and I'm telling you that's a problem, because people all over the country are turning to us and saying, well why do you have the Cuban Adjustment Act? But beyond that issue, let me tell you what we have here, the massive amounts of dollars that are going into the hands not of the Cuban people but of the Cuban government."

A related question is whether the Obama administration designed the changes to work this way. Realizing that the new Cubans being let in by the Clinton changes were less ideologically anticommunist than the earlier wave, President Obama lifted the cultural guillotine and encouraged more visits and remittances to the island. This also helps with the rapprochement with the communist government in Havana that Democratic policy makers have hankered for.

Whether by design or not, the result is that the Cubans who come today look more like immigrants from other parts of Latin America. Though eighteen times a year is probably more than a slight exaggeration, the fact that a portion of the Cuban-American population would travel back and forth between the United States and their Caribbean island would make the community resemble more the *vaivén* of Puerto Ricans than a group of dignified refuseniks. This is threatening to conservative-voting Cubans on several grounds, not least to their self-image as a group of political exiles rather than economic immigrants. As we will see in Chapter 11, cultural indicators have gotten much worse for Cuban-Americans over the last twenty years, catastrophically so in the case of the illegitimacy rate.

Cuban-Americans still voted for the Republican candidate in high numbers, but we shouldn't lose sight of the important fact that among Cuban-Americans in 2012 Obama improved on his 2008 performance by 6 percentage points. In other words, Cuban-Americans may have been the only group in which Obama—reelected with the thinnest support of any president since World War II—saw his numbers improve.

The fact that the president was able to slice and dice another Hispanic group is not remarkable. Barack Obama and his campaign have, to their credit, understood from the beginning not just that

Hispanics are not one group but that Cubans, Mexicans, and Puerto Ricans need to be subdivided further. They have been able, masterfully, to divide the Cuban-American community as they have the rest of the nation. One thing to bear in mind is that the new Cuban immigrants have a lower voting rate than do earlier Cubans. It is partly a function of the fact that they naturalize at a lower rate, but it may be something else, too. "They lack conviction," Claver-Carone told me. "Conviction is everything in politics."

It should still be a matter of concern for conservatives that this once reliably conservative group, which believed like José Calleja in a strong work ethic, a strong nation, and allegiance to country, could be molded to be another constituency for the welfare state.

But it's not just new immigrant waves with different outlooks that threaten Cubans' success in this country. As Charles Murray and others have demonstrated, the dividing line in our society is not racial or even ethnic; it's between socioeconomic classes. An educated new upper class intermarries (within its education level, not racially per se) and then strives to keep the family intact. These people work with their children at night when they're doing their homework and whenever possible provide additional tutors; they drive them to play dates and coach their soccer and baseball teams; they're involved in the PTA. In other words, this class manages to maintain and add to what Stuart Butler calls the human capital and social capital that are so necessary for success, whereas government intervention has led to their erosion among those whom the government intended to help.

Cuban-Americans new and old have to figure out how to keep themselves on the right side of our new socioeconomic divide. Republicans cannot take them for granted but must continue to send the right message to them.

Chapter 4

CENTRAL AMERICANS AND DOMINICANS

"I am Maya, not Guatemalan, nor Hispanic."

—Florida immigrant quoted in a research paper
by Berlin's Free University

T HE THREE GROUPS THAT HAVE BEEN DESCRIBED SO FAR—
Mexicans, Puerto Ricans, and Cubans—amount to almost 80
percent of the Hispanics in this country and an even higher
proportion of Hispanics' political and market clout. But the picture is not quite complete. Though we can't devote a chapter to
each nationality, as that would produce a tome of upward of twenty
chapters, we can't conclude an introduction to Hispanics without mentioning Central Americans and Dominicans, two groups
whose numbers have increased in the last three decades. With these
additions we will have covered about 95 percent of the Hispanic
population.

CENTRAL AMERICANS

Three nationalities account for the lion's share of the almost 4 million Central Americans in this country: Salvadorans, Guatemalans,
and Hondurans, in order of numerical importance. Together they
are estimated to be between 2.4 million and 3 million strong in this
country and would be the third largest group of Hispanics if they
were counted as one group.

These three countries are known as Central America's Northern
Triangle, a subregion that is a byword for poverty, drug trafficking,

and violence within Latin America. They supply by far the highest number of US immigrants south of Mexico, legal or illegal—in the case of Guatemala and Honduras mostly illegal. Even though the Northern Triangle's entire population amounts to only 27 million, there are more illegal immigrants from these three countries in the United States than immigrants from both India and China, which together have more than 2.5 billion people, or one-third of the world total. This gives new meaning to the real estate mantra of location, location, location.

Salvadorans, Guatemalans, and Hondurans started coming to this country in great numbers in the 1980s, when the region was torn apart by civil wars that became part of the larger global struggle between freedom and communism. They continue to come today because their countries are now ravaged by drug violence; their impoverished governments simply lack the resources to deal with well-financed drug mafias. Congressional sources briefed by the State Department told me as 2013 drew to a close that illegal immigration to the United States from Central America was up 100 percent that year.

Statistics alone cannot describe how dangerous the Northern Triangle countries are. To travel there is to be constantly surrounded by men with semiautomatic weapons lest you be robbed, kidnapped, or murdered. But statistics tell a frightening story, too.

The US homicide rate, 4.8 per 100,000 inhabitants, is considered high for a Western society; in Britain and France, the rate hovers around 1.0, for example. According to the United Nations, the rates for the Northern Triangle are the following: in Guatemala it is 39, in El Salvador it is 69, and *in Honduras it is 92*—the last two being the two worst rates in a world that also includes Somalia, Iraq, and Haiti.

The reason for bringing this up is that these very high murder rates are related to drug trafficking and gang-related violence, phenomena that push Central Americans to undertake a dangerous trek north to the United States–Mexico border. The violence has also engulfed many US cities with high concentrations of Central Americans.

Some of the gang activity first originated here and then was taken to El Salvador. One of the most ruthless gangs, the Mara Salvatrucha, or MS-13, is said to have been created in the early 1980s to protect Salvadoran immigrants in Los Angeles's impoverished Pico-Union district, where first-generation immigrants from Central America and Mexico live in an uneasy truce. From there, the MS-13 migrated to El Salvador, which was then teeming with weapons from the civil war. MS-13 is now a multinational organization, with tentacles in over forty states, including the leafy suburbs of Washington, DC.

"We decided to round up all these gang members and deport them back to their countries, so what we did was dump in El Salvador, Honduras, and Guatemala all these guys who knew about gang warfare. They were all tatted up," an FBI agent who's dealing with the problem told me. Our government is now working directly with the Salvadoran government to address the problem in both places.

The MS-13's cruelty—they have hacked victims to death with machetes—surprised even rival Mexican-American and African-American gangs. The MS-13 also has something close to an operating navy, which runs around our Coast Guard to land on California beaches as it conducts its operations in drug and human trafficking. The federal government no longer sees it as just a gang but has reclassified it as a "transnational criminal organization."

None of this is to say that Central Americans in this country, legal or illegal, should be suspected of gang-related activity. We shouldn't repeat today the mistakes that were made with previous generations of Italian-Americans, many of whom bravely opposed the Mafia in their communities. Some of the fairest, most honest people I have ever had the pleasure of dealing with are hardworking Central Americans trying to make a go of it in this country.

They come because they hate the violence. As bad as the gang activity may be getting in US cities, it is still preferable to the turmoil and the poverty over there. Thus, Central Americans keep hopping trains, getting on buses, and walking through the jungles of their countries and then Mexico to make their way to the Rio Grande.

The latest trend is that children are making this arduous and dangerous trip alone, braving gangs, the elements, and corrupt police and risking being robbed, raped, and murdered. As of January 31, 2013, there were 2,179 children from Guatemala, Honduras, and El Salvador in the care of the Office of Refugee Resettlement, which is part of the Department of Health and Human Services (HHS). According to ORR, this entitles them to certain services: classroom education, mental and medical health services, case management, socialization and recreation, access to religious and legal services, and family reunification services.

The Central Americans who make it to our border, cross it illegally, and evade the ORR quickly disappear into their communities. The trip is so arduous that once they are in, they don't go back to their home countries until they are ready to move back for good, something many do when they decide that they have made enough money.

But though they don't travel back and forth, they keep in contact with their home countries by constantly sending money back to their relatives—lots of money. The average Salvadoran sends home $340 a month, Guatemalans send $363, and Hondurans send $225.

The remittances they send are among those countries' biggest sources of foreign reserves, overshadowing foreign direct investment and overseas development assistance. It is a testament to the love they feel for the less fortunate family members they left behind that Central Americans send them a large proportion of the meager wages earned through backbreaking labor in our lawns and construction sites. But family values notwithstanding, these remittances have become a problem both here and there.

Here in the United States the remittances prevent capital formation in immigrant communities, delaying or even blocking a path to the middle class. It is very difficult to save for your daughter's college education or pay for a math tutor for your son if you're sending 10 percent of your earnings to your mother in Tegucigalpa.

But if remittances cause a problem here, in Honduras, El Salvador, and Guatemala they may be creating real long-term havoc. Yes, no doubt remittances solve day-to-day problems for a very impoverished people, but they also disincentivize work and investment.

"Some NGOs have decided that they flat out can't work in areas with high remittances flows because people don't want to do anything productive. People don't want to do anything except receive remittances," the Bread for the World Institute in 2012 quoted Erica Dahl-Bredine of Catholic Relief Services as saying.

Critics charge that the government and elites in Central America also have come to depend on immigrants and their remittances.

"As coffee, cotton and sugar prices have declined, traditional exports have shrunk. Increasingly, El Salvador's most important export is people, primarily to the United States. Remittances are now a critical source of national income and make up over half of all export earnings and more than 16 percent of GDP. Household survey data reveal that more than 40 percent of households in rural areas and 20 percent in urban areas have at least one family member overseas," wrote economist Sarah Gammage in a 2005 paper.

The lack of investment and destruction of social and human capital caused by remittances in turn creates more poverty. This in turn leads to renewed immigration to the United States. It helps account for the fact that 20 percent of Salvadorans and 6 percent of both Guatemalans and Hondurans live in the United States.

Most of them came here illegally. Almost half of Salvadorans, 60 percent of Guatemalans, and almost 70 percent of Hondurans in the United States are here illegally. After Mexico, the three countries were, respectively, the second, third, and fourth largest sources of illegal immigrants in the United States. The more than 1.5 million illegals from the Northern Triangle amounted to just under 15 percent of the illegal population. The United States rounded up and deported some 300,000 between 2008 and 2011, according to Bread for the World, but at least half of them intend to turn around and come right back.

Central Americans can be incredibly industrious, though they are still largely relegated to lower-end jobs in the construction and landscape industries. Those workers building your deck? Many people incorrectly assume they're Mexican. But if you engage them in a conversation when you bring them coffee or a Coke, you probably will find out that they're from Honduras or Guatemala. A persistent problem is that the burden of remittances prevents their strong work ethic from translating into generational success. Rather than setting a tradition of university educational achievement right now, with the second generation, Central Americans' urge to send money to their extended families back home may be postponing for many the educational leap immigrant groups must make to become upwardly mobile. It also postpones the feeling that their home is now here.

Negative phenomena such as illegal status, pervasive violence in the home countries, and deep poverty may have contributed to a positive outcome: because families are not constantly going back to their home countries, second-generation Central Americans assimilate fast. "I'm not going to take my children home if I can't come back," a Salvadoran father who is here illegally told me. This may explain why they marry out at a very high rate—tying the knot with non-Hispanic whites at a 20 percent rate in the immigrant generation, a rate that goes up to 42 percent in the second generation.

Salvadorans

Salvadorans are by far the largest group among the three. All by themselves, the 1.95 million Salvadorans residing in the United States accounted for 3.8 percent of the Hispanic population in 2011, the year in which they edged out Cubans as the third largest Hispanic group in terms of numbers.

Salvadorans are less likely to be here illegally than are immigrants of the other two groups from the Northern Triangle. Since 2001 Salvadorans have been able to receive Temporary Protected Status, which allows people from countries where conditions prevent a safe return to stay in the United States legally. Back home about 40 percent of Salvadorans live under the poverty line even though their country is the richest in the Northern Triangle, with a gross domestic product per capita of around $3,200. Salvadoran-

Americans are big contributors to that GDP, sending $2.5 billion annually in remittances, the country's main source of income.

Cuban-Americans provide a good context in which to describe Salvadorans, as the two groups are almost mirror images of each other in many categories. To start with the obvious, whereas Cubans fled communist dictatorship and tend to be conservative, many if not most Salvadorans who came in the 1980s fled a US-backed government fighting a Soviet-backed guerrilla war, and many tend to hold leftist views.

We saw shades of this in an infamous case that took place in the summer of 2012 in the village of Freeport, Long Island. Nassau County is home to 47,000 residents of Salvadoran origin, and as the county prepared to observe Salvadoran-American Day, August 8, local officials invited the country's vice president, Salvador Sánchez Cerén, to take part in a public ceremony in which he would be declared "Salvadoran-American of the Year." Many local officials were there, including US Representative Peter King, a staunch conservative, then chairman of the House of Representatives Homeland Security Committee.

But Sánchez Cerén is a leftist extremist with connections to gangs and drug traffickers, who also has a horrible past. Here's how Mary O'Grady at the *Wall Street Journal* put it:

> In the aftermath of the [9/11] horror, messages of sympathy poured in from democracies around the world. But there were a few exceptions. One occurred days after the crisis when El Salvador's far-left Farabundo Martí National Liberation Front (FMLN) political party turned a street rally in San Salvador into a celebration of the carnage. The leader of those festivities, which included burning the American flag, was a former Soviet-backed guerrilla commander by the name of Salvador Sánchez Cerén.

The Salvadoran-American politicians who put Sánchez Cerén's name forward feigned not knowing about his past. But how could they not have? In the 1980s the man led the FMLN, one of the most pro-Soviet, cruelest guerrilla movements in the history of Latin America. In March 2014, Sánchez Cerén became president in a hotly contested election he won with 50.1 percent of the vote and will probably be the most anti-American president in Salvadoran history.

This mishap in Long Island is only the tip of the iceberg when it comes to the interplay between politics here and politics there. Because such large percentages of Central Americans now live in the United States—remember, for Salvadorans it is one of every five— whatever happens here matters there.

President Obama certainly played an important role in letting Salvadorans both here and there know that he had no problems with them electing Marxist former guerrillas of the FMLN to the government. Like Sinn Fein in Northern Ireland, the violent guerrilla killers have become a political party, a change that came as a result of the end of the country's civil war in 1992.

Before Obama's intervention, the conservative party ARENA had successfully campaigned on the message that electing the FMLN—which is linked to drug trafficking and other criminal activities—might threaten both remittances and the Temporary Protected Status. President Obama's sudden choice of San Salvador on his 2011 trip to Latin America sent a strong signal of support.

Salvadoran-Americans are also known as militant union members here, playing a key role in the 1992 LA janitors' strike, in campaigns against passage of the Central American Free Trade Agreement, and in the 2006 and 2007 marches in several US cities demanding amnesty for illegal immigrants.

It's hard to understand how this helps Salvadoran-Americans with their assimilation process in this country. Much as the MS-13 has become not so much a local LA gang as a transnational crime organization and money that could be spent here is remitted to El Salvador, the leftist Salvadoran movement is some sort of transnational political machine that knows how to pull the right levers in Washington to get the desired results in San Salvador—at the expense of a commitment to this country's future. This form of "transnational organizing," which takes neighborhood organizing across borders, is cheered by the Left as the wave of the future. Not much was heard from the State Department on President Funes's extension of voting rights to Salvadorans here, however.

This does not mean that all Salvadoran-Americans are communist sympathizers. Most in fact appear to want to leave the past behind in the war fields of Central America, at least in everyday conversations. Many Salvadoran-Americans in the Protestant evangelical community, a growing slice, tend to hold conservative views. The younger generation especially has moved on. But the contrast with the very conservative Cuban-American community couldn't be starker.

The 2009 vote in El Salvador shows yet another area where Salvadoran-Americans and Cuban-Americans are the obverse of each other. The campaign showed that although Salvadorans have little say in politics here, they do flex their muscles back home. The weight of the remittances alone makes them a player. Cuban-Americans may influence American policy on Cuba but have no say whatsoever about what Fidel Castro and his brother Raúl do.

Whereas Cubans undoubtedly punch above their numerical weight, Salvadoran-Americans punch well below it. Though Salvadoran-Americans have just surpassed Cuban-Americans in numbers, there are no Salvadoran-Americans in the US House of Representatives, let alone the Senate. This is no doubt partly a result of the relative lack of engagement Salvadoran-Americans have with their new country, as they keep their focus on El Salvador.

Salvadorans have succeeded in politics at more local levels. For example, Walter Tejada is chairman of the Arlington County Board in Virginia and Ana Sol Gutierrez is a member of the Maryland House of Delegates from the leafy areas of Chevy Chase and Kensington; both are Democrats. The Washington, DC, area in fact is the only part of the country where Salvadorans form the majority of Latinos.

But even these elected Salvadoran-Americans sometimes let slip their ambivalence about their nationality. Gutierrez, for example, told NPR's Kojo Namdi in a 2007 interview, "Our country, unfortunately, is extremely poor." She didn't mean the United

States. As with other Americans who originate from Central America, Salvadoran-Americans who are influenced by liberal activists will vote for the Left, whereas the great middle will vote on the economy.

Guatemalans

Guatemala sometimes is referred to as the cultural capital of Central America, and certainly it is there that Indian languages and traditions thrive more than anywhere in all of Latin America outside the Andes Mountains and the Amazon Basin. There are some twenty-three different groups, all with their own distinct languages, though a majority are Mayan in origin, in Guatemala (and therefore in Guatemalan communities in the United States), alongside a minority that is descended from the Spaniards.

This gives the country its colorful and varied history. More than its neighbors, where the overwhelming majority is mestizo, or a mixture of Indian and European, with few who are full-blooded at either end, Guatemala is truly a diverse society.

Partly as a result of the strong indigenous communities, Protestants make up a higher percentage among Guatemalan-Americans than among any other Latino group in this country, a consequence of the success evangelical missionaries have had there. About a third of Guatemala is now Protestant, the highest proportion in any Latin country in the Americas or Europe. Guatemalans therefore have made an important contribution to the rise of Hispanic Protestants in the United States, an important movement with political implications because they tend to be more conservative than their Roman Catholic counterparts.

Also related to its ethnic makeup (though which way the causality cuts is unclear), Guatemala is extremely poor. The GDP per capita of over $3,000 is one of the lowest in Latin America. In the United States, about a quarter of Guatemalans live below the poverty line, compared with only about 10 percent of Americans of all backgrounds.

There are 1.04 million Guatemalan residents of this country, not all of whom can rightly be called Guatemalan-American as many are not citizens; in fact, 60 percent are here illegally. The majority live in Los Angeles (California has about a third of all Guatemalans in the United States), New York, and Houston. If you look at communities where Guatemalans form a large percentage of the population, however, you get odd findings such as Marydel, Maryland, and Brewster, New York.

According to Pew, 70 percent of Guatemalans in this country are foreign-born, which is higher than the already high Hispanic level of 40 percent. They also include a higher proportion of high school dropouts, more than 53 percent compared with under 40 percent for Hispanics and 15 percent for the United States as a whole. Not surprisingly, only 40 percent of Guatemalans report that they speak English proficiently; this means that 60 percent depend on the likes of Univisión for their take on what's happening in this country.

Only 35 percent of Guatemalans own their homes, compared with about half of all Hispanics and two-thirds of all Americans.

Hondurans

Honduran-Americans are the poorest of the three Central American nationalities from the Northern Triangle. They speak English less well than the average Hispanic (63 percent report to Pew that they speak English less than well, compared with 39 percent of all Hispanics). Consequently, median income is lower on average than for all Hispanics. They're also less educated. About 75 percent of Honduran immigrants in this country have only a high school education or less. About 7 percent have a four-year college degree.

The twenty-first century saw a surge in people from Honduras. This means that Hondurans are relatively new in this country: more than 70 percent are foreign-born. Indeed, the US resident population almost tripled between the 2000 and 2010 censuses, going from 217,569 to 633,401, accounting for the largest percentage increase in the immigrant population. The number of illegal immigrants from Honduras rose by 95 percent in that decade, the highest percentage increase of any country, according to the Department of Homeland Security.

Context is everything. The 320,000 Hondurans estimated to be illegal in this country account for more than 50 percent of the Hondurans here but are a tiny group compared with the 6,650,000 Mexicans thought to be here illegally. However, they send home a lot of money. Remittances account for almost 20 percent of Honduras's GDP, according to the World Bank, the highest percentage among the Northern Triangle countries.

Lastly, as a nation with a long Caribbean coast, Honduras has a higher percentage of people of African descent than do its neighbors. Along these lines, immigration from Honduras has brought to the United States one of the rarest ethnic groups and languages on earth, the Garifuna.

Descendants mostly of African slaves who mixed with Indian tribes in the Caribbean, the Garifuna speak a language that has different words for women and men; the women use Arawak loan words, and the men use loan words derived from Carib. This may be a living vestige of the fact that before Columbus, Caribs from South America used to raid the West Indies, kill the Arawak men, and take their women as their enslaved wives. Garifuna is now spoken in the streets of New York and Los Angeles.

DOMINICANS

Some people will argue that Dominicans should not be in a chapter with Central Americans, so different is one from the other. But perhaps it is fitting to have Dominicans in the same chapter with Central Americans in a book that tries to make the point that Hispanics are not one group, for there's no better way to show how different Hispanic groups are from one another than to juxtapose the mostly African-American Dominicans with the mostly Indian-American Central Americans.

Dominicans share some traits with Central Americans, such as having Spanish surnames and speaking versions of what once used to be a common language (a Salvadoran and a Dominican can understand each other in a conversation, but they will have to make some effort to get past wildly different accents and terminology).

Both groups are late arrivals to the United States compared with the more established Mexicans, Puerto Ricans, and Cubans. Although there are records of Dominicans arriving in New York as early as the 1600s and definitely in the 1930s, half of the Dominicans who live in the United States today arrived after 1990. According to the Census Bureau, there were 1.53 million Dominicans in the United States in 2010, almost double the number in 2000, making them the fifth largest Latino group.

Dominicans also resemble Central Americans in their habit of sending high levels of remittances back home. The Inter-American Development Bank says that in 2011 Dominican residents of the United States sent home as much as $3.1 billion, almost 8 percent more than the previous year. Remittances accounted for about 10 percent of GDP and about 37 percent of the money the country earned through exports.

Lastly, many Dominicans in this country are here illegally, just as with Central Americans. Though the number is unknown, it has been estimated to be in the hundreds of thousands.

In just about everything else, however, Dominican residents of this country are very different from Central Americans. They are Northeastern urbanites, about 90 percent of the ones in this country are of African ancestry, and unlike the soccer-loving Central Americans, Dominicans are great with a baseball bat in their hands.

In this country, Dominicans are highly concentrated in the Northeast, especially in New York and especially in that city's Washington Heights neighborhood. About 675,000 live in New York, with another 200,000 in nearby New Jersey and a further 100,000 in Massachusetts. In Rhode Island they are the largest Hispanic group.

In New York especially, they are seen as filling in the labor gap created by Puerto Ricans leaving for Florida. In fact, a strong rivalry between the two groups has arisen both at low-level jobs such as running bodegas and at the higher end such as enrollment at Columbia University and New York University.

Dominicans can also have an ambiguous relationship with African-Americans. Because many Dominicans are black, they often are identified as African-American, but Dominicans find ways to make the distinction clear. "The many second-generation Dominicans who are phenotypically indistinguishable from African-Americans, for example, 'speak Spanish' in order to counter others' assumptions that they are African-American," wrote the anthropologist Benjamin Bailey.

Dominicans have made their mark in baseball. Alex Rodriguez, the sport's highest paid player, was born in New York of Dominican parents, and his former teammate on the New York Yankees Robinson Canó and the power hitter of their rivals the Boston Red Sox, "Big Papi" David Ortiz, were both born in the DR, as were countless other players.

Many Dominicans bristle when their contributions to this country are limited to grown men who are able to hit curve balls. Baseball lover though I am, I do see such a refusal to be typecast as athletes as a healthy sign that the community is striving to improve itself.

And improvement the Dominicans have very much achieved, taking the best and most assured path out of poverty: education. Second-generation Dominicans have done relatively well, with 21 percent attaining a college degree, a higher success rate than that of Mexican-Americans and Puerto Ricans.

Dominicans are just as quick to point out writers like Junot Diaz and Julia Alvarez and the world-famous fashion designer Oscar de la Renta as they are to speak of baseball greats Albert Pujols and Pedro Martínez as examples of their contribution to our society.

Dominicans resemble Cubans in many ways except that they are liberal and vote Democratic. Polls put their support for Barack Obama in the 90th percentile in the 2012 election, which definitely is not Cuban-like. But like Cuban-Americans they are true baseball connoisseurs, fiercely political (a trait they bring over from their politicized island home), and aggressively determined to get ahead. Angelo Falcón, an iconic Puerto Rican figure in New York who heads the left-of-center National Institute for Latino Policy, told me, I think ruefully, "The first Latino mayor of New York won't be Puerto Rican but Dominican."

THE FOUR GROUPS discussed in this chapter—the three from the Central American Northern Triangle and the Dominicans from the Caribbean—share some traits besides speaking Spanish (albeit very different versions of it). They tend to vote for Democratic Party candidates and support liberal causes but remain more interested in politics in their home countries than in politics in their new home. They have also demonstrated a strong work ethic, but the rewards of that are eroded by the fact that all four groups are known for sending a considerable portion of their wages back to extended family members in their countries of birth. These remittances do next to nothing to revitalize the economies of the home countries but rob their children here of potential savings that could be put toward education. The four groups also bring us to around 95 percent in terms of the Hispanic groups in this country. The reader should by now have a deeper grasp of what a disservice we do ourselves when we look at people of such different backgrounds as an undifferentiated mass.

PART II

COLLISION
COURSE

Chapter 5

THE MAKING OF HISPANICS

LBJ's words reflected a fundamentally different philosophy,
Progressivism. Individuals do not pursue happiness
within a framework of rights. Government pursues happiness
for them or rather for "our" people.

—JOHN SAMPLES

THE LATIN AMERICAN IMMIGRANTS OF DIFFERENT NATIONALI-
ties who started streaming into America in the second half
of the twentieth century had in common regional variations
of Spanish but not much else. They came here for different reasons, moved to different parts of the country, and met with different rates of success. Some, such as Puerto Ricans and Cubans, had
much more things in common with Americans as a result of proximity, shared history, and regular contact than with South Americans such as Uruguayans and Bolivians. Mexican-Americans had
contributed to the weaving of the cultural and historical fabric of
the American West for generations.

Soon, however, bureaucrats, politicians, and the media would
defy nature and lump together people of different races and nationalities into one single, synthetically made "ethnic" group: *Hispanics.*
In the popular imagination, Hispanics became something more: a
racial group. And not just any race but one that became by law a
"protected group" with access to benefits such as affirmative action
in a country that became newly divided between whites and "minorities."

This metamorphosis has happened quietly over five decades,
noticed mostly by social scientists. The key pieces of legislation,
executive orders, and bureaucratic decisions that enabled the

transformation received surprisingly little attention from the public, however, and remain little known. If you asked someone in his twenties about his views on the subject, he might earnestly repeat some school-indoctrinated nostrum about the benefits of diversity, but it is very unlikely he would know that the Hispanic category is of very recent vintage or that people who originated in Latin America were not seen as minorities only a few decades ago.

Contrary to what our well-intentioned but uninformed Millennial might think, the Hispanic label and all that came with it may have done more to impede the progress of Latin American immigrants than those who came up with the term realized. Warnings like Linda Chavez's that "ultimately, entitlements based on their status as 'victims' rob Hispanics of real power" are too often ignored. Now that the huge influx of immigration that started at midcentury shows signs of leveling off and growth in the "Hispanic" population is coming mostly through native births, we will have to deal with the effects of those decisions. But how did this all happen? More important, why?

When I was a lineman in high school, Coach Ghormley used to bark at us in practice, "When in doubt, fire out!" My equivalent of that in politics is, "If you're not sure who's at fault, check the records of both the Johnson and Nixon administrations." In this case, that would be the right thing to do.

CONGRESS ACTS AND CHANGES US DEMOGRAPHY

The Johnson administration was the first to have to deal with surging numbers of immigrants from Latin America because it was during its tenure that Congress took two fateful decisions that would change American demographics dramatically. First, Congress eliminated the bracero program for temporary guest workers from Mexico; second, it almost simultaneously passed the Immigration and Nationality Act of 1965.

The bracero program had been put in place in 1942 to deal with wartime labor shortages and was consistently expanded in the 1940s and 1950s because it answered the demands of agricultural businesses. Hundreds of thousands of circular workers entered the United States from Mexico every year (and then left), peaking at around 450,000 a year at its height. Was bracero perfect? No: workers were reportedly harassed and housed in poor living conditions. Could it have been improved? Of course. Did it need to end? No. The unions hated it, however, and so Johnson and Congress shut it down. "Guest workers don't pay union dues," said former GOP California chairman Ron Nehring, adding, "The bracero program ended, but the economic need for it did not." We will see where that imbalance led us.

No less important than ending the bracero program was the Immigration and Nationality Act of 1965, also known as the Hart-Celler Act, which had a profound impact on immigration patterns. It is important to understand the act's history, as conservatives who care about this subject know it all too well and often refer to it. The Immigration and Nationality Act was driven not by Latin Americans or Asians but by Italians, Poles, Portuguese, and other Europeans from Southern and Eastern Europe. It was indeed at a speech to the American Committee on Italian Migration in June 1963 that President Kennedy notably said that the old quotas were "nearly intolerable."

I would be remiss not to point out as well that in announcing the policy on October 3, 1965, President Johnson directed one of his agencies "to immediately make all the necessary arrangements to permit those in Cuba who seek freedom to make an orderly entry into the United States of America." As a young Cuban who came to these shores seeking freedom nine short years later, I salute President Johnson.

The law was a turning point, "a vast social experiment" in the words of the liberal Harvard sociologist Christopher Jencks, and not just demographically. Considering family reunification as a reason to grant immigrant visas started what many on the right refer to as chain migration. To University of California at Santa Barbara historian Otis Graham, the 1965 law would be seen as "the Great Society's most nation-changing single act," one that would in the end affect our history even more than the Civil Rights Act of 1964.

These immigration decisions and others to follow were in the hallowed tradition of our legislative branch: Congress acted out of political expedience and with little regard to the potential consequences. As Professors Douglas Massey and Karen Pren wrote in a 2012 Princeton paper, "The crux of the problem is that Congress routinely makes consequential policy decisions with scant consideration to the underlying dynamics of the social processes involved. . . . Congress took little notice of the long history of recruitment in the hemisphere, the high degree of circularity that historically had prevailed; the strong connection of flows to the dynamics of supply and demand."

Latin American immigration surged after these decisions, but it's important to understand that it did so *despite* the intent of the legislators, something that often gets lost today. This is yet another reminder that the only law that Congress ever gets right is the law of unintended consequences.

The immigration law replaced by Hart-Celler had been on the books since the 1920s and had sought to limit the immigration of Italians and Jews and ban entry to Africans and Asians. There had been no limits on Latin Americans. Between 25,000 and 50,000 Mexicans entered the United States every year with legal resident visas—hardly a stampede.

Hart-Celler changed all that, imposing an annual cap of 120,000 visas for the entire Western Hemisphere. It was later amended to a 20,000 annual cap per country and a worldwide cap of 290,000. In other words, Mexico went from at most 50,000 per year—90 percent of them temporary—to a ceiling of 20,000 overnight.

Something that always holds true with immigration is that nature abhors a vacuum. What happened next was that illegal immigration from Mexico went through the roof. Estimated at around 18,000 per year in the early 1960s (there was very little need to cross the border illegally while the bracero program was in place and there were no quota limits on visas), illegal immigration shot up to 101,000 in 1968, 224,000 in 1971, and 408,000 in 1974.

As illegal immigration rose, the cost of illegal border crossings increased as well. This had little impact on inflows but dried up outflows. Once in, the illegal immigrants didn't want to chance leaving; they hunkered down. As opposed to braceros, illegal immigrants were not circular. The illegal Mexican population in America began not just to build up but also to bottle up. The peaks for annual entries of the temporary Mexican workers under the bracero program and the illegal Mexican immigrants, in 1960 and 1980, respectively, were nearly identical at around 450,000, according to Massey and Pren. The economic forces were the same in both countries, but Congress was oblivious to these facts.

The legal population also went up. Remember that Hart-Celler exempted parents, spouses, and children of citizens from the resident visa cap of 20,000. Thus, the number of visas legally granted to Mexicans each year became a multiple of 20,000, going up to 101,000 in 1981. It has been in excess of that every year but one since 1993.

But that's not all. Congress throughout the 1980s and 1990s, sometimes for all the right reasons, took decisions that made it more palatable for permanent residents to become citizens. This resulted in increasing the number of residents who applied for citizenship, according to Massey and Pren. Mexican residents, who traditionally had had one of the lowest naturalization rates, soon were raising their right hands in legions. In the two decades between '65 and '85, Mexicans became citizens at the relatively low average rate of 8,200 per year. Between 1986 and 1996, however, that number went up to 29,000, growing afterward to an annual average of 169,000 naturalizations per year. Naturalizations stabilized at around 100,000 annually in the 2000s, ten times what they had been up to 1985.

What might have happened in 1986 to occasion this turnaround? It was Reagan's Immigration Reform and Control Act in 1986, which within five years turned 3 million formerly illegal immigrants into legal residents who could become citizens. Many of these were now not just Mexicans but people from throughout Central America, whose republics were undergoing civil wars at the time. And remember, every one of those new citizens could bring in relatives.

After that, all it took to grow the Hispanic numbers was a higher fertility rate than the national average. In the case of Mexican-Americans, each woman had an average of three children during most of these years, a much higher rate than that of non-Hispanic whites, which was below 2.0 (the replacement rate is 2.1). Central American rates were also high. The Mexican-American fertility rate has begun to slow with the recession, but it remains higher than that of any other group.

Hispanics haven't just grown in absolute numbers in the past half century; they have also grown at a much faster rate than the population around them. In terms of percentages, Hispanics have quadrupled. Since the turn of the twenty-first century, Hispanics have accounted for over half of the population growth (50.5 percent), and this growth has been due mostly (60 percent) to natural increase, not immigration.

That's how we got from fewer than 7 million Hispanics in 1960, or less than 4 percent of the overall population, to 50 million today, accounting for 16 percent. Congress obeyed the unions' command and ended a guest worker program that was working; it thereby created overnight an illegal immigrant problem that is still with us, bottled up the border by convincing people that it was in their interest not to leave, convinced residents who previously had been content not to naturalize to become citizens, and gave amnesty to those who were here illegally—and then it made it possible for all these people to sponsor relatives. It wasn't magic.

The composition of Hispanics in this country has changed. Mexicans, already 60 percent of the Hispanic population, have grown to around 66 percent today, and Central and South Americans have doubled from around 6 percent to more than 13 percent. Those from the Caribbean—Puerto Ricans, Cubans, and Dominicans—have dropped in proportion significantly, from 25 percent to 15 percent.

HOW HISPANICS BECAME A PROTECTED GROUP

Our ruling institutions—Congress and the executive agencies—weren't done. After deciding to alter America's demographic outlook dramatically, they determined that the way to deal with the new immigrants was to amalgamate them into one "colored minority" group, declare that they had been victims of past wrongs, and therefore extend to them affirmative action benefits that would create the habit of looking to the government for help.

Three remarkable things happened simultaneously to the identity of these immigrants and the descendants of Mexicans or Cubans who had been here for a century or more. First, the bureaucracy lumped them all into a single monolithic group, which soon became known as Hispanics, a term that was not used in Latin America. Second, this group became one of four minorities officially recognized by the government and then by civil society. Third, Hispanics became a "colored people." The impact these changes had on the way these immigrants would see themselves and how others would see them was immense.

Affirmative action was originally a benign push for "race-blind" employment practices, a remedy for a century of de jure segregation of African-Americans in the South and de facto segregation in parts of the North. It was clear from the start that the Civil Rights Act of 1965, as well as its Title VII, which prohibits employment discrimination, and the Equal Employment Opportunity Commission, which enforces Title VII, were created to help African-Americans.

Over time, however, affirmative action became a malign push for legally mandated proportional representation in employment, university enrollment, and politics—malign because it threatens concepts that are essential to liberal democracy, such as meritocracy, equal representation under the law, and property rights. It is also patronizing.

The first Equal Employment Opportunity form (EEO-1) bureaucrats sent out to employers under the Civil Rights Act's Title

VII required that they gather statistics on the employment of "Negroes," "Spanish-Americans," "Indians," and "Orientals," but even then the emphasis was on African-Americans. EEO-1 was, however, a giant first step in making Hispanics a protected minority group. "For the first time there was an official government document that stated the identity of the nation's minority groups, separating them from the 'majority' and joining this designation to policy with real impact and implications," wrote John Skrentny in *The Minority Rights Revolution*. All government agencies and in time civil society actors such as colleges would come to use these four minority groups.

It is important to note that it was Washington elites and leaders of Mexican-American pressure groups that fought for the inclusion of Mexican-Americans in the list of minorities. Rank-and-file Mexican-Americans, who had suffered some discrimination for decades, though never as much as black Americans, had shown a strong aversion to being seen as minorities. Leo Grebler, whose massive study of Mexican-Americans we first saw in Chapter 1, *The Mexican-American People: The Nation's Second Largest Minority*, wrote, "Indeed, merely calling Mexican-Americans a 'minority' and implying that the population is the victim of prejudice and discrimination, has caused irritation among many who prefer to believe themselves indistinguishable white Americans."

In fact, Mexicans had been officially designated as white in the 1850s, when thousands of them became US residents, or as citizens after the Mexican War and the annexation of Texas. Efforts starting in the 1930s to designate Mexican-Americans as nonwhite had met with strong opposition from the Mexican-American population, and when the Mexican Embassy protested, Washington desisted and Mexican-Americans continued to be white before the law. (In fact, the first instance of a US court striking down a ban on marriage between whites and blacks was in Perez v. Sharp in 1948, a case involving a Mexican-American woman, Andrea Perez, and an African-American man, Sylvester Davis. County clerk W. G. Sharp had refused to issue the license because Perez was white, but the California Supreme Court voided the law in question on the grounds it violated the religious freedoms of Perez and Davis.)

Puerto Ricans in New York soon were added to the list of minorities that qualified for help. The Small Business Administration in fact stated, "These minorities are Negro, American-Indian, Mexican-American and Puerto Rican." Another group, "Orientals," was added later. In 1973, the SBA identified African-Americans, American Indians, Asians, Spanish Americans, and Puerto Ricans as five groups "presumed" to be socially or economically disadvantaged and thus eligible for the Section 8(a) program, under which the SBA provides management, technical, financial, and procurement assistance.

In 1977 Congress passed Representative Parren Mitchell's amendment to Public Law 95-28 setting aside 10 percent of government contracts for businesses owned by "Negroes, Spanish-speaking [*sic*], Orientals, Indians, Eskimos and Aleuts." It was the first congressional act since 1854 to designate beneficiaries by race, and nobody batted an eye. In twelve short years since the passage of the Civil Rights Act, the nation had gone from segregationist laws that benefited the white race to laws that benefited other races. Scant attention was paid to this important shift.

After examining the evidence for which groups were covered under the "minority" label, University of Maryland professors George R. Lanoue and John C. Sullivan concluded that "there was no consistent rationale for group admission other than a vague 'people of color' ideology" that did not correspond to formal congressional mandates, economic realities, or people's actual races. Even though many Hispanics were Caucasian and "most Hispanics identify themselves as white," say Lanoue and Sullivan, they had to be designated people of color to be a minority.

"Brown" was then added to the rainbow of colors that came to make up the minorities in this country—the others being black, yellow, and red—but the assignment of brown to Hispanics was for many linked more to their last names than to their pigmentation. The blond, blue-eyed Mexican-American congressman Bill Flores is no more brown than is his fellow Texan George W. Bush. Senator Marco Rubio could be Irish, Italian, or Polish to someone who doesn't know his name, but that didn't prevent a small-minded big-time liberal like Donny Deutsch from calling the Republican Rubio a "coconut" when he was running for the Senate in 2010.

In 1976 Congress passed another remarkable piece of legislation, Public Law 94-311, which maintained that because "a large number of Americans of Spanish origin or descent suffer from racial, social, economic and political discrimination and are denied the basic opportunities they deserve as American citizens and which should enable them to begin to lift themselves out of the poverty they now endure," several government departments would start collecting data on them. The purpose was to "implement an affirmative action program within the Bureau of the Census for the employment of personnel of Spanish origin or descent." In other words, the new law isolated those groups of immigrants which had Spanish in common and said that unlike previous waves, they needed government intervention to deal with the discrimination that immigrants always endure, everywhere. The law also had national significance. It was nothing less than "the first and only law in U.S. history that defines a specific ethnic group and mandates the collection, analysis, and publication of data for that group," according to Rubén Rumbaut of the University of California at Irvine.

Additions were made on another front. At the instigation of the Mexican-American Legal Defense and Education Fund (MALDEF), Congress in 1975 extended special protection under the Voting Rights Act to Hispanics, mostly Mexican-Americans in Texas. Because the law encouraged the creation of districts where the newly designated minorities were in the majority, this "affirmative gerrymandering" led after the 1980 Census to the creation of gerrymandered Mexican-American majority districts where the elected representative has little if any incentive to reach out to all his constituents. In fact, because a high proportion of the district may not be citizens and thus not able to vote, the elected leader is even further distanced from the needs of most of her constituents.

The experience of comparatively well-organized Mexican-

American voters had been very different from the plight of black voters in the South. Moreover, as voting rights scholar Abigail Thernstrom wrote in *National Affairs* in 2010, the act's "literacy test was redefined to include English-only ballots, as if they were equivalent to fraudulent literacy tests in the Jim Crow South." The extension of the act to Hispanics, concluded Thernstrom, was "indefensible," and the act over time became a barrier to racial progress.

It is important to note that black leaders, including the Congressional Black Caucus, fought against the idea of extending affirmative action to other groups. The political calculus was strong, however. Johnson had been the principal at a Mexican-American school in Cotulla, Texas, and knew the power of that vote in the Lone Star State. Nixon, too, saw naked electoral profit in all this, says British historian Kevin Yuill in *Richard Nixon and the Rise of Affirmative Action*. Indeed, an ominous Nixon reelection strategy memo quoted by Skrentny read: "We should exploit Spanish-speaking hostility to blacks by reminding Spanish groups of the Democrats' commitment to blacks at their expense."

Once the growing numbers of Latin Americans had been pushed into this "colored person protected group," the bureaucrats needed to come up with a new name, as "Spanish-speaking" no longer would suffice. After all, as Professor Jonathan Bean asks, quoting the Small Business Association, "How is racial background proven? Who is a Spanish-speaking American?"

HISPANIC IS BORN

Not many people today know the name Grace Flores-Hughes, and she should indeed be allowed the restful anonymity that is the reward of all hardworking bureaucrats were it not for her single contribution to our lexicon.

In the early 1970s Flores-Hughes, a Mexican-American, toiled at the Department of Health, Education and Welfare (HEW) under Caspar Weinberger. She was tasked with developing racial/ethnic definitions that "all federal agencies could use in meeting their data-gathering requirements and in more clearly identifying the underserved people that were the target of their various programs," as she put it in an article in the *Harvard Journal of Hispanic Policy*.

Her contribution: the term *Hispanic*, blessed from 1980 with inclusion in the US Census.

The term *Hispanic* has some ancient relevance. The one thing that the different peoples of Latin America have in common is that they were colonized by Spain or Portugal. Hispania was Rome's name for the Iberian Peninsula. But all that is (very) old history and irrelevant today. Latin Americans don't use *Hispanic* as a term for themselves.

The bureaucratic designation of Hispanic was meant to do two specific things. First, purposely and explicitly, it was intended to create a separate group that was American—not foreign. Second, it was meant to make it easier for the government to racially profile members of this group for the purpose of handing out benefits and thus expand the state.

In her article for the *Harvard Journal of Hispanic Policy*, Flores-Hughes clearly stated that she saw her action as a natural consequence of the 1965 Civil Rights Act. The mission of the Ad Hoc Committee on Racial and Ethnic Definitions within HEW, she wrote, "was to develop racial/ethnic definitions for Hispanics and Native Americans as well as for Asians, Blacks and Whites that HEW and all federal agencies could use in meeting their data-gathering requirements and in more clearly identifying the underserved people that were the target of their various programs."

Or, as she told the *Washington Post*, "How can we argue for more federal funds or more federal help if we don't know how many they are?"

The die was cast in 1976 when Congress passed Public Law 94-311, which by magic created the Hispanic population for official use. In 1977 the Office of Management and Budget issued Directive 15, which mandated the two-dimensional classification we have today for government records: five races—whites, blacks, Asians,

Indians, and Hawaiian or Pacific Islander—and two ethnicities—Hispanics and non-Hispanics.

One has to have some empathy for a Mexican-American from South Texas like Flores-Hughes, especially one who grew up in an age when people suffered real discrimination.

Flores-Hughes wrote about those experiences in her article in the *Harvard Journal of Hispanic Policy*: "From the start, I was a fervent proponent of the term 'Hispanic.' It was the term that I strongly believed would begin to close the door on the kind of discrimination that I came to know firsthand while growing up in South Texas. At least in my world in Texas, a Mexican American or any other person of Spanish lineage could count on being often addressed in derogatory terms. References to us as 'wetbacks,' 'dirty Mexicans,' or 'beaners' could be an everyday occurrence. The terms 'Latin' or 'Mexican American' were often used in public, *but each was meant to focus on our differences from Anglos rather than to include us as an American ethnic group. I cannot count how many times I heard, 'Why don't those Mexicans go back where they came from?'*" [my italics].

Thus, one reason for using the term was to create an American ethnic group that could be identified not only for the purposes of affirmative action but also to give it a certain Americanness. A Mexican belongs in Mexico; a Hispanic belongs here.

It is easy to see how Flores-Hughes reached that conclusion. One can argue, however, that the Hispanic label achieved exactly the opposite of its avowed intention: it hacked a cleavage in society that separated Hispanics from all others.

In other words, this bureaucratic decision only reinforced the impression that Hispanics are separate, the opposite of what Flores-Hughes wanted to do. As Marta Tienda and Faith Mitchell explained in their 2006 study for the National Academy of Sciences, *Multiple Origins, Uncertain Destinies*, over time the children of immigrants have come to believe in this new racial construct:

Children of immigrants exposed to American culture and its definitions of race during their formative years and later classified as Hispanic or Latino at school internalize the belief that they are members of a racial minority. They render their Hispanicity racial by expressing their national origin in those terms. This has far-reaching consequences for the contours of minority group boundaries and potentially, therefore, for inter-group relations.

The government, in other words, has created an unprecedented situation. "Among earlier immigrants, particularly those from southern and Eastern Europe, social acceptance and cultural assimilation often involved shifting racially from nonwhite to white," Tienda and Mitchell wrote. With Hispanics, the government has worked really hard at achieving the opposite effect.

Perhaps even worse, by succeeding at helping Hispanics benefit from affirmative action programs, the bureaucratic label has held Hispanics back. Affirmative action is not a time machine that allows us to redress past cruelties. It does the opposite—it creates new grievances for future generations.

Perhaps even worse is in store. As we head into the 2020 Census, word began emerging in early 2013 that the Census Bureau was planning even greater mischief: "creating" a Hispanic race by taking away Hispanics' ability to tick off white, black, Indian, or other categories.

This would be the next logical step in what has been a long process of habituating the entire country, especially Hispanics themselves, to the idea that despite what the biology books may say, what the naked eye sees, and what they know themselves, Hispanics are a race, and a single one at that. There was evidence of a backlash against the move among Hispanics, but as we have seen, bureaucrats have never been dissuaded by the feelings of the subjects in question. In fact, if the decision is eventually taken, it will be the bureaucrats' way of punishing Hispanics for continuing to declare themselves white in large numbers on the census form.

Chapter 6

THE MAKING OF LATINOS

Aegrescit medendo. (The remedy is often worse than the disease.)

—LATIN PROVERB

I N EARLY NOVEMBER 2004 I WAS SITTING IN MY HONG KONG OF-
fice sifting through the results of the just completed elections
when I saw that two Hispanics had been elected to the US
Senate: a Mexican-American from Colorado, Ken Salazar; and a
Cuban-American from Florida, Mel Martinez. Even more eye-
popping was the fact that Hispanics had given George W. Bush
43 percent support across the country. As editor of the editorial
page of the *Wall Street Journal*'s edition in Asia at the time, I usually wrote about Asian matters, but I decided this time to write an
op-ed celebrating all these trends. The result was "Hispanics for
Jorge," published on November 8, 2004.

While the piece was in editing I received a phone call from some
guy on the news side of the paper in New York who had noticed
the piece in the queue and informed me that I had to change all the
references from Hispanics to Latinos. My response was something
like "Huh?" Something seemed to have changed stateside during
the nine previous years, when I had been posted to Hong Kong and
Brussels. Yes, he went on, he had convinced the news-side editors at
the paper that the politically correct way to describe Hispanics was
as Latinos, because "this is what they themselves use."

Surely when they speak Spanish they do, I responded, but
why are we going to take a phrase from Spanish and pluck it into

English? We don't say "I'm going to *Paree*" or "Berlusconi is the *Italiano* prime minister" unless our purpose is affectation. Worse, the purpose was more of the same politically correct minority coddling that was doing so much damage to the coddled.

The little martinet at the other end of the line would not be persuaded. Finally, I used the last arrow in my quiver. "You know," I said, "I'm one of these Hispanics you keep going on about, and you're not. Shouldn't my opinion matter in this?" Nope, came the reply. He had looked into this matter for years and had met with several ethnic group leaders, and this was the right approach, he said.

I called my editor at the editorial page, George Melloan, and he reassured me, "No, you don't need to change anything." That silliness applied only to the news side, not to the editorial page. I'm happy to report that as of this writing, Dow Jones has dropped its only-Latinos rule, probably one of many salutary changes that came after Rupert Murdoch bought the company. Using *Hispanics* as an agglutinative label for different cultural groups was bad enough; groping now for another term struck me as replicating with Latin American immigrants the same endless iterative process that we have seen with African-Americans (the latest iteration at the time of this writing); this silly search for new labels did nothing to address real issues.

There was a replay in 2010, when, having become vice president of communications at the Heritage Foundation, I wrote a piece for *Politico*, also on Hispanics and politics. The verdict was the same, except this time I couldn't get around the rules. In the *Politico* piece I could not use *Hispanics* but had to write *Latinos* every time. I don't know what ethnicity my *Politico* editor was, but I remember that she was very nice and listened to all my arguments, but she was not Hispanic.

These two instances constituted my own individual exposure to how those in charge of the culture pretty much ignore the desires of the people in question and forge ahead with their decisions because they know what's best.

The federal bureaucracy obviously felt it *had* to create Hispanics out of whole cloth to make sense of many disparate groups, and once formed, the group had to be given the contours of race, because to have protected status for the purpose of civil rights legislation, a group had to fall under the vague heading of people of color. The fact that Hispanics didn't see themselves as one group and that the people themselves had expressed no interest in being considered as members of a minority—not even Mexican-Americans, the group that had been most discriminated against and the only ones who could claim a prior history of economic and social disadvantage— did not seem to matter to the Washington crowd.

It was even sillier, then, that West Coast academics suddenly opined that *Hispanics* was a "colonial" term because it harked back to Spain's colonization of Latin America, and we as a nation needed a new one. What this made clear once again is that to claim sensitivity to other cultures does not necessarily mean to know anything about them. Of all the terms that can be used, *Latinos* might be the silliest.

The Spanish-language term *Latino America* from which *Latino* derives was in fact created by the French, and what's more, in one of Europe's most blatant colonial misadventures in the Western Hemisphere: France's attempt to forge an empire in Mexico, which it invaded in the 1860s while the United States was busy fighting the Civil War.

What the French were trying to do by popularizing a new phrase was to deemphasize the region's ties to Spain and Portugal and create a larger connection to the Latin peoples of Europe—not just the Spanish and the Portuguese but also the *French themselves*. Up to that point, *Latin* had referred exclusively to the peoples of southern Europe who were conquered by the Roman Empire and adopted a version of their language, which was, to wit, Latin.

The French imperial exercise in Mexico was more tragicomedy than anything else, an operatic interlude in the history of the region. The Mexicans did not react well and promptly overthrew the empire and executed the French puppet Emperor Maximilian within three years, installing in his place their first Indian president, Benito Juarez, to boot. The term *Latin America* stuck, however.

This was not the first time an inappropriate name had been imposed on people of the Western Hemisphere. When Columbus arrived, he famously called the natives of the place *Indians*, a term that is still with us to this day, also causing great confusion.

Of course, one could go even farther back in history to discover the other, older "imperialistic" meaning of the word *Latino*. It harks back to the even earlier conquest of Spain, Portugal, Italy, and France by Latin-speaking Roman soldiers—not a nice colonial era if you could interview my rock-throwing ancestors in Spain and Portugal back then.

It is therefore surprising that anyone would ever have considered the term *Latino* less colonial and more PC than *Hispanic*. Many corporations have bought into it, however, as we can see from Dow Jones and *Politico*, if only to buy peace.

Whether Hispanic or Latino, it is clear that today's generation feels some pressure to identify itself as members of a panethnic group. This came home to me in a conversation I had with a very young anchorwoman from Los Angeles who was of Central American origin and who identified herself as Latina in conversation with me in mid-2013. I asked why she did that, and she gave me a sheepish look. "I feel this is what I'm supposed to say," she said.

One of the biggest ironies of this story is that an identity wholly crafted by members of the bureaucracy is being foisted on people who may or may not be ready to accept it but who certainly did not initiate the effort. Generally, it is assimilation and integration as an American that are popularly derided as coercing immigrants into "losing their identity." Apparently no one has thought that forcing people to accept an identity they had never thought of—as Hispanics—also may be coercive.

The knowledge-making elites in the academy, the culture, and the media—always the handmaidens to the federal bureaucracy in liberal endeavors—have strongly nurtured the panethnic group identity. The Spanish-language media are one such strong force working to create a Hispanic or Latino identity fit for a people who would vie for power not as individuals but as an ethnic group. We must turn our attention now to this other phenomenon that has mushroomed in the last twenty-five years.

TV LAND

Spanish-language TV networks have a direct commercial interest in seeing a Latino or Hispanic ethnic group emerge, since such a group would retain a separate identity and continue to demand differentiated Hispanic entertainment. The cultural element of this separateness becomes much more important as the Latin American immigrants and their children switch to English, as they inevitably do. It's to be expected, therefore, that they would use shrewd marketing to help government conjure up such a Latino or Hispanic entity.

Any discussion of Spanish-language TV has to feature prominently one word: Univisión. The Spanish-language network headquartered in New York and Miami is wildly successful and has gotten there by selling itself as the protector of the group it has a financial stake in seeing grow. Its rise has paralleled the post-1965 Hispanic boom. The network also exerts its power to ensure that this new group will be liberal and vote Democratic.

Univisión not only has the largest Spanish-language audience in the United States; it has the largest audience of Spanish speakers *in the world*. At the time of this writing it had 70 percent of the Spanish-language market in the United States. Univisión's pure audience numbers still trail those of CBS, NBC, ABC, and Fox overall, but that understates reality.

No wonder Univisión's president, Cesar Conde, has told the *Miami Herald* that he expects his network to be number one in the United States by the 2016 presidential elections. If anyone has the ability to turn Directive 15 and Flores-Hughes's dream into reality, it is Univisión.

Univisión is not without rivals. Telemundo, which belongs to NBC, is the second largest Spanish-language network and is also competitive, commanding a 21 percent audience share. It is more middle of the road, though it supports allowing illegal immigrants to become citizens.

To these two in 2012 was added MundoFox, whose slogan was the more assimilation-conscious *"Americano como tu"*: "American like you."

The addition of a Fox channel (a joint venture with Colombia's RCN) in Spanish was a source of comfort to conservatives who care about connecting to the Spanish-speaking world. Jorge Mettey, executive vice president of news at MundoFox, said that when the network got started, it would focus on Latinos "who are involved in the culture of this country, who know this is the land of opportunity and who want to improve their quality of life."

Those reassuring words came not a minute too soon. Univisión and Telemundo have achieved their wild success with telenovelas, daily soap operas that run every night—365 fresh runs a year, no reruns—but it is news broadcasts that play a big part in the way that Hispanics who prefer to get their news in Spanish begin to grasp the land in which they're now living. These broadcasts are, for many, the only interpretation they get of what happened each day in America. On these two channels, it is a liberal interpretation more often than not and one that tends to reinforce the pan-Hispanic view. That Univisión and Telemundo are slanted to the left was confirmed by a major study released in the spring of 2014 by the Media Research Center, which found a 6/1 left to right slant.

Univisión explicitly brands itself as a network offering a "Latino perspective" on the news. The network's president says that Univisión's market leadership owes a lot "to the unique relationship we have with our community. There has been this void of leadership nationwide, and I think in many ways Univisión has filled that void in the Hispanic community, as far as being its defender, being its advocate."

The son of a Peruvian cardiologist and a Cuban-American academic, Conde perhaps embodies that Hispanic or Latino yet to emerge. He is a privileged one, to be sure: a product not just of

Harvard and Wharton but also of Miami's elite Belen Jesuit Preparatory School, where the children of the Cuban-American upper middle class are sent. He is unsurprisingly not what one would call modest, saying once: "Second to the Church, Univisión is the most recognized and trusted brand among Hispanics."

Despite what it might think about its divine mission, Univisión is not above using gutter journalism to politically drag down the man the network obviously considers a threat to its political mission here on earth: Cuban-American Florida senator Marco Rubio.

Politicians like Marco Rubio and Ted Cruz—Cuban-American conservatives who speak vividly about love of America and succeeding not through group set-asides but through individual initiative—are nightmares for the forces that have an interest in cultivating a group identity that sets Hispanics apart from the national conversation. Next to politicians and parties that want votes delivered in blocs, no other force has a greater interest in perpetuating the use of Spanish—or of identity in case it ever has to migrate to English-only broadcasts—than a Hispanic network such as Univisión.

Therefore, it shouldn't come as a shock that in 2011 Univisión was accused of trying to blackmail the Republican Rubio into appearing on its signature Sunday news show *Al Punto*, which is hosted by the anchor of Univisión's nightly news, Jorge Ramos. Not one to hide his Latino chauvinism, the Mexican-born Ramos is a pro-immigration activist who believes the United States should be officially bilingual. The reported Univisión deal offered to Rubio was that if he agreed to be grilled by Ramos on *Al Punto*, the network would kill an investigative piece on the senator's brother-in-law's decades-old drug bust.

The story did not damage Rubio's career. Once the *Miami Herald* published the backstory, few other news outlets picked up what was clearly a hit piece without merit. But the moral of the story is clear: Univisión is the protector of Hispanics, but only those Hispanics who agree with its vision of Latino identity. Conservative Cuban-American politicians on the rise need not apply.

In my own experience I have found most of their journalists

professional and courteous on both TV and radio. But Univisión does take a pan-Latino view, no question.

The principal owner of Univisión, Egyptian-born Israeli billionaire Haim Saban, is also a major Democratic donor. According to the *Miami Herald*, he openly exposed his bias in an e-mail when Republican presidential candidates boycotted a Florida debate to protest the network's report on Rubio and his brother-in-law.

"The fact that Rubio and some Republican presidential candidates have an anti-Hispanic stand that they don't want to share with our community is understandable but despicable," Saban wrote in the e-mail, according to the *Herald*. It also emerged in February 2014 that Saban told the Israeli newspaper *Yedioth Ahronoth* that he views Hillary Clinton as Obama's "natural successor." Without mentioning his network, he said, according to the *Daily Caller*, "She would be a wonderful president. If it happens, we will of course pitch in with full might. Seeing her in the White House is a big dream of mine."

Univisión's uniformly liberal stand goes from top to bottom. When Rubio was chosen to give the Republican response to President Obama's 2013 State of the Union address, an official at Univisión went very public with her distaste for the Florida senator, writing on Rubio's congressional staffer Alex Burgos's Facebook page: "Oh, wow, the loser is going to speak after our president." The *Miami Herald* observed that "sentiments like that reflect the prevailing political feeling among Univisión's higher-ups at its Doral headquarters, say Univisión insiders."

None of this means that conservatives should boycott Univisión any more than they should boycott MSNBC. Obviously, conservatives can't expect an even break from Chris Matthews, but they can get one most mornings on *Morning Joe* and even, once in a while, from the Reverend Al Sharpton. Conservatives should therefore agree to do interviews on Univisión with its cadre of professional journalists and even go on Jorge Ramos's *Al Punto*. They should just know what to expect.

In a sign that Univisión realizes that its future is in English-language broadcasts, in 2013 it joined forces with the ABC network to launch a new cable network called Fusion. The two partners said the joint venture would cover pop culture, immigration, food, music, and entertainment in English but in a way that would "resonate with the Hispanic community, one of the fastest growing and important demographics in the U.S." To succeed, Univisión needs to have a segment of the population that will demand content that is Hispanic-specific.

Fusion's marketing is very interesting. It targets not just Hispanics but Millennials in general: people born between 1980 and 1995. It does this for two reasons. First, it finds that young Hispanics don't like to be marketed to as Hispanics; second, because the Millennials are a new breed. Pollster John Zogby calls them "the First Globals" because they are the first generation of Americans to be globally conscious and have a global sensitivity. The obverse side of this, of course, is that they may not consider the national interest first. Fusion wants to aim programming at them.

BUCKING UNIVISIÓN

The truth is that at least so far, Hispanics are being stubborn about not seeing themselves as Hispanic or Latino.

"The universality of the language has created an illusion of ethnic unity among Hispanics that is belied by their diversity: there is no monolithic Hispanic population with a common history or common problems," write sociologists Marta Tienda and Faith Mitchell. The Pew Hispanic Center consistently finds that "the labels are not universally embraced by the community that has been labeled."

Pew finds that 52 percent of Hispanics describe themselves by their country of origin first; 21 percent generally call themselves American on first reference; and only 22 percent use the term *Latino* or *Hispanic*. That means 78 percent do not refer to themselves as Hispanic or Latino. Among the third generation or higher, the percentage that uses Hispanic or Latino goes down to 15 percent. The terms the bureaucrats wanted Latin American immigrants and their descendants to use have not stuck, in other words. For those who do use the labels, only 14 percent preferred *Latino*.

Marriage patterns are also not going in Univisión's direction. When Hispanics marry, they marry members of their own nationality group in the first generation and non-Hispanic whites in the following ones.

Ten percent of first-generation Cubans marry non-Hispanic whites, as do 20 percent of first-generation Central Americans. But by the second generation, fewer than a third of Cubans marry Cubans and half marry non-Hispanic whites. Almost half of third-generation Central Americans do the same. Puerto Ricans don't change as much through the generations, going from 21 percent to 29 percent in marrying non-Hispanic whites from the first to the third generation.

The exception—and it is an important one—are Mexicans, who marry other Mexicans at the extremely high level of 91 percent in the first generation and descend only to 72 percent by the third. In the third generation, Mexican-Americans' rate of intermarriage with other Hispanics is an abysmally low 1.8 percent.

But even the groups that do marry out don't do so with other Hispanics in great numbers; they marry non-Hispanic whites.

Salvador Oropesa, Nancy Landale, and Christina Bradatan, from whose groundbreaking 2006 National Research Council paper "Hispanics and the Future of America" I take these figures, conclude that "several features of ethnic mixing among Hispanics are consistent with the idea that Hispanics will be classified with whites" in a new racial dualism to emerge in the future.

Oropesa, Landale, and Bradatan do observe that the Mexican exception is worth considering, if only because Mexican-Americans are so numerous. The fact that Mexican-Americans tend to marry other Mexican-Americans "will undoubtedly contribute to the persistence of a Mexican ethnic identity and culture," they write. This will mean that Mexican might endure as a category for many years or perhaps that the term *Hispanic* may come to denote a Mexican identity in the future. Over at *Slate*, writer Jamelle Bouie asked this question in April 2014:

To say America will become a majority-minority country is to erase these distinctions and assume that, for now and forever, Latinos will remain a third race, situated next to "non-Hispanic blacks" and "non-Hispanic whites. Going forward, will white Hispanics see themselves as part of a different race—light-skinned, but distinct from whites—or will they see themselves as another kind of white?

WHAT IT ALL MEANS

The last two chapters have sought to illustrate how over time immigrants from Latin America and the Caribbean became an official minority and then were shoehorned into a group that now, confusingly, has two different labels. Also discussed are the forces working to nurture this synthetic identity. We should not forget that these changes were as dramatic for the whole country as they were for Hispanics, signaling a radical philosophical departure from the past. Skrentny put it best in *The Minority Rights Revolution:*

> It was through affirmative action that policy makers carved out and gave official sanction to a new category of American: the minorities. Without much thought given to what they were doing, they created and legitimized for civil society a new discourse of race, group difference, and rights. This new discourse mirrored racist talk and ideas by reinforcing the racial difference of certain ethnic groups, most incongruously Latinos. In this discourse race was real and racial categories discrete and unproblematic. By dividing the world into "whites" and "minorities" (or later "people of color") it sometimes obscured great differences among minority groups and among constituent groups within the pan-ethnic categories, so that Cubans and Mexicans officially became Latino, Japanese and Filipinos became Asian, and Italians, Poles, and Jews joined WASPs as white. Most profoundly, the minority rights revolution turned group victimhood into a basis of a positive national policy.

Skrentny obviously did not mean that there had been no discrimination against blacks, Asians, Indians, or Mexicans—or against the Irish, the Italians, the Jews, and the Catholics for that matter. What was new was the creation of minorities, one of which was named Hispanic, and the brand-new understanding of minorities versus whites. Many see these labels as necessary tools for sociologists, required to assess how different policies affect diverse groups. But that in itself implies thinking in terms of the "disparate impacts" that policies have on these groups, rather than hewing to color-blind policy making. And, to boot, the labels don't even do a good job of assessing disparate impacts, since they conflate very different groups under overly broad labels. There seemed to have been no consideration of potential adverse consequences for the new "minorities" involved from this novel interpretation of life. These changes resulted from actions that were taken by our government initially to alleviate the conditions of African-Americans. They were extended to the "Spanish-speaking" population without much if any public debate and mostly only with the experience of Mexican-Americans in the Southwest in mind. But because new immigrants started streaming in starting in the mid-1960s, these millions of people entering the country from Mexico and the rest of Latin America were caught up in the maelstrom.

One problem with extending to immigrants and their children preferential access to university enrollment, jobs, and government contracts, all in the name of affirmative action remedies for past institutionalized discrimination, should be obvious: immigrants came here of their own volition, and many of us have no history of past discrimination to be remedied.

As Nathan Glazer put it in "The Affirmative Action Stalemate," a 1988 essay for *National Affairs*, "We had seen many groups become part of the United States through immigration, and we had seen each in turn overcoming some degree of discrimination to become integrated into American society. This process did not seem to need the active involvement of government, determining the proper degree of participation of each group in employment and education."

The presumption of social or economic disadvantage is also borderline offensive. Sure, my family had no money when we arrived here, but we never felt disadvantaged, just lucky. As for history, my Cuban grandfather came to boarding school in this country and the other, a Spanish immigrant who made good in Cuba, vacationed here whenever he could. In fact, most beneficiaries of these programs tend to be socially advantaged. In one case I looked at a business owned by Ernesto Zedillo, a Mexican who stood to gain from a quota program, never mind that he had a PhD from Yale— and was once president of Mexico.

Moreover, as Hugh Davis Graham put it in the book *Color Lines*, "the immigrant success ethos, however, with its emphasis on hard work, merit and social assimilation, clashed with hard affirmative action's emphasis on historic victimhood, reparations and racial entitlements."

One harmful impact on the growing numbers of Latin American immigrants is that this new discourse made it much harder for them to follow in the steps of previous immigrants and join the melting pot. The government basically drew a line and put WASPs, the Italians, the Poles, the Jews, the Irish, and so on, on one side and then put the Latin Americans on the other side with African-Americans. This despite important similarities between the new Hispanic immigrants and the old ones: the Italians, the Jews, and the others had all faced severe discrimination when they arrived here and had to scratch for everything they got. The government was now officially telling the arriving Latin American immigrants and their children, along with those who had been here before them: No, you're not like previous waves of immigrants, so don't aspire to the same experience.

In his 1961 classic *Who Governs?* sociologist Robert Dahl articulated three evolutionary stages of generational ethnic politics. In the first, most of the new ethnic immigrants belong to the same stratum, usually low-skilled labor, which strengthens the class bonds that unite them. In the second, the immigrants start to differentiate as some individuals become successful in this country, and so leaders in their communities emphasize ethnic bonds in order to maintain group solidarity. In the third, full assimilation takes place and the ethnic immigrants integrate individually into American society.

The problem with setting a minority off from the rest is that it can get stuck in the second stage, never assimilating or doing so very slowly. This can become an even bigger problem when you have the high numbers we have seen with Hispanics.

Lost on the rules makers was the fact that federally enforced racial differences, even those which did not exist, had the same harmful effect on assimilation as the racial policies that they replaced.

Telles and Ortiz unwittingly make this point in their book *Generations of Exclusion*. They emphasize the barriers to assimilation that are erected by the process of racialization, which they define as "designating people by race, thus implying their position in a social hierarchy." They write:

> [T]he strong force of assimilation in American society may be slowed or even halted by the counterforce of racialization. Racialization may act to maintain or strengthen ethnic boundaries, despite the forces of assimilation.

They are completely right: designating people as members of minorities would keep them in a lower social hierarchy and slow down assimilation—and the fact that it was the government doing the racial designation gave it an official imprimatur. But what did any of this do for Hispanics? Precious little; in fact, it set them back. Extending university admission quotas to Hispanics (one of the reasons that the ethnic group was created by bureaucrats in the first place) amplified the crater that bilingual education had created between the children of immigrants and the rest. No policy could be better designed to create a bigger wedge than telling parents worried about their children's future that their chances are worse because a Hispanic kid with poorer grades will be put ahead in line in the admissions process or that someone else will have a better chance at a job because of his or her race or perceived ethnicity.

Many Americans see some common sense in affirmative action for African-American students, the overwhelming majority of whom are the descendants of slaves who were kidnapped in Africa and brought to this country against their will (Barack Obama being a well-known exception to this rule). The history of segregation against African-Americans is well known and does not need to be retold here.

One can even plausibly extend that line of argument for those few Hispanics who are descended from the people who were in the Southwest when the United States took over those lands in the mid-1800s and who have experienced discrimination.

But for the overwhelming majority of Hispanics in this country, most Americans see little or no justification for affirmative action. It is truly hard to comprehend that people who willfully came here searching for a better life as well as their descendants should benefit from policies meant to remedy past injustices. This is one reason why grouping African-Americans and Hispanics together across many issues, something many politicians do, especially on the left, makes no sense. There is nothing in the Hispanic experience that compares with the repulsive system of slavery.

Even supporters of affirmative action can get this. As Ricky Gaull Silverman, vice chairman of the Equal Employment Opportunity Commission (EEOC), put it, immigrant participation is "the ultimate nightmare of affirmative action. It is its Achilles' heel." The creators of affirmative action seem not to have considered, however, that it would be corrosive to the concept of a meritocratic society or that it would foment anti-Hispanic sentiment.

Most Americans have found the idea insufferable, and the quotas system has caused acrimony that has played out not just in difficult relations on the person-to-person level but in cases that have gone to the courts.

Affirmative action doesn't just institutionalize racism—it is the federal government constantly reminding you, "You are a member of a group that is so threatened, it needs protection." I worry more about impressionable minds that may come to buy into this victimhood narrative and start self-stereotyping than I do about the damage any bigot may inflict on people's self-image.

But ultimately, affirmative action may even prevent advancement, the act that will lead others to admire Hispanics. Linda Chavez, the highest-ranking woman in President Reagan's White House and a New Mexican whose ancestors have been in the Southwest for hundreds of years, once wrote:

> The rationale for treating all Hispanics like a permanently disadvantaged group is fast disappearing. . . . It is inherently patronizing to assume that all Hispanics are deprived and grossly unjust to give those who aren't preference on the basis of disadvantages they don't experience. Whether stated or not, the essence of affirmative action is the belief that all Hispanics—or any other eligible groups—are not capable of measuring up to the standards applied to whites. *Ultimately, entitlements based on their status as "victims" rob Hispanics of real power. The history of American ethnic groups is one of overcoming disadvantage, of competing with those who were already here and proving themselves as competent as any who came before* [my italics].

THE NEW MAJORITY

The divisive impact of promoting a minorities-versus-majority mind-set and the harmful effect it has on Hispanics' ability to assimilate are never really considered by politicians looking for an edge with a group. Just as Johnson and Nixon acted with narrow political interests in mind, President Barack Obama has given every sign that he intends to cull from different minority groups to fashion a minority-majority nation, one with a stake in the entitlements state. Hispanics are the linchpin of this strategy.

The Obama political machine understands full well that many Hispanics still don't see themselves as one group. Obama operatives therefore must be seen to be buying into the Hispanic identity at the national level even while differentiating among the different groups at the local level.

One of the biggest endorsements the Obama campaign sought and won in 2012 was not that of Oprah but that of Cristina Saralegui, or simply Cristina to her legions of Spanish-language fans on television and radio. Twelve-time Emmy winner Saralegui might be the most important American television personality Americans have never heard of. The Cuban-born, blond and blue-eyed, sixty-six-year-old Saralegui's show, *El Show de Cristina*, which ran in the United States for twenty-one years on Monday nights at 10 p.m., was seen throughout Latin America and Europe. Her impassioned pleas from the stage at the Democratic National Convention in September 2012 for Hispanics to cast their ballots for Obama was invaluable in getting the Latina vote.

At the same time, Obama's 2012 campaign succeeded wildly not just by being able to tell a Puerto Rican from a Cuban but also a Puerto Rican in New York from one in Florida.

While Mitt Romney's befuddled campaign translated English-language ads into Spanish, the Obama campaign and its super-PACs launched a Spanish-language operation that microtargeted people. The ads in Florida's I-4 corridor had Puerto Rican actors speaking with the appropriate accents, tones, and expressions, whereas those in the Rockies used Mexican-Americans.

And now that he's won, it is clear that Obama wants to use the support of Latinos to transform the country increasingly into a European-style social democracy. In exchange for votes to allow this transformation, the president and the progressives hold out the promise not just of protected status but of the redistribution of wealth.

But is that good for Hispanics, and is it good for America?

Affirmative action did good things, to be sure, but it also divided the country between whites on one side and minorities to be protected on the other. It also had harmful consequences for all. It has been used by those who seek a bigger government to the detriment of all Americans and has played a part in preventing some Hispanics from succeeding in this country, as we will see in the next few chapters.

It will be up to future administrations and voters to decide whether we will view our society as the Ottomans did theirs, as a compendium of discrete confessional and ethnolinguistic groups such as Jews, Turks, Circassians, and Armenians, the non-Islamic elements of which were called *dhimmis* and had semiautonomous but inferior places in society, or if we want to try to assimilate Hispanics and all immigrants to the national culture in ways that will benefit them and enrich or at least preserve the American experiment.

Although there may be some who think becoming a European-style social democracy is not the worst of fates (having lived in Europe, I'm not one of them), not many Hispanics came to this country to be part of a multinational Ottoman-like future. They came here with dreams of one day joining the mainstream and sharing in all of America's bounties, not to be limited to the role of *dhimmis* living under imaginary millets. Multiculturalists have done their best to send Hispanics the message that this diversity, this multiculturalism (this salad bowl versus melting pot idea that is already being taught to my elementary school–age daughter) is in their interest, but there's no reason for conservatives to accept this narrative. A truly inclusive message that welcomes immigrants to become Americans and join the mainstream (while retaining their ethnic pride, as others have successfully done and enriched the country by it) will always be a surprisingly winning one.

Chapter 7

THE PERFECT STORM

> *We know that we have made no discoveries; and we think*
> *that no discoveries are to be made in morality, nor many in the*
> *great principles of government, nor in the ideas of liberty,*
> *which were understood long before we were born.*
>
> —EDMUND BURKE

THOUGH IT WAS ALMOST EXACTLY FOUR DECADES AGO, I REMEM-
ber vividly everything about the day I arrived in this country.
Everything was oddly familiar because like most people around
the world, I had seen America, especially New York, on both the
small and the big screen. At the same time, everything was new and
foreign. Even the relatives who came to get us at the airport were
strangers to me; I had only heard about them while growing up.

Unbeknownst to me at the time, I was at the spearhead of a massive Hispanic immigrant wave that started to come to this country
in the mid-1960s. Little did I know that this influx coincided with
contemporary forces transforming the nation I was joining in un-
foreseen ways, which in time would curtail the upward mobility the
immigrants sought. It all added up to a perfect storm.

The 1960s are known especially for two phenomena that altered
society: President Johnson's Great Society and the sexual and cultural revolutions. Proponents of the Great Society promised that
this raft of social programs would help the poor gain access to the
middle class, and those who gleefully promoted the Age of Aquarius
said it would liberalize us from the shackles of our inhibitions. Iron-
ically, the desertion of economic self-reliance and cultural mores
tore up the family, the community, and society at large, shackling

millions to something worse than our own self-discipline: poverty and government dependency.

There was another force at work. Less noticed but no less harmful was that one of the country's key institutions, the once-sturdy and no-nonsense American schoolhouse, suddenly abdicated its historical assimilating responsibility and stopped instructing Americans on what constituted an upstanding, virtuous, and civic-minded citizenry.

But it wasn't enough that the schools stopped teaching values. Almost immediately our politicians, policy makers, administrators, regulators, educators, and media moguls, and even in time our military leaders—everyone in charge of opinion making—started to erect roadblocks to assimilation without giving a thought to the fact that it is by agreeing to the norms of a community (that is, assimilation) that one can gain access to the social capital networks that have been so crucial to success in America.

In other words, they didn't just stop teaching Hispanics how to assimilate into the American values of hard work, religiosity, honesty, and civic-mindedness that built this country; they went further and started teaching that those values had created a racist society in which Hispanics, who as we saw in Chapter 6 had been newly created as a minority, needed protection in order to succeed. Assimilation over time became a dirty word and was officially jettisoned.

Assimilation had been what my Heritage colleague Matthew Spalding calls "the long-standing resolution" of the seemingly irreconcilable conflict between the replenishing advantages of immigration and the potential dangers posed by large concentrations of foreigners. Absent that resolution, the conflict would fester.

Millions of Hispanic immigrants, then, suddenly arrived in a country that was casting off nearly all its norms. If this abandonment of age-old standards took a toll on the whole nation, it hit immigrants especially hard, as they had no memory of what the country had been like.

THE SEXUAL REVOLUTION

Sex being the fountainhead of life, we might as well start there. The 1960s saw a revolution in sexual attitudes and a questioning of gender roles that America had never seen before. The sexual revolution was accompanied by a new militant feminism that set out to shatter the millennia-old institution of marriage, the most durable of social arrangements.

If any single statement came to symbolize the new attitude it was "a woman needs a man like a fish needs a bicycle." Though usually attributed to the American feminist Gloria Steinem, it actually came from Irina Dunn, one of Steinem's feminist sisters Down Under. It is even more interesting where the Australian got her inspiration:

> I was paraphrasing from a phrase I read in a philosophical text I was reading for my honours year in English Literature and Language in 1970. It was "A man needs God like a fish needs a bicycle." My inspiration arose from being involved in the renascent women's movement at the time.

The relationship between man and God being probably the only one older than that between man and woman, the provenance of this feminist phrase highlights just how wide the reach of the countercultural revolution was and how much it was imbued by teachings at universities.

It wasn't only feminism that unleashed the sexual revolution. All conventions regarding premarital sex, marriage, and divorce were cast to the wind, rhetorically by some, in practice by many. The overthrow of taboos bloomed in the free love movement with its rejection of the marriage ethos, culminating in the Summer of Love of 1967.

This produced consequences that we live with today. Any chart that plots the rise of illegitimacy, broken marriages, or societal acceptance of premarital sex will show low rates in the 1960s and then a steep rise to today's levels. In the mid-1960s, only 6 percent of American children were born out of wedlock. By 2010, that rate had ballooned to 41 percent. These changes can be blamed squarely on the split between marriage and childbearing brought about by the sexual revolution of the 1960s. As Kay Hymowitz of the Manhattan Institute put it in *Marriage and Caste in America:*

> The sexual revolution and feminist movement of that era changed American society in myriad ways, but what interests us here is their profound effect on marriage. For the first time in history—not just American history but the history of known human society—people began to toy with the idea that children and marriage were really two distinct life phenomena. If they wanted, if it made them happy, why shouldn't men and women have children without being married?

This "unmarriage revolution," as Hymowitz terms it, and the consequential rise in single mother–led families, also fed the rise of poverty and dependence on social welfare programs, and those programs in turn perpetuated single parenthood, producing a vicious cycle. As even the left-of-center Brookings Institution has reported, the unmarriage revolution and its attendant ills directly led to $229 billion in welfare expenditures from 1970 to 1996. Another study, this one from the Institute for American Values, estimates that divorce and out-of-wedlock childbirth have cost the taxpayers $112 billion a year.

As Brookings found, a child born to a married mother who is age twenty or over and has at least a high school education has only an 8 percent chance of falling into poverty. The chances of becoming poor grow steadily with each new risk factor till they reach almost 80 percent for a child born of an unmarried teenager who did not complete high school.

The unmarriage revolution had a deep impact on Hispanic families; we will see in Chapter 8 just how deep. As University of Southern California sociologist William Vega said with the usual scholarly detachment in 1995: "Changing family structures, including marital disruption and cohabitation, could represent the most important issue for Latino family theory and research in the decade ahead."

Indeed, Hispanics come to this country exhibiting high levels of what sociologists call familism: strong families in which everyone more or less acts responsibly toward one another and the interests of the individual are secondary to those of the family. Within a generation, however, these strong units erode. This is why it isn't true that Hispanics don't assimilate; it's just that many are assimilating downward.

There were strong variations among the different groups of Hispanics, as we shall see, but overall every group was affected; family breakup and illegitimacy have grown among Cubans, Puerto Ricans, Mexicans, and so on. "Although there are some inconsistencies across national-origin groups, the pattern for several Hispanic subgroups suggests declining familism across generations. This is especially the case for Mexican-Americans, a group that exhibits lower levels of family-oriented behavior on every indicator among the native-born compared to the foreign-born," write Oropesa, Landale, and Bradatan.

Again, I don't need the research to write this as I remember well how hard my immigrant family had to fight against the world that Gloria Steinem and the sisterhood had created for us, in other words, not to fit into the conditions we found.

WELFARE DEPENDENCY

Just around this time, government set out to expand the welfare state massively, further transforming the national character. Among the programs created or greatly enhanced in the '60s by Johnson's Great Society were Medicaid, the Special Supplemental Nutrition Program for Women, Infants and Children (WIC), food stamps, Project Head Start, and what today is known as Temporary Assistance for Needy Families (TANF), or simply welfare.

In 1964, one year before the Great Society was launched, income transfer payments accounted for well under 30 percent of the federal government's total outlays, according to Nick Eberstadt of the American Enterprise Institute. This was the same fraction it had been in 1940, just after the New Deal had been put in place and while the country was suffering with 15 percent unemployment and was still in the grip of the Great Depression.

By 1975 transfer payments accounted for half of government outlays. By 2010 those payments took up 66 percent of federal government spending.

"In some basic respects—its scale, its preoccupations, even many of its purposes—the United States government today would be scarcely recognizable to a Franklin D. Roosevelt, much less to an Abraham Lincoln or a Thomas Jefferson," writes Eberstadt.

It was no coincidence that the rise in illegitimacy happened at the same time as the War on Poverty. As the Heritage Foundation's Robert Rector, one of the country's foremost experts on welfare, reminds us, "when President Lyndon Johnson launched the War on Poverty in 1964, 93 percent of children born in the United States were born to married parents. Since that time, births within marriage declined sharply. In 2010, only 59 percent of all births in the nation occurred to married couples."

Means testing welfare programs, a practice understandably aimed at limiting them to the poor, may have contributed to illegitimacy. Mothers can lose their eligibility for the program once they marry and the family receives a new source of income. As Rector says, "All income-tested welfare programs are inherently anti-marriage and produce what has been termed 'household-splitting effects.'" Indeed, the fact that a family or an individual can lose most or all government benefits after a certain threshold of income has been reached can lead them to make all sorts of bad long-term choices, not just not marrying and stabilizing a family but also refusing to take a job or do well enough in one to be promoted. The fact that the amount lost in benefits is often much greater than the immediate gain of marrying or taking a job has led people to call it the cliff effect: you fall off a cliff economically if you do something that is beneficial in the long term.

An antimarriage bias was hardly the sole antisocial effect that federal social programs had on the country. All means-tested income-transfer programs, especially those that do not demand behavior modification on the part of the recipient, become at best enabling processes that permit dysfunctions to continue and fester. At worst, these programs deepen and expand problems.

Just as social welfare programs discouraged marriage, they also discouraged finding a job. Since most people who qualify for one program qualify for others, getting a job means that recipients lose income from multiple sources. But the individual, not just society, pays a high price.

As Heritage's David Muhlhausen and others have explained, the longer a recipient is out of work, the more his or her skills deteriorate, further limiting the ability of the poor to rise economically. Lastly, families, churches, civil society organizations, nongovernmental organizations, and the like, reduce their assistance to the poor or, worse, channel their efforts into lobbying government to give more public assistance rather than relieving indigence outright.

The damage does not end with the individual but becomes generational. As Heritage's David Muhlhausen explains, a combination of factors—from the lowering of the stigma related to assistance, to being less aware of work behavior and job-search skills, to learning how to game the welfare system—hinders the ability of the offspring of aid recipients to become economically self-sufficient.

These results can be harmful to both human capital and social capital. Both individuals and civil society respond to government expansion by reducing their efforts to improve themselves. This has had unhappy consequences for working-class families, including many Hispanics.

The upshot is that the whole welfare edifice as we know it now may have been created with the best of intentions but has been a signal failure at moving people out of poverty. In many ways, it has only ensured that even if the poor may be materially better off, they remain poor.

The fact that America was embarking on such a massive welfare expansion and lowering taboos on government dependence just as hundreds of thousands of Hispanics were coming in did not bode well for the new arrivals.

The Office of Family Assistance reports that Hispanics are greatly overrepresented on the welfare rolls—or Temporary Assistance for Needy Families. Hispanic families account for 30 percent of families on TANF even though Hispanics make up only 16 percent of the population. (African-Americans and whites account for about 32 percent each.) Hispanics are also overrepresented among food stamp users, though at a much lower rate. All in all, about 40 percent of all Hispanic households now receive benefits from one of over eighty welfare programs.

The issue of Hispanic representation on the welfare rolls has been needlessly politicized. We should take time here to counter the notion that immigrants come to this country because it is a generous welfare state. This dim view of humanity does not correspond to people as I have met them. Even the anti-immigration Center for Immigration Studies acknowledged in 2011 that "an unwillingness to work is not the reason immigrant welfare use is high."

Rather, CIS attributes the use of welfare to the fact that immigrants have on average a low educational level, which is linked to income underperformance, which leads to welfare use because the government will promote social assistance to Hispanics, in Spanish, not as a safety net for those who need it but as an entitlement or right that anyone who qualifies would be foolish to pass up. What the government ads don't say is that welfare use is linked to the destruction of the social and human capital that Hispanics need to succeed. This is a message that urgently needs to get out.

WHEN SCHOOLS THREW IN THE TOWEL

It wasn't just that the government and the culture were telling you that you were different, a people apart, and that it was your right to use assistance if you met certain economic criteria. Nobody was telling Hispanics the opposite view. Just around then the United

States stopped trying to assimilate newcomers to traditional values either by design or because it had lost confidence in its values.

The push for bilingualism and multiculturalism, which are corrosive to national cohesion, became a feature of this, but the signs of cultural surrender were even more pervasive. American institutions in fact stopped assimilating even the native-born into the founding values of the country, not just immigrants from Latin America.

Until then, the American schoolhouse had for nearly two centuries taught all Americans not just the three Rs but also how to be good Americans. For over a century and a half schools unabashedly instilled in students the values that created a civic-minded populace and had built a republic that attracted immigrants from around the world. These values are so deeply felt—or were—that they have often been called America's civic religion.

The American Enterprise Institute's Charles Murray lays out four founding virtues without which America would not be what it is today, or at least what it was by the mid-twentieth century: industriousness, honesty, marriage, and religiosity. "Until well into the twentieth century, all four of the founding virtues were seen much as they were in the first half century of the nation's existence. They were accepted as well by the children of immigrants within a few years of getting off the boat."

All cultures that have left a mark on human history and contributed to progress have had a standard to which citizens subscribed. Rome, a model the Founders assiduously studied, had its personal and public virtues: authority, courtesy, mercy, dignity, tenacity, frugality, gravitas, respectability, humanity, industriousness, piety, prudence, wholesomeness, severity, and honesty. The Middle Ages famously had a code of chivalry. Our schools' growing relativism, with its constant undermining of tradition and morals (which goes under the label of teaching students to think critically), by contrast, gives you no platform on which to stand.

Schools taught America's civic religion for two reasons. From the start, America was a nation of immigrants who needed to understand the basic tenets of the country, and the schoolhouse was the easiest way to give their children this instruction. The more important purpose, however, was that the founding generation and its nineteenth-century descendants, Lincoln above all, worried about the survivability of the American experiment.

"The reason that our 18th century founders and their 19th century successors believed schools were crucial to the American future was not only that the schools would make students technically competent. That aim was important, but their main worry was whether the Republic would survive at all," writes E. D. Hirsch Jr., who takes a liberal perspective in his 2009 masterpiece *The Making of Americans.*

The anxiety was real and was openly discussed throughout the first century and a half of our nation's history. Republics, after all, were famously unstable in the eighteenth and nineteenth centuries. Rome had been dissolved by its elites' selfish decision to put their interests ahead of those of the republic. Relentless schooling in civic virtues was the only thing the Founders thought could keep the republic together, because it would instill from an early age a devotion to the common interest. It was not coincidental that both Washington and Jefferson left parts of their estates for the construction of schools.

Instruction in values, incidentally, allowed the religious and ethnic heterogeneity of America to thrive in the private sphere, because the public sphere would be unified. Thus, the textbooks of Noah Webster and Hugh Blair on grammar and American English usage, William McGuffey's Eclectic Readers, Horace Mann's histories, and their intellectual successors all had their deficiencies, to be sure, but they all brought Americans together from the eighteenth century to the mid-twentieth century. Some 120 million copies of the McGuffey Readers textbooks were sold between 1836 and 1960.

But then, sometime around the mid-twentieth century, Murray writes, "the idea that the school was a place to instill a particular set of virtues through systematic socialization had been rejected." And gone with it has been "some of the coherence in the idea of what it meant to be a good American."

For newly arrived immigrants, who were at this time increasingly Hispanic, this was nothing less than a tragedy.

Unlike the native-born, they knew little or nothing about an ancient republic founded on self-reliance; they had no tales of great-grandparents breaking out through the plains on wagons with nothing but a few tools, the nuclear family, and grit. Just as millions of Latin American immigrant children started attending our schools, fewer and fewer teachers were passing on America's civic virtues. For newly arrived Hispanic kids, not being plunged into American history and values meant that they had nothing to turn to for value absorption but the boob tube, the radio, the movies, and the union hall.

Why did America do this to itself? Hirsch chalks it up to several things. Progressives at the turn of the twentieth century had decided on a child-centered curriculum rather than one based on subjects. More important, self-confidence about the durability of the American project overcame the anxiousness that had haunted our leaders in the eighteenth and nineteenth centuries. Our schools therefore began to lose some of their civic purpose. "By the 1950s, they no longer conceived their chief mission to create educated citizens who shared a sense of public commitment and community," writes Hirsch.

This overconfidence is as unfounded as it is dangerous, however. As we know from Reagan, who shared the anxiety of Lincoln and the Founders about the potential instability of republican government, "freedom is never more than a generation away from extinction."

Sociologist Nathan Glazer, writing in the mid-1990s, made an additional point that we see again and again with other momentous decisions: no one at the time seemed to notice that social Rubicons were being crossed. "The American public school, originally established to mold Americans of all backgrounds into a common culture and fully devoted to this task until perhaps two decades ago, has undergone a remarkable change in the last twenty years. The change has received almost no public notice as recently as a few years ago," Glazer wrote.

Hirsch has an additional insight worth exploring. An added problem with this major change in education—apart from the fact that it left immigrants in the lurch and the nation at risk—is that it put in jeopardy the very ability to learn.

It turns out that shared knowledge is key to our ability to comprehend any passage either in literature or in an owner's manual. That is, you may know all the terms in a text, but unless you have some acquaintance with the subject, you cannot start making out what you're reading or hearing.

"The tacit intergenerational knowledge required to understand the language of newspapers, lectures, the Internet and books in the library is inherently traditional and slow to change," Hirsch writes.

We have this tacit knowledge less and less in our society these days, because when schools stopped instilling shared values, they also stopped instilling shared knowledge. This current deficit in knowledge that we share nationally, says Hirsch, is the reason reading comprehension scores have fallen substantially for the last few decades despite many attempts to teach technical aspects of reading in such programs as No Child Left Behind.

Race-conscious leaders who have demanded these changes are willing to accept this cost because they stubbornly believe that "privileged knowledge has to be replaced in order to reduce the power and status of dominant groups," Hirsch writes. In other words, rather than teach black and Latino children the shared knowledge of previous generations, we must atomize society and teach each subcommunity its own subdivision of shared knowledge in a new version of cutting off one's nose to spite one's face.

Thus, at the time of this writing the Tucson Unified School District was trying to teach eleventh- and twelfth-graders a curriculum filled with "critical race theory" and "Barrio pedagogy." The *Daily Caller* reported that "courses were taught from a pointedly Mexican-American vantage point. (There will also be a separate, analogous African-American curriculum.)"

We all got a memo of sorts in 1994 that the evolution had been completed when a decision by the school board of Lake County, Florida, caused a furor in that state. The board had decided "to instill in our students an appreciation of our American heritage and culture, such as: our republican form of government, capitalism, a free-enterprise system, patriotism, strong family values, freedom of religion and other basic values that are superior to other foreign or historic cultures."

This was, of course, exactly what American schools had taught for over a century and a half, a practice that no doubt contributed to America's success as a nation. But some local papers wrote scathingly about this dastardly act, calling it bigotry. Even the *New York Times* reported on it.

Nobody of course bothered to ask the opinion of the largest Hispanic group in the state of Florida, Cubans, the vast majority of whom agree that "our republican form of government, capitalism, a free-enterprise system, patriotism, strong family values, freedom of religion and other basic values" are superior to those of others, and in fact their exodus to this country is a testament to that fact. The curriculum was withdrawn.

Today, not only are we *not* teaching American values to young Hispanic students in our public schools; we are teaching them that those values produced an oppressive, racist society that discriminates against them as people of color. A raft of "Chicano/Latino studies" or "diversity studies" throughout the country, not just at universities but also in K–12 classes, emphasizes a consciousness of "white privilege" and "minority oppression." As columnist George Will wrote in 2013, "no corner of this country is immune to propaganda pretending to be pedagogy."

The perfect storm of growing welfare dependency, ending the unique role the family had in national cohesion, and the assimilating function of schools has left a divided nation in which Hispanics all too often find themselves trapped in the bottom half.

For the truth is that the whole country hasn't gone into a discard pile of dysfunction, and neither have Hispanics. The problem has become one of class rather than ethnicity. Americans with the right academic degrees, intact families, high levels of industriousness, and the other attributes of success have clustered themselves into a new high-income class, for lack of a better term, and into functioning communities with high levels of human and social capital. These neighborhoods, called Super-Zips by Charles Murray, are oblivious to race. If you have all these attributes, including of course the financial capital needed to buy in, you're more than welcome no matter your color or your last name. Gone, mercifully, are formal and informal barriers that kept groups such as African-Americans and Jews out of certain neighborhoods.

To be sure, after the '60s and '70s, all classes did seem to be headed into a pit of dysfunction. Single-parent homes skyrocketed among all groups. Soon, however, those in the middle class who remained stubbornly aspirational twigged on to the fact that single parenthood results in poverty, and a new appreciation for marriage appeared.

The college-age children of the 1960s baby boomers, the so-called Generation X, who saw firsthand the wreckage from casting away conventional marriage and child rearing, led the way. Writes Hymowitz:

> From the vantage point of those who were children in the 1960s, '70s and '80s, when these ideas were at their zenith, the matrimonial revival is not so startling. Where social revolutionaries had promised more freedoms, the children of those years experienced troubled parents, disordered homes and diminished prospects. Feminist professors might continue to scowl at bourgeois marriage, but their young students longed for the stable homes their generation had been denied. They judged that marriage, for all its contradictions in an individualistic age, offered the best chance for deep bonds, for rootedness—and most of all, for the rearing of successful children.

The Gen Xers also found institutions to impart values to their children. Even liberals who dislike many aspects of the Boy Scouts, from its religious dimensions to its refusal to admit gay scoutmasters, still put their children in it because as a lawyer in New York once told me, "it's one of the last institutions in America that imparts civics."

The bad news was for those in the working-class neighborhoods, where immigrant Hispanics almost always move. There the breakup of the marriage culture, the separation of marriage and childbirth, continues to wreak havoc to this day. Thus we have today the situation that the rates for nonmarital births and for children of broken marriages living with a single mother are much lower for mothers with college degrees or above than for those with only a high school degree or below, in other words, those who are least equipped to deal with these problems.

As we shall see in Chapter 8, this has created two Americas, and Hispanics are overrepresented in the bottom one. It's important to understand that their problems with relative mobility are not the same as the inequality trumpeted in 2011 by Occupy Wall Street protesters.

The income-support programs that liberals advocate for Hispanics increase material comfort, but do nothing to help the intended beneficiaries exit the cycle of poverty; in fact, it can trap them there. The problems are parents who in far too many cases are nonexistent, have bad habits to impart when they do exist, or work all day and cannot provide the support a child needs. Add to that poor and/or dangerous neighborhoods that do not provide the social structures that can make up for bad parenting or actually fritter away the benefits of good parenting.

Government programs may at best resolve some day-to-day issues, but they disincentivize the creation of human and social capital and crowd out civil society efforts that have a proven record of success. Immigrant communities especially must rely on complex social webs and structures, as do ethnic enclaves at the margins, such as the Mexican-Americans of South Texas. Extended family networks and country-of-origin or regional associations produce a skein of self-help organizations that slowly develop organically. Government programs, especially large-scale endeavors such as the War on Poverty, splinter those efforts. As Charles Murray put it in *Losing Ground*: "Any teenager who has children and must rely on public assistance to support them has struck a Faustian bargain with the system that nearly ensures that she will live in poverty the rest of her days."

Any storm leaves wreckage behind, and so did this perfect storm that began to gather force in the 1960s. Hispanics have been among the worst hit.

Hispanic immigrants do fairly well across a number of indicators, performing better on average than non-Hispanic white natives on such key markers as married motherhood and industriousness. Subsequent generations lose ground, however.

The nexus is clear between family breakup and welfare use on one side and the creation of minority consciousness, protected classes, and ethnolinguistic groups with separate rights on the other. In both instances the result is that the people depend on the state, not their individual talents or the strength of their communities. Dependence on government action for university acceptance and hiring, or welfare for those who do not get into schools or find a job, is in the end destructive of individual ability, community involvement, and national cohesion.

We will get the full measure of where this leads in Chapter 8.

Chapter 8

THE AFTERMATH

The role of the family in shaping character and ability is so pervasive
as to be easily overlooked. The family is the basic social unit of
American life; it is the basic socializing unit.

—Daniel Patrick Moynihan

I N THE LAST THREE CHAPTERS WE REVIEWED HOW HISPANICS
came to be socialized in this country after starting to arrive in
large numbers in the 1960s. We have seen the environment they
came into as well as how they were grouped as one of the official
minorities of the United States, with access to benefits such as affirmative action and, because of their relative poverty, the income
transfers of the vast social welfare programs. In the next two chapters we will assess some of the issues affecting these communities in
the last quarter century.

In the first decade of the new century, Hispanics as a group
crossed a threshold that foretells dire consequences in almost every
social marker. More often than not, Hispanic babies are now born
illegitimately. As with everything else, this has happened at different rates for different nationality groups and different educational
levels. *All* Hispanic groups have experienced a dangerous rise in
out-of-wedlock births, however.

As always seems to be the case, with illegitimacy Hispanics find
themselves at a midpoint between whites and African-Americans.
Out-of-wedlock births among Hispanics are now about 24 percentage points higher than they are in the white community and about
19 points lower than they are in the African-American community.

No other cultural indicator could be more concerning for those of us who want Hispanics to succeed and join the American main-stream. Rampant illegitimacy ravages future generations, destroying hopes of upward mobility, harming the overall culture, and therefore increasing xenophobic reservations about Hispanics. As Cynthia Harper of the University of Pennsylvania and many others have amply demonstrated, children who grow up without a father in the home have much higher odds of getting caught up in serious delinquency and ending up in prison.

It is also a trend that becomes habitual and thus very, very hard to reverse. Although much attention is paid to illegal immigration, the thornier issue of illegitimacy gets swept under the rug. And although self-appointed ethnic leaders continue to bang on about affirmative action, that does nothing to solve illegitimacy and all the other pathologies it entrains. As Roger Clegg of the Center for Equal Opportunity put it, high illegitimacy rates are such a key cause of social pathologies that one would expect academics to be discussing them widely. But this isn't happening:

> Among academics and the media, it has long been oh-so-politically-incorrect to suggest that there might be something wrong with having children without getting married. . . .
>
> It is also politically incorrect to point out the disparity in illegitimacy rates between whites and Asians versus blacks, Hispanics, and Native Americans. What is especially galling to the left is that the gap can hardly be attributed to discrimination.

According to the Centers for Disease Control and Prevention (CDC), for years the out-of-wedlock birthrate among Hispanics had held steady at around 40 percent in the 1990s; then, in 2001 the rate started a steep incline until it crossed the fateful halfway mark in 2007, rising at a faster rate than it did for both whites and blacks. Since 2008 the rate of illegitimacy has refused to budge, plateauing between 52.6 percent and 53.4 percent, where it was in 2013.

The rate is much higher for black Americans, who have an out-of-wedlock rate of 72 percent. But because Hispanics now outnumber blacks, 2003 became the first year in which the total number of illegitimate births for Hispanics was greater than the total number for African-Americans.

Illegitimacy is not a word we hear very often anymore. It's not nearly as bad as *bastardry*, which is gone altogether, but social scientists still prefer not to use it, opting instead for the less judgmental *out-of-wedlock* or the *unmarried birthrate*, which is the term in Department of Health and Human Services statistics. In the view of many, no baby should be considered illegitimate because of decisions his or her parents made. In our more tolerant, value-neutral age, we tend not to judge and abstain from pejorative terminology.

Such linguistic squeamishness may be a symptom of the problem, which is that we've become more socially tolerant of out-of-wedlock births despite solid evidence that their rampant growth is killing communities and families. Cleansing our vocabulary of all judgmental words may actually enable the underlying realities to proliferate.

These realities can be disastrous. Children born out of wedlock will be at a disadvantage compared with those raised by two parents in almost every way. As Heritage fellow Patrick Fagan puts it: "Social science literature is replete with robust findings on the harmful effects of broken families, particularly for children. Juvenile crime, abuse and violence, and lowered income are often associated in the research with single-parent families. Children born out of wedlock have an increased risk of death in infancy, higher incidence of retarded cognitive and verbal development, and higher rates of drug addiction and out-of-wedlock pregnancy as teens. As adults, they have higher rates of divorce, work at lower-wage jobs, and abuse their children more often."

It's not just Heritage saying this. On this verdict we have a rarity: an almost universal consensus among social scientists cutting across the ideological spectrum that illegitimacy and single parenthood produce bad results for the offspring. As James Q. Wilson once quipped, the data on this are now so strong "that even some sociologists believe it."

"We know the statistics—that children who grow up without a father are five times more likely to live in poverty and commit crime, nine times more likely to drop out of schools, and twenty times more likely to end up in prison," said candidate Barack Obama in June 2008.

The apparent disability of not being raised by a mom and a dad, incidentally, is noticeable even after controlling for race, income, and socioeconomic status. It also extends to areas in which causality is harder to explain. Children of unmarried parents have, for example, higher mortality rates as well.

The point is not to finger wag; politicians discussing these matters with Hispanic audiences must take great care not to engage in reprimanding. It is human nature to err and much in our culture encourages behavior that leads to out-of-wedlock births. The point, rather, must be to show how the growth in illegitimacy can drag down the Hispanic community and how striving to keep the family intact will lead to success for their children not just in terms of economic achievement but also in terms of leading more meaningful lives. Politicians must inspire, not scold, and show the way forward with solutions that help the family stay together and then start the process of rebuilding the community around them. We will see in Chapter 10 what solutions can be offered.

At the other end, the admittedly anti-immigration Center for Immigration Studies reports that Hispanics have seen "the largest increase in out-of-wedlock births." In a 2007 study, CIS noted that one of every seven unmarried Hispanic immigrant women had had an out-of-wedlock birth compared with one of thirty-three for non-Hispanic white natives.

The latest CDC numbers at the time of this writing, those for 2012, did paint a worrisome picture. Mexican-Americans were at the midway point among Hispanics, with a 52 percent illegitimacy rate. At the high end among Hispanics were Puerto Ricans, with an illegitimacy rate of 65 percent, about tied with American Indians and Alaska natives and second only to African-Americans; at the low end were Cuban-Americans, with a 49 percent rate.

The case of Cuban-Americans has been particularly worrisome. Their rate jumped by a full percentage point from 2010 to 2011.

The rise was meteoric from 2001, when the Cuban-American illegitimacy rate stood at 27.3 percent, not much higher than the rate for non-Hispanic whites, which that year was 22.5 percent (today it is 29 percent). This must be a function of the change in the immigration makeup among Cubans reviewed in Chapter 3, combined with the adaptation paradigm discussed in Chapter 7.

In the ten years between 2001 and 2011 the rise in out-of-wedlock births for other Hispanics was less precipitous but still very concerning. Mexican-Americans, the largest group and therefore the one in which the rate means the most, saw an increase of 10 percentage points from a 2001 rate of 40.8 percent, or a 25 percent rise. The rate for Puerto Ricans rose 6 percentage points from 58.9 percent in 2001, but it started from a much higher level.

Critics of immigration such as the Manhattan Institute's Heather Mac Donald, who has for years been raising the alarm not just about the illegitimacy rate but also about the fertility rate among unwed Hispanic mothers, make the point that these rates will impose an additional burden on the public dole. This is hard to argue against. If their out-of-wedlock rates continue at these levels, let alone rise, Hispanics will grow increasingly dependent on government services. Mac Donald writes:

> The government social-services sector has already latched onto this new client base; as the Hispanic population expands, so will the demands for a larger welfare state. . . . Not only has illegitimacy become perfectly acceptable, they [social workers] say, but so has the resort to welfare and social services to cope with it.

African-Americans may have much worse rates of illegitimacy, she concludes, but the black population is not going to triple in size in the next few decades.

Nor does the situation improve with the number of generations in this country. In fact, it can become worse. Pew reports that only 18 percent of Hispanic children who have come to this country as immigrants live in a household led by a female, which is only slightly higher than the 16 percent rate for native whites. That number, however, worrisomely rises to 38 percent for third-generation Hispanic children, that is, those not only born in this country but with both parents born in this country.

Much of this has to do with the new cultural norms learned in this country, which challenge the more traditional views of marriage brought by immigrants from their home countries, as we saw in Chapter 6. The National Resource Center for Healthy Marriage and Families tool kit for social workers trying to strengthen marriage culture among Latinos thus observes that "the benefits of marital stability are more apparent to first generation immigrants and diminish with subsequent generations."

Hispanics, who started out with fairly good numbers in 1980 across all indicators, have seen deteriorating numbers in recent years and also from one generation in this country to the next. Sociologists have found a decline in familism and a rise in the rate of households led by a single mother both over the years and generationally. It turns out, for example, that the rate for mothers of children under five who are divorced, separated, or never married is about the same for Hispanic immigrants and for non-Hispanic whites at about 21 percent. That rate almost doubles to 40 percent for second-generation Hispanics and rises further still for third-generation Hispanics.

It is this generational decline that rightly worries many observers. The *Examiner* newspaper spoke for many when it wrote, "America's legendary 'Melting Pot' has assimilated millions of immigrants from around the globe into our society, and in process greatly improved their lot, usually by the third generation. But that's not what's happening with Hispanics, who represent the largest inflow of immigration into the United States since the 1920s."

Much of this lack of generational mobility boils down to high rates of illegitimacy. CIS was insightful when it observed: "Children of immigrants are often caught between two worlds, torn between their parents' culture and that of the country of their birth.

They have traditionally relied on a strong family to help them navigate life in their parents' adopted country. If a large share of these children now have to also adjust to life in single-parent households, then the problems they face could be substantial."

These trends become a powerful argument for those who want zero or more limited immigration. Heather Mac Donald knows, for example, that her starting premise of a sudden improvement is unlikely to happen when she writes, "Unless the life chances of children raised by single mothers suddenly improve, the explosive growth of the U.S. Hispanic population over the next couple of decades does not bode well for American social stability."

Her warning here is clear: the rapid growth of the Hispanic population, immigrant and nonimmigrant, legal and illegal, is dangerous to our nation's well-being because the increased societal problems related to illegitimacy affect everybody. She's not wrong, incidentally, that if we don't do something about this worrying trend it will engulf us all in myriad ways: higher taxes, the erosion of the national culture, and bigger government and thus fewer freedoms. But this is an argument for taking the issue of illegitimacy seriously and trying to reverse it.

Our political leaders, in other words, have no choice but to engage Hispanic audiences in this admittedly prickly issue. The more pro-immigration they are, the harder they must work at this, because a continuation of these trends will call into question our country's tradition of being a land that welcomes immigrants. Anti-immigration politicians who use this issue as fodder to make the case that we should close the border will inevitably say something nasty that will be played on an endless loop by Univisión.

Pro-immigrant leaders will find much to work with. Attachment to family values is a real feature of the Hispanic community; it is one trait about which we really can talk in terms of Hispanics. Cubans, Mexicans, Puerto Ricans, and others do indeed share a deep commitment to family, Mexican-Americans especially.

The link between unmarried births and education is strong. Illegitimate births happen more often among the least educated and ensure that this undereducation is perpetuated in future generations. Illegitimate children beget more illegitimate children. Out-of-wedlock births are thus both a consequence and a cause of high dropout rates. Given the intense demand for high-skilled labor in the knowledge economy that is America in the twenty-first century and the poor wage prospects for low-skilled labor, these statistics can only be described as dire. So are the ones related to education.

THE EDUCATION GAP

Much scholarship has been devoted to the education gap. Even with recent improvements among all groups, almost 37 percent of Hispanics in America, including those who've come here as adults, have not completed high school, the highest rare for any group. Fully a third of foreign-born Hispanics have not gone beyond ninth grade.

High school graduation rates have improved markedly for Hispanics brought here as children and especially for generations born here. There are still problems, though.

Three-fourths of Hispanics who have attended school in this country have completed high school, a lower rate than those of the African-American population (81 percent), the non-Hispanic white population (88 percent), and the Asian population (90 percent). The Hispanic dropout rate—officially the percentage of sixteen- to twenty-four-year-olds who are not in high school and have not earned a high school degree, so it is a different number from the total percentage of people without a degree but shows what's happening at the present—was also much higher than for other groups at 14 percent compared with 5 percent for whites and 7 percent for African-Americans.

There was good news on educational performance in 2013. A record 69 percent of Hispanics who did graduate high school enrolled in college in the fall of 2012, 2 percentage points higher than the white performance, according to the Pew Hispanic Center. The high school dropout rate also fell by more than 2 percentage points.

For two years now Hispanics have been the largest minority group on the nation's college campuses, accounting for 16.5 percent of all college enrollments, roughly their share of the nation's population, according to Pew. Hispanics also accounted for about 24 percent of all pre-K–12 public school enrollment.

The rising college enrollment rate referred to above is due in part to high enrollment in two-year colleges. In 2011, Hispanics' share in two-year community colleges was 25.2 percent and their share in four-year colleges was 13.1 percent, below their share of the population. "Hispanic college students are less likely than their white counterparts to enroll in a four-year college (56% versus 72%), they are less likely to attend a selective college, less likely to be enrolled in college full time, and less likely to complete a bachelor's degree," said Pew.

As the Bill and Melinda Gates Foundation–funded Migration Policy Institute noted in 2011, Hispanics are indeed enrolling in college, but many drop out and do not earn a degree.

It isn't just a question of completing college. The National Assessment of Educational Progress (NAEP) report, a congressionally mandated project known as "the nation's report card," shows in its last report, 2011, that there is a persistent educational gap between Hispanics and white students. For both fourth and eighth grades, the gap in reading and mathematical skills is significant and, if anything, slightly expanding over the last twenty years. The NAEP's long-term data also show that non-Hispanic white eighth-graders scored only one point below Hispanic twelfth-graders.

The picture that is emerging is therefore mixed. Hispanics, like all other groups, are reacting to the recession by dropping out of high school less because there are fewer jobs to lure them, and those who completed high school in 2012 enrolled in college at a rising rate. They tend to go to two-year colleges, however, and drop out of both high school and college at an unacceptably high rate (their high school dropout rate is twice that of African-Americans). They also show a persistent educational gap with white students. Latinos are therefore still the least educated group in the country in terms of school years and are only slightly ahead of African-Americans in the NAEP-measured comprehension gap.

School performance has a direct impact on mobility, as education is the surest path out of poverty, and so all eyes will be on how Hispanics perform in the second decade of this century. Americans with a college degree will make on average much more over their lifetimes than will those without one, let alone high-school dropouts.

A Georgetown University study put the lifetime earnings for high school dropouts at $973,000; those with a high school diploma, $1,304,000; those with some college, $1,547,000; those with an associate degree, $1,727,000; those with a bachelor's degree, $2,268,000; and those with a master's degree, $2,671,000. Those with a doctorate can expect to earn $3,252,000 over a lifetime, and for those with professional degrees such as lawyers and medical doctors lifetime earnings go up to $3,648,000.

Conservatives sometimes show a certain aversion to higher education, and it's easy to see why. The Left has such a death grip on the academy that universities have become mere factories producing liberals such as Sonia Sotomayor. Tuition has experienced a price inflation all of its own: since 1985, while general prices have risen by 115 percent, college tuition has risen by almost 500 percent, according to Timothy McMahon at InflationData.

But life being what it is, education is still the best ticket out of the barrio, and conservative leaders would be doing a disservice by not emphasizing education when they speak to Hispanic audiences. We will see in Chapter 10 what solutions they should offer.

Illegitimacy can be only a partial explanation for high dropout rates among Hispanics, as black Americans have more out-of-wedlock births but still drop out of high school at half the rate of Hispanics (though they have a higher NAEP gap). There are myriad other reasons, starting with the low educational level of many Hispanic parents as well as the fact that Hispanics don't know the system.

"I didn't understand how important it was to stay involved with your child's education, how important it is for the child to succeed," a Salvadoran-born woman in the heavily Hispanic Columbia Heights neighborhood of Washington, DC, told me. "We Hispanic women need to learn how to work with the school system. We need to know what they're teaching so we can reinforce it at home."

Perhaps more important, Hispanics generally go to inner-city public schools, which nearly always are academically behind the suburban schools where many non-Hispanic whites tend to go, a subject we will take up in Chapter 11.

A 2012 Brookings study shows that Hispanic children start out not far behind non-Hispanic white children in such measures as basic reading and math skills but keep falling further behind so that by age twenty-nine, 66 percent of whites have successfully transitioned to adulthood (living independently, having graduated from college, and maintaining a salary at least 250 percent of the poverty rate) compared with only 47 percent of Hispanics.

Academic theories abound to explain the source of the education gap. What is clear and indisputable is that Hispanics, especially Mexican-Americans, show a vast improvement in high school graduation rates from immigrant parents to their children but that progress stalls thereafter.

It seems that religiosity is among the highest determinants of academic success. Merely attending church services once a week adds about a year of schooling for Mexican-American children. Attending parochial school is an even stronger determinant, leading Telles and Ortiz to refer to it as "a Catholic private school bonus," partly because these schools impart a "common sense of values based on religious beliefs." Skin color, in contrast, doesn't seem to play a role in schooling. In other words, white, European-descended Mexican-Americans do no better or worse than their bronze-skinned counterparts.

Other social scientists have emphasized the taboo against "acting white" that is seen also among African-Americans as one of the reasons some Hispanic kids academically underperform their white and Asian peers. There is also the question of low expectations by educators and the negative impact that can have on students (though it can also act as motivator of success, as we saw with

Jonathan Espinoza of the "I'll show my teacher I can do it" variety in Chapter 1).

The NAEP cited such family breakdown factors as "out-of-wedlock births [and] two-parent versus one-parent families" as probable causes of the persistent educational gap, mentioning also "family income, home literacy development, child care, educational resources in the home, and the parent-school relationship."

Telles and Ortiz conclude that discrimination is probably the culprit, stating that "our research supports the claim of many educators that public school failure for many Mexican-Americans derives from a racialized system that stigmatizes Mexican-American children in various ways. Racialization through schooling seems to help cement their low status in American society." Once again, they seem to be ignoring that official consignment to minority status, barrio pedagogy, and other forms of victim mongering can pigeonhole Hispanics into roles that depict them as being in a lowly status. When your government and your school are constantly telling you that you're a victim of a racist society who needs protection, you may start believing it at some point.

INCARCERATION

Given the breakup of the family and the education gap, it should not be surprising that Hispanic males are about three times as likely to be incarcerated as white males, though only one-third as likely as African-American males. More worrying is that according to Pew, "native-born Hispanic males are significantly more likely to be in prison or jail than foreign-born Hispanic males"—another statistic in which generations born in this country do worse than immigrants. It also means that the prison population is not affected by illegal status in the United States.

DEPENDENCY

The issues laid out above have led to a large and growing Hispanic dependence on government support, which hinders their mobility and produces bigger government and thus less freedom for everyone. According to the Census Bureau, 53 percent of Hispanics live in households that receive means-tested noncash assistance and 44 percent live in households in which at least one person is covered by Medicaid.

As for the main cash-assistance program, Temporary Assistance for Needy Families, known by policy wonks as TANF and by everyone else simply as welfare, the Office of Family Assistance at HHS says that "Hispanic children comprised 34.7 percent of recipient children in FY 2010; while 31.4 percent of TANF recipient children were African-American, and 27.1 percent were white."

Among adults, Hispanics were also overrepresented: 37 percent of TANF adult recipients are white, compared with 33 percent of African-Americans, 24 percent of Hispanics, and 2.4 percent of Asians.

In another program, the Special Supplemental Nutrition Program for Women, Infants and Children (WIC), about 41 percent of recipients were Hispanic in 2008, the last year for which the US Department of Agriculture has figures. The department is notoriously bad about releasing demographic figures for WIC and the related food stamp program.

These assistance programs are available to anyone who fulfills the required criteria, and this is one of the problems with welfare entitlements given by state or federal governments compared with assistance given at a more local level. Communities are best positioned to consider families' true needs. When assistance programs are administered from on high, abstract requirements must be set, and once they're met, individuals are made to feel like fools if they don't take what's coming to them.

Recently it has been the US government itself that has been actively trying to wear down people's natural resistance to going on the dole.

Take the case of food stamps. The US Department of Agriculture (USDA) says about one-fifth of the recipients are Hispanic, only slightly above Hispanics' proportion of the population. But the Obama administration has been aggressively recruiting Hispanics to go on food stamps on Spanish-language TV.

To be sure, the Obama administration has been going after every group to get on food stamps, using a Clinton era loophole known as "broad-based categorical eligibility," which weakens income limit requirements and waives asset limits entirely. As Heritage puts it, "Food stamps has been transformed from a program for the truly needy to a routine bonus payment stacked on top of conventional unemployment benefits." Many states have gotten in on the act and started hiring "recruiters" to bring people into the food stamp program. According to an April 13, 2013, *Washington Post* story, one recruiter in Florida had to deal with many people reluctant to be a burden on the government. One told the recruiter, "I don't want to be another person depending on the government," to which she answered, "How about being another person getting the help you deserve?" Unsurprisingly, as of March 2014 there were 47 million people receiving food stamps, one of every six Americans, a record.

The recruitment of Hispanics into the program was nothing but brazen. The online news site the *Daily Caller* caught the Obama administration trying to persuade Hispanics to get over their innate pride and go on food stamps by subliminally placing messages in Spanish-language adverts that were surreptitiously made to sound like radio soap operas, or telenovelas. To top it off, the USDA was working in tandem with the government of Mexico to promote food stamp use.

In one of the USDA-produced soaps, one of the characters fights back when her friend suggests that her family accept the aid, saying, "I don't need anyone's help. My husband earns enough to take care of us." Her friend mocks her, saying, "Ay, girl. When are you going to learn?" Eventually the woman gives in and enrolls her family for food stamps.

Senator Jeff Sessions of Alabama took to the Senate floor and asked:

> Is this the right approach for America? We need to work to help people with pride, help people to assume their own independence, and to be successful, and take care of their own families and move them from dependence to independence.

The furor became so great that the Obama administration withdrew the soap operas. But as of the writing of this book, it was still working with the government of Mexico to increase participation among Mexican-Americans. The USDA was still was saying on its website, "USDA and the government of Mexico have entered into a partnership to help educate eligible Mexican nationals living in the United States about available nutrition assistance. Mexico will help disseminate this information through its embassy and network of approximately 50 consular offices."

The Obama administration and the assistance lobby generally respond that the government has a responsibility to, as the USDA puts it, "reach out to underserved groups to raise awareness of the nutrition benefits of SNAP." Indeed, the Obama administration always goes to great lengths to point out that many Hispanics "are missing out on benefits" (in the words of a sympathetic group, the Center for Budget and Policy Priorities) as only about 56 percent of SNAP-eligible Hispanic families participate in the food stamp program.

But food stamps in particular are known as the "gateway drug" of government dependence because they are so easy to receive and they get people accustomed to relying on government help. The Obama administration's efforts to get Hispanics hooked on government is pervasive and is both explicit and concealed. Thus, the face of the woman on the Obamacare.gov website for the first few weeks of its failed launch looked vaguely Hispanic, and it turned out that she was an immigrant from Colombia. It is a cautionary tale that "Adriana" in the end begged to have her face taken off the website and broke into tears while telling ABC News what it was like being the face of such a monumental failure.

Even if we accept that the bureaucrats are acting with the best intentions, we must demand that they think twice before they lure Hispanics into dependence on government.

In general, when we look at the rates of illegitimacy, education, incarceration, and government dependence, what should really concern us is that second-generation Hispanics fall short of closing the gap with non-Hispanic whites and that the third generation plateaus even further. We see this generational deterioration across the board; with family breakdown, incarceration, education, income, and other measures, the longer Hispanics are in this country, the worse they perform.

Generational progress in the all-important poverty indicator is also scant. A quarter of Hispanic immigrants are poor, compared with 10 percent of white Americans. That rate goes down to 17 percent in the second generation *but hardly moves in the third.*

IT'S NOT JUST HISPANICS

I have so far recounted a circular tale of pathologies leading to dependence leading to further pathologies among the Hispanic community. It is important to note, however, that all these problems are present and rising not just among Hispanics and African-Americans but also among working-class whites. These problems are less racial and ethnic than cultural and economic. Class is the new race.

There is no consolation in stating that fact, as it provides further evidence that too many Hispanics are assimilating downward. It is a necessary reminder, however, that the adoption of these pathologies has less to do with ethnicity or Latin American culture than with the general direction in which our country is going, and it underlines how habits and values matter. As the Heritage Foundation's Stuart Butler wrote in a groundbreaking *National Affairs* article in 2013 laying out the importance of having the right habits to succeed:

[T]he more important feature of America's market economy is that it rewards other traits typically passed from parents to children—traits like perseverance, far-sightedness, love of education, prudent risk-taking, and raw intelligence. The transmission of these crucial qualities, rather than simply silver spoons in children's mouths, explains why success in America is tied so closely to one's parentage. In many other countries, one's economic advancement is determined much more by factors less related to upbringing, such as conformity to social norms and seniority in the workplace. Because of these different priorities, the correlation between a parent's success and his child's is much weaker in these other countries.

Like whites, Hispanics and African-Americans who escape the self-perpetuating treadmill of family breakdown, illegitimacy, lack of education, criminality, and incarceration and start a virtuous cycle of strong families, hard work, perseverance, education, and honesty can and will succeed in America. It may take more grit and determination to thrive when one starts out with the handicaps of bad and dangerous neighborhoods and schools, but success is within the reach of those who strive for it by making the right choices.

It is Charles Murray's findings at the other end of the societal spectrum, those related to the "new lower class," that deserve our attention, however. For there we find among whites many of the same pathologies we find among many Hispanics.

"The separation of the new lower class from the norms of traditional America would be interesting but not alarming if it represented nothing more than alternative ways of living that work equally as well as the old ways of living," Murray writes, adding immediately, however, that this is not the case. The choices being made by the new lower classes "affect the ability of people to live satisfying lives, the ability of communities to function as communities, *and the ability of America to survive as America*" [my italics].

This is not hyperbole. We increasingly have two Americas, a country newly divided by lifestyles and values. The top income quintile of the population is made up mostly by people with intact families who are professional, are mainly white or Asian, and live in suburbs or city neighborhoods with healthy social capital: an active PTA, Boy Scouts, church groups, swim teams, and the like.

At the other end are those in the bottom two quintiles, the working class, where Hispanic overrepresentation may if anything grow, living with growing rates of divorce and out-of-wedlock births with the attendant ills of poor school performance, truancy, and criminality.

This cleavage makes it harder for all children at the bottom— again, increasingly Hispanic—to compete with those at the top. They start out not only with less material wealth but, much more important, with less social and human capital. This is happening just as our society ramps up a new economy that increasingly re- wards those who work with their minds analyzing and process- ing symbols—people such as lawyers, professors, journalists, and scientists—and ramps down manual labor jobs by exporting them to other countries or putting downward wage pressure on those it cannot export.

Compounding the problem is that as a result of these factors, the ability to move up and down the income ladder may have be- come calcified in America. According to the Pew Economic Mo- bility Project, 43 percent of children raised in the bottom income quintile will be stuck there *their whole lives.* A further 27 percent will make it only to the second quintile. Only 9 percent will make it to the fourth quintile (keep in mind that it is only in the fourth quintile that people's after-tax income begins to rise above mean income levels), and only 4 percent are expected to make it to the fifth quintile. Though there is still debate among economists as to whether mobility has become even stickier over time, many believe it has. The Federal Reserve Bank of Boston was definitive in 2011, saying, "a variety of measures indicate that US family income mo- bility has decreased over the 1969–2006 time span, and especially since the 1980s. . . . families have become increasingly less likely to change rank." If this is accurate, it means that the rags-to-riches stories that were once the staple of American writing are now rarer.

Is this a situation Hispanics cannot break out of? Not at all. But they must be given access to the knowledge that the habits they see in the popular culture are not always conducive to success. Conservatives especially should understand that these bad choices are all too often incentivized by government.

Chapter 9

BATTLEGROUND

> *Know thyself, know thy enemy. A thousand battles,*
> *a thousand victories.*
>
> —SUN TZU

N
O TWO STATES SYMBOLIZE THE SPIRIT OF AMERICA BETTER
than California and Texas. From diametrically opposed perspectives—culturally, socially, geographically, and politically—
they embody our character in ways that are instantly recognized
nationally and internationally. A moviegoer in dusty Karachi or
sunny Seville may not know much about our Constitution but
can tell a surfer from a cowboy, a Hollywood mogul from an oil
baron. These two states—regions, really, comparable in size, population, and importance to New England, the Old South, and the
Midwest—are united in one country based on individual liberty.
But if California and Texas were countries, they'd be seen to be as
different as France is from Germany.

California and Texas stand for two radically different faces of
the Hispanic experience in this country or, more to the point, the
Mexican-American experience. They are the two largest states in
the union, with 38 million people and 27 million people, respectively. They both also have an equal percentage of the population
that is Hispanic, 38 percent, and both are majority-minority states,
or states where no one group has an outright majority (the only two
other such states in the Union are New Mexico and Hawaii). Both
California and Texas were settled by Spain and were briefly part of
Mexico after its independence from Madrid in 1821.

There the similarities end. Texas went its own way after it broke from Mexico and became an independent republic in 1836; California was annexed by the United States at the end of the Mexican War in 1848 and very quickly became a state, never going through the territorial stage. One is deep red, giving Romney an 18-point margin in 2012, the other deep blue, giving Obama the same margin. One has no income tax, a small welfare state, and low regulation. The other—well, you know.

The question now is about the future: Will California and Texas point the way to two future different Mexican-American subcultures in this country or will the Golden State, as it often has done for the rest of the country, be a trendsetter whose integration (or disintegration) model will be adopted soon in the Lone Star State?

If they really want to take the country back, as they repeatedly say they do, conservatives will have to win Hispanics back. To do that they would do well to understand the duel between two models playing out in Texas and California.

The conservative political class, including the donors, should take this duel seriously.

TEXAS'S WAY

"We are kind of in a race in Texas over what direction the state will go," warns Joshua S. Treviño, a multigenerational Texan who also knows California firsthand from living there for years. He is in the thick of this duel as vice president for communications at the Texas Public Policy Foundation.

One road leads to a continuation of Texas's culture of economic growth, self-help, small government, low regulation, patriotism, and entrepreneurship, all of which apply also to the state's large Hispanic population. The other road leads to the California model of large transfer payments, significant portions of the population on the dole, economic paralysis, identity politics, and ethnic conflict.

If you don't know there's a paradigm fight at hand in Texas, the Left does. The Democratic Party is going all out to flip Texas from red to purple and then to blue. But many fear the effort doesn't stop at politics. Liberals play for the long term; they understand that politics stands downstream from culture, and it is there that they want to make their mark. They've done this before—changing the country with the counterculture of the 1960s—and think they can do it again.

The fight therefore is not just about Texas but about something much larger—the entire country. Big money is involved in the effort. Liberal donors, GOP strategists say, are more patient than conservative ones. They are less interested in seeing the TV ads they paid for—which, as the 2012 race showed, produce less bang for the buck than people once thought—and keener about the slow but inexorable turning around of the ship of state. Conservatives would be wrong to be lulled into complacency by the dismal 2014 campaign for governor by Democrat Wendy Davis.

Hispanics are the central players in this effort to turn Texas into the next California. There is no similar effort to flip California and turn it red. As former California party leader Ron Nehring told me, "the Republican party will not win another statewide election until we can win at least 40 percent of the Latino vote, and that won't happen until the national brand improves." The reason liberals think they can flip Texas is that there is a large and growing Hispanic population there. And if they can flip Texas, they can convert the country to their progressive image.

The progressives' political strategy is this: early in 2013 a handful of veterans of the successful effort to reelect President Obama headed to Texas and firmly planted their flag, creating an organization called Battleground Texas whose aim is to change the state.

The motivating idea behind Battleground Texas is that the state's Mexican-American population is not turning out to vote in the numbers at which they should be voting.

"Battleground Texas is a grassroots organization that will make Texas a battleground state by treating it like one," the organization's head, Jeremy Bird, told RealClearPolitics in February 2013, after the organization got off the ground. "Over the next several years, Battleground Texas will focus on expanding the electorate by registering more voters—and by mobilizing Texans who are already registered voters but who have not been engaged in the democratic process."

A memo prepared for the rollout spoke about how the electoral college vote–rich state—its 38 votes are second only to California's 54—could "virtually remake the presidential campaign map. But the current political landscape in the state is keeping Texas—and its residents—from meeting its promise and being relevant at a national level." The priority, as it has been in other states where Obama succeeded, would be "voter registration and engagement efforts," according to the memo.

Implied in all this is the recognition that the Texas Democratic Party had just about given up and needed national reinforcements. The party's communications director, Tanene Allison, confessed as much to RealClearPolitics when she said, "The [state] party has not been leading—clearly."

The national players include Alex Steele, a veteran Obama campaigner who became Texas field director; Jeremy Bird, national field director for the 2012 reelection, who will lead the Texas effort; Jenn Brown, the campaign's Ohio field director; and Christina Gomez, digital strategist at the Democratic National Committee.

The operative words here are *Ohio* and *digital*; the Obama campaign's get-out-the-vote effort in that Midwestern state was nothing short of masterful, as was a digital operation that ran circles around Romney's snakebitten electronic effort. Also, both Steele and Brown are native Californians.

A visit to the Battleground Texas website reveals who the target of the outreach is: just about every photograph is chock-full of smiling Mexican-Americans wearing Barack Obama T-shirts and waving signs that read "Vote Democratic." The "About Us" tab, meanwhile, leads to a statement that does not leave much to the imagination, starting with the headline "Texas at a Crossroads":

> The Lone Star State is changing—and with its size and diversity, our state should be a place where all elections—from local elections all the way up to the President of United States are hotly contested.

To do that, we need Texans in every corner of the state—
from Amarillo to Brownsville and El Paso to Beaumont—to
stand up and say that they're tired of not being heard, tired of
not being represented in Austin and in Washington, DC, and
tired of the same Republican playbook which is failing our
communities and ignoring the needs of countless Texans. . . .

The strategy is based on the demographic fact that Mexican-
Americans will soon pass the tipping point of parity with non-
Hispanic whites, just as they probably will have done in California
by the time this book is printed.

"It is not a question of if Texas will become a swing state but
when," Matthew Dowd, a Texan and former George W. Bush strategist, told Bloomberg News in 2013. "Demography is inexorably
pushing Texas from solid Republican state to swing state over time.
And it is a serious problem for Republicans in putting together a
winning electoral coalition as Texas does move to a swing state."

The effort did not begin in 2013 but before the 2012 election.
It was not for nothing that the keynote speaker at the Democratic
National Convention was none other than San Antonio's photoge-
nic mayor, Julián Castro.

A Stanford and Harvard Law graduate, Castro comes from a
family steeped in politics. His identical twin brother, Joaquín, represents San Antonio in the US House of Representatives, and his
mother, Rosie, was a political firebrand who founded the Chicano
nationalist party La Raza Unida. Like Los Angeles Mayor Antonio
Villaraigosa, Castro comes from a broken home. His father, Jesse
Guzman, never married Rosie and ran out on the family when the
twins were six. The articulate and bright Castro is clearly being
groomed for bigger things. Since his speech at the convention he
has become a habitual Democratic spokesman on the Sunday news
shows. Castro, in other words, is the Democratic Party's answer to
Marco Rubio.

Time will tell, of course, but not everyone is immediately buying into the Castro as savior narrative. A Republican strategist
told me before Wendy Davis decided to run for governor that he

was salivating at the thought of Castro running for that office, because he thought Castro wasn't ready for Austin. Evidently, Castro agreed and let Davis go unchallenged as the Democratic nominee for governor, appealing to the other group Democrats want to scare off from ever supporting conservative causes: women, especially single ones. This much Davis was doing in early 2014, though in a campaign that got off to a very rocky start.

With regard to Hispanics in Texas, however, it is hard to ignore that Republicans have increased their margin of victory at the same time that the Hispanic population has been growing in the state in terms of numbers and percentage and as Hispanic voter turnout has grown.

There is a difference between Mexican-Americans in Texas and those in California. Their background tells a big part of the story. From the beginning, they have been very different. Conservatives who think they can hold the line at Texas are also placing their bets on Hispanics, in fact. In Texas, Mexican-Americans are an organic part of society, deeply interwoven in the state's history and cultural fabric. This is less the case in California.

A BIT OF HISTORY

The preexisting Hispanic populations were very different to start with. Texas's Mexican population was large, between 15 percent and 25 percent of the new state, so there could possibly have been as many as 50,000 of the so-called Tejanos. California's Hispanic population at the time Mexico ceded the state, by contrast, was small, around 10,000 when it was admitted to the Union in 1850. These so-called Californios were swiftly overwhelmed by the hundreds of thousands who flocked to the state in the Gold Rush of 1848.

"California Hispanics have a very tenuous thread to the past," says Treviño. "I lived in California for several years and cannot remember a single time when someone said to me, 'Oh, I'm a descendent of one of the original Californians.' They're all recent imports, going back at most to the 1920s."

In Texas, Mexican-American mutual aid societies were often patriotic and religious in character. One, the *Orden Hijos de America* (Order of the Sons of America), stated in its constitution that the group's goal was to use its influence "to realize the greatest enjoyment possible of all the rights and privileges and prerogatives extended by the American Constitution."

The OSA in time joined other groups to form the League of United Latin American Citizens (LULAC), often compared to the National Association for the Advancement of Colored People in its early days in that its thrust was to hold the US government to the promises of the Declaration and the rights enumerated in the Constitution. Leftists have often disparaged the early LULAC as an establishment group that sought normalcy for its constituents—read equality, not separateness. (LULAC has since then turned sharply leftward.)

Texas's harsh rural poverty combined with an even harsher clime and topography to breed a frontier mentality in which neighbor helped neighbor. Mexicans in Texas, and especially the people who spoke for them, were unabashedly patriotic, joined the army, and fought segregation tooth and nail as they sought not a separate identity but a piece of the great American pie.

It is very difficult to find parallels to any of this in California. The Colonial-era Franciscan friars who established missions to convert Indians and tend to the needs of the Spanish soldiers in the presidios never strayed far from the coast. The missions left little mark on the California of today. Even Florida's Spanish period has left a more enduring imprint.

California's path to equality emphasized less patriotism and more separation and identity politics. Its more militant Chicano Movement was about sit-ins, bilingual education, and "Chicano studies." California is also the home of the United Farm Workers and its 1960s founder, Cesar Chavez. Unlike the OSA, the Chicano Movement emphasized pride in Mexicans' distinctiveness and a refusal to assimilate. Like President Obama, Chavez was influenced by Saul Alinsky, the radical whose *Rules for Radicals* was a manual for subverting society.

Telles and Ortiz's book, which compares Mexican-Americans

in San Antonio with those in Los Angeles, the two emblematic
Mexican-American cities in Texas and California, concludes with
what may be a paradox: "Mexican Americans are more Mexican in
lifestyles and behaviors in San Antonio but are more Democratic
and politically liberal in Los Angeles." Those in San Antonio are
more likely to identify as white and vote Republican, the researchers found. Assertions of an aggressively nonwhite racial identity
emerged, however, in Los Angeles, which, the authors say, "provided a fertile ground for progressive political activism, including
the Chicano movement."

WELFARE

As we can see, history sets apart Texas and California more than
one might think. Its progress through nearly two centuries has
made Hispanics in one state more conservative and in the other
more progressive. When one gets right down to it, however, the
biggest difference between the two states is the size and the mentality of the respective welfare states. This has also had an impact
on the two states' Hispanic populations.

California's overly expansive welfare state has landed a higher
percentage of its population on public assistance than has been the
case in almost any other state in the Union. Texas, in contrast, has
consigned fewer of its people to public assistance. With 12 percent
of the total US population, California has 34 percent of the welfare
caseload, for an overrepresentation of 238 percent. That means that
though only one of eight Americans lives in California, the state
is home to more than one of three welfare recipients in the entire
United States. By contrast, Texas, with 8 percent of the US population, has only 3 percent of the country's welfare caseload, for an
underrepresentation rate of 35 percent.

To put it further in perspective, California's 34 percent is not
just the highest; California is the only state in double digits. The
state with the second largest percentage of active welfare cases,
New York, with 19 million people, has only 7 percent of the nation's caseload. Texas's 3 percent, meanwhile, is the third lowest

in the country, undercut only by thinly populated Wyoming and Idaho.

California also has one of the highest monthly cash transfers to the average family on welfare, $638, according to the *San Diego Union Tribune*. Of course, all this profligacy has left California cities staggering under the massive weight of municipal liabilities.

Overly generous welfare programs that keep families on the dole longer and give them more money incentivize lifetime dependency instead of providing temporary relief. It is therefore unsurprising that California's unemployment rate is much higher than the national average—9 percent in April 2013 compared with 7.5 percent for the country—whereas Texas's, at 6 percent, is much lower. For Hispanics, the comparison is even stronger. California's Hispanic unemployment rate runs about 3 percentage points higher than the national average, whereas Texas's runs about 2 points below the national average.

What has all this produced? According to the US Census, California's poverty rate is 23.5 percent, the highest in the nation, and Texas's is 16.5 percent. "Proportionately, there are 42 percent more poor people in California than in Texas," says the Texas Public Policy Foundation.

Californians singed by the comparison with Texas are always quick to point out that the Lone Star State is rich in oil. They neglect to talk about all the attributes that God has given the Golden State, including not just a gorgeous coast and weather but oil, which California regulations make it difficult to extract.

Probably as a result—though again it is difficult to assign causality—Texas's Hispanic population is also much more entrepreneurial than California's. Texas's Hispanics are much more likely to start businesses than are California's, for example. Texas's rate of Hispanic-owned businesses as a percentage of the Hispanic population is 57 percent, whereas California's is 45 percent.

The stereotype that Texas's success is based on low-paying McJobs that trap the poor is also untrue, says the Dallas Fed's Pia Orrenius. Low regulations and taxes have attracted businesses, and that has led to labor demand and therefore competitive wages. "On an adjusted wages basis, Texas has relatively high wages among the least-skilled, compared to the rest of the nation," she said.

At the high end, Texas has outpaced the United States in terms of job growth in the highest wage quartile, 26.1 percent to 7.3 percent, according to the Current Population Survey.

Although it may be a chicken and egg question which phenomenon caused which, the reality is that Texas's frugality does go together with a culture of self-help. According to a *Houston Chronicle* article in November 2012, many poor Texas families that might qualify for cash assistance don't apply. Shannon Perry, manager of social service outreach for the Houston Food Bank, told the paper, "People are resourceful. They go to churches, food pantries, friends and neighbors. These people find ways to get by."

Or as the former Texas state representative from Hidalgo County Aaron Peña puts it, public assistance "can be hazardous to the culture of a people. I don't object to giving a certain amount of assistance, it's when it becomes sustained that it ruins communities. Our history taught us to survive on our own."

Peña, a lawyer today, recalls that the Mexican-American community in the Rio Grande Valley even had its own medicinal system, a mix of European and Indian practices. "We had *curanderas*, who practiced folk medicine," he said. "I saw my grandparents practice it and depend on it, and great-aunts and great-uncles. We had to depend on each other because it was all we had."

When the Great Society programs came in, those interlocking networks started to fray. Peña commented, "After the '60s a lot of the self-sustaining institutions broke down. A lot of the old family structures and institutions that we had here just broke down."

Peña remembers real racism—his family was not able to go to certain restaurants because they didn't let Mexicans in—and he is very glad those days are gone. He is certain that Presidents Johnson and Nixon were motivated by the desire to end the scourges of racism and poverty.

But the programs didn't become a temporary hand up to pull people out of a hole but a permanent handout. "The problem with sustained help is that people become dependent," he said. "Human beings adapt to it. It can be hazardous to the culture of a people. I don't object to giving a certain amount of assistance; it's when it becomes sustained that it ruins communities."

Today, he says, "the self-support system is gone. Today's generation is less independent, less self-sustainable. The difference between the generation of my grandparents and today's generation is enormous, unbelievable. I was so lucky that I got to see the old generation. They were supermen and superwomen, fighters. They had character."

The two states' different history and welfare dependency status have had an impact on family formation, religiosity, and the educational gap, three important cultural indicators that are associated with stability, ability to move upward on the income scale, and conservatism.

According to the Census Bureau, Hispanics in Texas are 10 percent more likely to be married than those in California (47 percent to 43 percent) and close to 20 percent less likely never to have been married (36.9 percent to 43.5 percent), less likely to have had a child out of wedlock in the previous year (39.8 percent to 42.6 percent), one-third more likely to have served in the military (4.1 percent to 2.8 percent), and one-third less likely to have received Supplemental Security Income (SSI) public assistance income (2.4 percent to 6.2 percent). One of the most eye-popping statistics I have come across is that Hispanics in Texas are almost one-third more likely to live in an owner-occupied home than those in California (56.8 percent to 42.9 percent).

In terms of religiosity, the General Social Survey shows that Hispanics in Texas are far more likely to attend church services regularly.

The National Assessment of Educational Progress is pretty definitive about which state has done better by its Hispanic students. The educational gap between Hispanics and non-Hispanic white students is much smaller in Texas than in California, where it is statistically significantly higher than it is in the rest of the nation.

The fourth-grade mathematics gap for Texas was 20 points, below the national average; in California it was 28 points. For the eighth grade, the Texas gap was 24 and California's was 33. In reading comprehension, the fourth-grade Texas gap was 22 and California's was 31, and for eighth-graders, Texas's gap was 22 and California's was 28. In all four measures Texas outperformed the rest of the nation; California was among the worst performers.

If California's aim was indeed separatism, it seems to have succeeded—and failed its Hispanic population. Texas's approach appears to be working, however.

CULTURE CLASH

Conservatives in Texas are starting to wake up to the fact that their culture of self-help, entrepreneurship, relative family stability, and religiosity among Hispanics may be in the crosshairs of the Democratic Party's campaign to turn the state blue. Liberals know much better than conservatives that if you change the culture, the politics will follow. Conservatives do fret about cultural trends, but they put the emphasis on local community and family, and so they don't think as often about changing the entire culture as liberals do.

"There's a quite aggressive effort to replicate in Texas the California experience, which has been disastrous for Hispanics in California, who are being ghettoized, especially in the Central Valley," says Treviño. "California has a very well-developed welfare state, and whenever you have a welfare state, a community that is given privileges, it cleaves society."

In California, he says, "it's possible to grow up with a separatist identity. You can be in Sacramento for Cesar Chavez Day and hear all this separatist talk. It's almost like the Palestinian question grafted on the California Hispanic population."

If you're a Hispanic in California, then, you will go through twelve years of primary education hearing about repression against you as a Mexican; if you go to college, the message will only be amplified. That's sixteen years of indoctrination. Then, when you get out, if you're an entrepreneur, there's a huge array of benefits. In Texas you get some of that, but to a much smaller degree, especially in K–12. In Texas students also spend a long time studying Texas history, to a degree that doesn't happen in California.

Indeed, an attempt to indoctrinate young Texans with relativism and leftist economics just ran afoul of lawmakers in Austin, who, spurred by popular criticism, were trying to scuttle it in mid-2013. The K–12 curriculum, called CSCOPE, advocates teaching lessons that support wearing the Muslim hijab, or forcing women to cover their faces in public, all the while disparaging Christianity as a cult. The curriculum also called for sixth-graders to create communist flags and taught that communism was a higher-order economic model than capitalism. Another fun part of CSCOPE was disparaging the Founding Fathers.

Texans fighting CSCOPE know full well that relentless grievance mongering in California accounts at least partly for the huge vote differential between Hispanics in Texas and those in California. Hispanics, after all, make up an equal proportion of the population in both states, 38 percent, and have similar shares of the vote turnout (Texas's Hispanic turnout is, if anything, slightly higher than California's), yet they vote very differently.

Hispanic numbers in Texas have been respectable for the GOP. In 2008, for example, McCain got 35 percent of the Hispanic vote in Texas. In 2012, Romney also took 35 percent, much better than the 29 percent he won nationwide among Hispanics (in Texas, Hispanic voters are nearly all Mexican-American). Ted Cruz, meanwhile, got 40 percent of that vote in his successful run for the US Senate.

You might say that 60 percent of Hispanics voting against Cruz is not so great given that, well, he is Hispanic himself. But let's not forget that Cruz is Cuban, and only half Cuban at that. Forty percent of the Mexican-American vote for a very conservative politician is an extremely good sign for Hispanic conservatives.

Now consider California. In 2008, when McCain captured 31 percent of the Hispanic vote nationwide to Obama's 67 percent,

California Hispanics gave McCain only a paltry 23 percent. In 2012, California Hispanics gave Romney 29 percent, the same as the Hispanic vote nationwide.

This is a 6-point differential in the 2012 election versus a 12-point one in 2008. What accounts for that? Some of the history we've just been through in this chapter, to be sure. But history is not the only thing that affects culture. Conservatives who worry that a culture of dependence will create more liberal voters have a point, and they must keep a wary eye on efforts to increase government-run social services in Texas.

"You look at California, where Obama won by 18 points, and you look at Texas, where Romney won by 18 points. That's a 36-point differential," says Chuck DeVore, a former California assemblyman who finally had enough of liberal policies and transplanted himself to Texas. "If that is the case, it is because those damn Texans are too damn self-reliant. Somehow they think that the ability to have a roof over their heads and have the basics of life is enough. So you have to make them think that they need benefits."

The fact that the US Department of Agriculture has teamed up with the Mexican government to spread information on how people of Mexican origin can apply for food stamps unsettles many for a variety of reasons. First, food stamps are only one government assistance area in which Texas leads California. "It's a gateway drug," says DeVore.

Second, it is worth asking whether the government should be in the business of spreading dependency. This strikes many Americans as corrupting the populace. What the government should be doing, Americans who take this view would say, is fostering the self-reliant spirit that refuses to accept aid as much as possible, not undermining it.

Third, current immigration law makes it clear that "public charges" are not eligible for immigration visas. Bureaucrats have redefined food stamps so that recipients are not deemed public charges for the purpose of immigration law, but that only makes critics more furious, as they charge that it is a clear violation of the spirit of the law because it makes the definition of a public charge a technical, bureaucratic one.

Fourth, the fact that the USDA says on its website, "Mexico will help disseminate this information through its embassy and network of approximately 50 consular offices," is a bit of a last straw and makes many wonder whether there isn't a political end in mind.

"The federal government is trying to promote welfare dependency in the Rio Grande," sums up Treviño. "It's a deliberate effort to create a coalition of dependency among Hispanics. If you got control over the money, you got political power."

Turning Texas blue will not be as easy as many Democratic strategists believe, but Republicans should not be as confident as they tell me they are. If the state's thirty-eight electoral college votes ever go to the Democratic Party, the game is over. There just isn't a way the GOP can win a national race without Texas's votes unless it so remakes itself that Illinois and New York become competitive again, in which case the party would be unrecognizable.

Conservatives are right to worry, too, about spreading welfare reliance. The link between the growth of government, problems such as the breakdown of the family, and support for liberal causes is well established and circularly reinforcing.

One of the best ways to protect self-reliance is, of course, to make sure that the needy are taken care of through private means. It is important to emphasize to all the principle that self-reliance does not mean "you're on your own" but rather "we'll take care of our own." It is important, too, to make the case again and again that the welfare policies pursued by California have hit Hispanics the hardest. It is not Hispanics who have failed California; it is the state's philosophy that has failed all its citizens.

Endeavors such as bilingual education and Chicano studies have not helped. "It's not good for Hispanics to be separate; America is a great place, capitalism is a great system," says Treviño.

Conservatives concerned about taking back the country should examine policies that will help make upward mobility a reality. The culture is the big prize, however. Learning to celebrate Hispanic culture, especially the aspects of Mexican culture that are key to the American spirit, while conserving the all-important principle of E pluribus unum could be the trick that saves the country.

The next part of the book will be about why it is both desirable and feasible for conservatives to address the challenges we have covered in earlier chapters to help Hispanics who have fallen behind climb the ladder of success. Most important, we will discuss how to get that done.

PART III

THE
WAY
FORWARD

Chapter 10

THE ULTIMATE FORMS OF SOCIAL CAPITAL: THE FAMILY AND THE COMMUNITY

The first bond of society is marriage.

—Cicero

IN MARCH 2004 THE LATE HARVARD HISTORIAN SAMUEL P. HUN-tington published in the journal *Foreign Policy* an article (also expanded into a book) that set off waves that are still with us. Huntington's main premise was that Latin American immigration, especially from Mexico, posed a special challenge to American national identity that no other immigrant wave had ever presented. The piece upset many people, especially Hispanics who write about such things from a liberal perspective.

"In this new era, the single most immediate and most serious challenge to America's traditional identity comes from the immense and continuing immigration from Latin America, especially from Mexico, and the fertility rates of these immigrants compared to black and white American natives," wrote Huntington, who had served in the Reagan administration's National Security Council but did not share the Gipper's optimistic outlook.

Huntington pressed all the usual buttons. He called the Mexican presence in the Southwest part of a *reconquista* (a favorite term of such anti-immigration groups as NumbersUSA) and worried about whether the descendants of Mexican immigrants will ever speak English. The tone of the book and the article can be best described as scholarly grousing. Huntington ended the article with this polemical line: "There is no Americano dream. There is only the American dream created by an Anglo-Protestant society. Mexican Americans will share in that dream and in that society only if they dream in English."

Telles and Ortiz rightly chided Huntington, who died in 2008, for being "misinformed" about the history of Mexican-Americans. The Peruvian-born Carlos Lozada, at the time of this writing the editor of the *Washington Post*'s Outlook section but Huntington's *Foreign Policy* editor in 2004, complained in a 2013 piece that Huntington never asked him if his feelings were hurt.

Huntington's book and article serve better as a Rorschach test for conservatives' misapprehensions about Hispanics than as a look at the challenge posed by Mexican immigration. He pretty much cites everything in the conservative arsenal: the Immigration and Nationality Act, the public use of Spanish, regional concentration, and Mexicans' historical presence.

Huntington did not get everything wrong. He was right on some fronts, especially when he worried about the "failure of third- and fourth-generation people of Mexican origin to approximate U.S. norms in education, economic status and intermarriage rates." But Huntington offered no practical solution, restricting himself to griping.

Conservatives don't have the Huntingtonian luxury of limiting themselves to grumbling about Hispanics. They must offer policy solutions for these problems in the third and fourth generations. The way to do that is to offer proposals that restore the family and the community of which it is a part. We turn now to how we can do that.

LA FAMILIA

In 1965, when the US surgeon general issued a landmark study on the harmful effects of smoking tobacco, close to 60 percent of American males smoked. Today that figure is closer to 20 percent. This has been the result of a determined campaign on the part of nearly all our institutions to stamp out the habit.

The dogged struggle to persuade Americans not to light up used all the levers of power: policy making, taxing authority, and moral suasion. It is all the more remarkable that it has succeeded to the degree that it has when one considers that smoking was once seen as both glamorous and manly, a result of Hollywood's love affair with cigarettes and a residual association of smoking with the heroes of World War II.

I was once a heavy smoker who used newsrooms' floors as ashtrays with abandon. If anyone had told me in the late 1980s that one day smoking would be banned from newspapers, bars, and all public buildings and that it would be frowned upon socially, I would have found it amusing and misguided.

Yet the public relations effort against smoking has succeeded. Indeed, America is now embarking on a downright silly public relations effort against, of all things, sodas and fast food.

If we can have successful campaigns against Marlboros, Coca-Cola, and McDonald's, we can certainly do something to save that most fundamental of social capital structures, the family. Slowing down runaway Hispanic illegitimacy and family breakdown and then helping intact families get off welfare so that they can become avid contributors to the social network in their communities should be a national priority. Smoking kills you, and grease and sugar make you fat. The breakdown of the family will destroy not just us but our progeny and the nation they will inherit. On the importance of social capital, especially the family, there's a consensus that encompasses Berkeley, Harvard, and the Heritage Foundation: "Some of the strongest predictors of upward mobility are correlates of social capital and family structure," said a Harvard-Berkeley study in 2013.

Addressing the ills that ail the family should be the main mantra of any leader venturing out into the Hispanic community. Don't wear a sombrero and ask them for their vote a week before the election; show them even in off years that you care about what's happening in their lives. Conservative leaders should speak to Hispanic audiences years before elections, do it often, and express their support for the policies and institutions that are doing something to create thriving families and neighborhoods.

Our efforts must start with the nucleus of social capital, and that is the family, at the center of which is a solid legal marriage. There's no question that getting the out-of-wedlock rate down and bringing back the family will be a big task. It should, however, not be impossible. Hispanics care deeply about the family, and both Hispanic men and Hispanic women understand the responsibility of providing for it. They will be receptive to a message on these fronts if it is pitched the right way. It may be hard, but it is certainly not impossible.

The first step is slowing down family breakup and out-of-wedlock births and then reversing the process through public awareness. As the invaluable Charles Donovan wrote in 2011 when he was still with the Heritage Foundation—he left soon afterward for the Charlotte Lozier Institute—the value of marriage should be part of "what everyone knows." We need nothing less than a full-fledged public relations campaign, with public service announcements and more, that gets the word out to everyone, from the academics in the faculty lounge to children in schools in at-risk areas. Political leaders can play a very useful role in spreading the word. Everyone must get the message that marriage and child rearing cannot be separated.

Heritage's Robert Rector put it this way:

> To combat poverty it is vital to strengthen marriage, and to strengthen marriage, it is vital that at-risk populations be given a clear, factual understanding of the benefits of marriage and the costs and consequences of non-marital child-bearing.
>
> To develop this understanding, government and society should establish a broad campaign of public education in low-income areas.

After African-Americans, Hispanics are the leading at-risk population, and no effort should be spared to get them the word on marriage. As with education, the collision between a massive immigrant inflow and the unmarriage culture will be explosive and difficult for our society to handle. Some efforts are being made, but they are just a start; they need to be ramped up.

The only government programs in existence today that are aimed directly at strengthening the institution of marriage were begun by the Bush administration (in which I served in a very mid-level capacity).

In 2006, the Office of Family Assistance started a five-year initiative called Healthy Marriages and Responsible Fatherhood, which gave grants to groups working to foster stronger families. Under Bush, two-thirds of the money, or $100 million, was granted to groups that promoted marriage, for example, by teaching relationship skills and advising couples to wait till after they were wed to get pregnant. Groups working to teach men how to be good fathers got $50 million.

Organizations that receive these marriage grants, usually non-profits with a tax-exempt status, teach such relationship skills as communication, conflict resolution, and the ability to make lasting and exclusionary commitments.

It may be easy to dismiss these efforts as not accomplishing much, especially given the size of the problem. That would be looking at things from the wrong perspective. One must remember that even small changes improve the lives of children and make their futures brighter. As with the antismoking campaign, small first steps are needed to create a tidal change in the culture.

It shouldn't surprise anyone that one of the biggest recipients of the Healthy Marriages grants is the Chicago-based Family Bridges/Lazos de Familia, which caters largely to Hispanics, mostly Mexican-Americans and Puerto Ricans. Some 70,000 individuals have been served since Bridges opened its doors in 2006, counting only those who have completed the course, and it receives about $2.5 million a year in federal money.

"We go where people are," the executive director, Alicia La Hoz, told me in an interview. "We go to specific demographic areas of need" in eight counties in the Chicago area.

The vast majority of the Latinos she encounters want to marry, says La Hoz. In fact, one problem is that they have an ideal that is hard to realize, and as they wait for Mr. or Mrs. Perfect, they settle into cohabitation patterns. Rather than settle down, they settle for less as they wait.

"People have this ideal wedding—big, to someone good-looking, who's rich, who loves them. Then they slide into circumstances that limit their dream. They hook up with someone, get pregnant, so then they think, 'Now I have to live with this guy.' Then the guy leaves and they hook up with someone else, maybe for economic reasons, but that guy turns out to be a jerk," said La Hoz. The spiral is unending, and it leads downward.

To counter that, Family Bridges/Lazos de Familia teaches "good decision making, why marriage matters, how to avoid unhealthy relationships," said La Hoz. "We even have a program called How to Avoid Marrying a Jerk or a Jerkette."

Obviously, finding oneself in an alien environment puts added pressure on Latino immigrant families. When a husband and wife are both working, sometimes more than one job each, and are surrounded by a new language and isolated from their extended family, this can stress couples. But not all family breakups can be explained by the stress of immigrating. In fact, as we saw in earlier chapters, immigrants tend to have stronger families.

Some generalizations can be made about Latino patterns. An important one is that rates of cohabitation are lower among Mexican-Americans and Cuban-Americans (though, as noted earlier, they are ramping up rapidly) than they are among Puerto Ricans, whose rates are close to those of African-Americans. Another is that church-attending evangelical Protestants, a growing proportion of Hispanics in America, have lower cohabitation and out-of-wedlock rates than church-attending Catholics.

The programs that work best with Latinos, according to those with knowledge of the situation, are those that take a full family-inclusive approach. The father, whether already married to the mother of their children or not, must regularly attend the educational sessions or workshops if the program is going to succeed. It is also important to take a holistic approach to the family. Attendance will be lower if the parents must find baby-sitters and bear the cost. It therefore is effective to offer child care. Offering food for the children as a lure for participation is even better.

Not all the cultural traits brought over from Latin America are positive, to be sure. For example, part of the machismo practiced by Hispanic immigrants can include expectations of complete subservience from subordinates (which can include wives) that are clearly out of place in American society. Hispanic men can take the old dictum that a man's home is his castle to extremes, reacting badly to any questioning of authority by their wives or children. The division of labor is strong. A man's responsibility is to shoulder the main financial burden and keep the lights on. He will seldom engage in housework, whether cooking or cleaning. Of course, these strong gender archetypes begin to fade the longer immigrants are in this country. But as Roberto Reyes wrote for the Department of Health and Human Services in 2006, men who exhibit macho traits may "feel justified in engaging in destructive behaviors such as infidelity and substance abuse as long as they are fulfilling their cultural obligations to provide for their family economically."

But Hispanic immigrants' mix of strong discipline and deep nurturing is recognized by experts as the ideal combination. Children raised with the benefit of this formula show strong advantages in "psychosocial development, mental health, social competence, academic performance and avoidance of problem behavior," according to the National Resource Center for Healthy Marriage and Families tool kit for social workers. As the children of these immigrant families become Americanized, however, parents start to see the loss of parental authority.

Family Bridges has several success stories that I found gripping. One of them, involving a couple named Patricio Briceño and Norma Alfaro, illustrates how the marriage programs can work when they are at their best:

"Thirteen years into their marriage, Patricio and Norma were about to call it quits. Their relationship was plagued by fights and domestic violence. In a last attempt at change, they began attending St. Pius V Church where they were referred to a Family Bridges couples workshop.

"Patricio was impressed with the classes. Everything the instructor said applied to his life. The teachers challenged him to change and gave him tools for more peaceful and productive communication.

"Norma also started attending a women's group where she was finally able to talk about the difficult realities of her marriage. Through the classes, she learned to better understand men— especially the 'machismo' mindset. She met other women with similar struggles in their marriages, they were able to encourage and learn from one another.

"With all this training and counseling, Patricio and Norma experienced improved communication and restored trust. They even started going on dates again! As their bond with each other strengthened, Patricio and Norma were also able to restore their entire family. They asked their daughters for forgiveness for their old behavior patterns, and a new healing work began in their family.

"'Before, I was completely unhappy,' Patricio says. 'Now, I am happy.' Norma added, 'Before, I lived in darkness. Now, I have a light and safe way to the future.'"

These programs are paid for by the taxpayer to the tune of $150 million a year. Consider the potential savings, though. A 2008 study led by the economist Ben Scafidi said that if divorces across the country were reduced by even 1 percent, the resulting savings to the taxpayer would amount to $1.1 billion a year. The savings obviously come from the fact that even with child support a single mother with children nearly always will end up in a poorer status compared with a family that is whole, and therefore she is more likely to use social programs.

Marriage and relationship education is a new field, and not enough data have been gathered on its effectiveness, but we can be optimistic. In fact, one of the largest measurements of results, the Supporting Healthy Marriage Evaluation program conducted in 2012, said that "some evidence suggests that the positive estimated impacts of SHM are somewhat larger and more consistent for Hispanic couples." Conservatives seeking to make their case to Hispanics can point to these early rays of hope.

Typically, these programs were almost eliminated when the Obama administration first came in. This was either because the liberals in the administration don't like family promotion—as Bush officials charge—or because, as with democracy promotion overseas, the Obama people simply didn't like anything that had the imprimatur of the Bush administration.

The entire scheme was zeroed out in Obama's 2011 budget, when the five years would come up, and replaced with a new $500 million Fatherhood, Marriage, and Family Innovation Fund, 3.3 times the amount that had been earmarked for the Healthy Marriages and Responsible Fatherhood program. It very soon became clear that marriage promotion would not be a priority of the new fund.

The Innovation Fund, in fact, was to be a grab bag for every liberal priority in this policy area. "The Obama administration wanted to go in a different direction: help single moms, do job training, early child care, domestic violence. It was dropping the ball," Bill Coffin, the Bush era special assistant for marriage education at the Administration for Children and Families, said in an interview with me.

But people who had been doing marriage work swung into action to save an initiative they thought was vitally important to the nation. The National Association for Relationship and Marriage Education (NARME), a group devoted to promoting healthy marriage skills, went to bat to save the Healthy Marriages funding rather than supporting the Innovation Fund.

The NARME people went around the Obama administration and appealed directly to Congress. "We went to DC, hired a lobbyist, and we were successful," said Maggie Russell of NARME in an interview. "NARME made sure that folks on the Hill knew that this work was important. We said, don't end it now, we're starting to see results," said Russell.

Under pressure, the Obama administration scuttled the $500 million Innovation Fund. The price of getting the Obama people to change their minds? Splitting the $150 million originally slated for the Healthy Marriages and Responsible Fatherhood program with the fatherhood initiative 50–50; each side would get $75 million a year.

At first blush it would appear that healthy marriages and good fatherhood are complementary, but Washington is the capital city of euphemisms, a place where large ideological differences can hide behind small differences in innocuous-sounding titles. The healthy marriage people put the emphasis on abstinence before marriage, in-wedlock births, and exclusivity, and the good fatherhood people want to teach fathering skills to men whether they are married to their children's mother or have multiple arrangements.

This emphasis, scoffs Coffin, is necessary because of "multiple-partner fertility and complex family formation."

Liberals think of the family people as having an old-fashioned, if not obsolete, view of the world and lacking an understanding of poor people. "They always think that we just want to hook up low-income women to any Tom, Dick, or Harry," said Coffin. "They frame it in terms that we want to promote marriage to a low-income guy just out of prison. They thought we wanted men to marry women that didn't like them. They think that conservatives don't get poverty, low-income people, the inner city. Their position is that poor people can't make a promise for a lifetime. That poor people have to be established to get married. They have it backward; many of us, the way we got established was by getting married. We grew up together in our twenties."

Coffin also leveled a charge that goes to the heart of the issue, adding: "Obviously the Obama administration folks, being liberal, were going to stop most of the marriage stuff because they don't want to promote marriage."

For Russell, it is clear. The Left now is "accepting that this is just part of life, that people are going to have children out of wedlock."

"There is just this huge split between the fatherhood guys and the marriage guys," she said. "We emphasize the importance of fathers, but not all the fathers. Ideally, the fathers should be in a marriage, but not all the fatherhood guys believe that. They accept fathers who have five children with three different women."

This split is very important for the Hispanic community because of the need to address the acceleration in marriage breakdown we're witnessing. Most out-of-wedlock births in the Hispanic community result not from chance encounters but inside "complex family formations" in which cohabiting partners even plan many of the pregnancies, as a 2006 study by Ellison, Wolfinger, and Ramos-Wada illustrates.

Conservatives who understand the value of marriage to culture and our society, especially those who want to engage in improving the lot of Hispanics in this country, should be aware of the importance of good marriage programs and demand that candidates for office support them.

The government can make several policy changes that would give marriage in America a fighting chance. A paper issued in 2012 by the Institute for American Values offered ten policy recommendations to help reinvigorate marriage culture:

1. End the Marriage Penalty for Low-Income Americans: This proposal would end the disincentives to marry that result when welfare benefits are lost because a single mother marries. Obviously, many programs need to be means-tested to prevent abuse, but one recommendation is to give couples in the initial years of marriage a tax refund for the value of the loss of benefits incurred when two incomes are added together.

2. Triple the Child Credit for Children Under Age Three: The authors wrote that "research conducted in the U.S. shows that married couples have more children when they are able to protect more family income through child tax credits."

3. Help Young Men Become Marriageable Men: "Recent popular analyses have suggested that we are seeing the 'end of men,'" wrote the researchers, offering a series of recommendations on how to teach lower-income males husband—not just fatherhood—

skills. Included were good recommendations on how to use the resources of the criminal justice system to help young men locked up for minor offenses turn their lives around and become good husbands once they are free again.

4. End Anonymous Fatherhood: This recommendation, one of the more offbeat ones, calls for ending the anonymity of sperm donors, calling out the "cultural power of the idea that it's acceptable deliberately to create a fatherless child." Most adults created through donation want anonymity ended.

5. Enact the Second Chances Act to Reduce Unnecessary Divorce: Citing research that shows that in 40 percent of couples deep into the divorce process one or both partners want to reconcile, the authors call for steps such as lengthening the waiting period to at least one year, giving the divorcing couple an opportunity to reconsider. Nobody should spend a lifetime living with someone they despise. But where children are concerned, society does have a stake in helping couples stay together. This isn't just conservative advice. "A successful marriage is a decision; you decide it's going to work," said San Francisco liberal Nancy Pelosi.

6. Require Premarital Education for Persons Forming Stepfamilies: Though not crazy about the mandatory aspect of this proposal, I can see where it's coming from. In the study by the University of California's Cynthia Harper cited in Chapter 8, children raised by stepfamilies have higher rates of incarceration and criminality later in life compared with children raised by the original mom and dad.

7. Encourage Federal and State Policy Makers to Invest in and Evaluate Marriage and Relationship Programs: We saw above how important those programs are.

8. Engage Hollywood: Nobody who knows the movie industry and its lusty embrace of family breakup can have much hope for this recommendation. But if a president, especially a liberal one, made the case to Hollywood that lower-income people such as

Hispanics are seeing their communities ravaged as a result of marriage breakup, maybe there could be some hope.

9. Launch Community-Oriented Campaigns About the Facts and Fun of Marriage: In other words, promote marriage as a conduit to the good life, one that though it may seem harder at times ends up being more meaningful.

10. Find Your Marriage Voice: All of us can and should become vocal proponents of the marriage agenda and have the facts about what family breakup has done to minorities. Eventually, the private sector will need to get involved in the effort to reverse the unmarriage culture in the Hispanic community. Productivity and ultimately profit maximization depend on the quality of human capital, and so it is in companies' interest to chip in. They are essential for another reason: only nongovernmental organizations (NGOs) using private capital will be able to invoke God in this field because religion must be kept out of any activity that uses federal dollars. As we see from myriad organizations that work—from the Salvation Army to Alcoholics Anonymous—the toughest challenges are more easily tackled when we realize we're working for a purpose that is higher than ourselves.

These are policy proposals conservative political leaders can get behind. High-profile appearances at centers that provide these services to a majority-Hispanic community will telegraph to audiences watching on TV not only that a leader cares but that he or she cares about this mission. Marriage is key to the continuation of the American experiment in freedom. From all perspectives, the family must be strong if government is going to remain small. This is why from the very beginning marriage has been a hallmark of life in America. No less an observer of the American experience than Alexis de Tocqueville wrote in 1835, "There is certainly no country in the world where the tie of marriage is more respected than in America, or where conjugal happiness is more highly or worthily appreciated." The strength of this institution has endured.

Less than a hundred years later, in a book published in 1912, the Cuban sociologist Ramon Maria Alfonso praised the United States for seeing marriage as the way "to constitute honest and reproductive families that help the national well-being." Alfonso, my great-grandfather, compared the situation in America with that in Cuba, where the presence of a high number of single male immigrants from Spain was leading to a rise in illegitimacy, which he called "a dangerous social state which becomes a menace to the nation." My great-grandfather also praised the high level of civic engagement in the America of the 1910s, its deeply religious practices, charitable giving, and aversion to regulation, all habits of mind that may be under threat because of the breakdown of our culture of marriage almost a hundred years after my great-grandfather wrote.

THE COMMUNITY AROUND THE FAMILY

Working to ensure that low-income Hispanics grasp the primacy of the family as much as their forebears did just twenty years ago is only a start. The welfare system may provide a safety net for people in crisis, but it does nothing to propel families to get back on their feet and off assistance, change negative habits, or acquire new skills. For that, we must broaden our scope and include the community that surrounds the family. Luckily, nonprofit institutions are emerging that make sure that families can get off welfare and succeed in a thriving community again. One is the Family Independence Initiative headed by Mexican-born Maurice Lim Miller.

Lim Miller watched his Mexican single mother struggle against the system to raise him and his sister in Palo Alto. The sister got pregnant at sixteen, and his mother took her own life rather than see Lim Miller quit graduate school to become her primary caregiver. He graduated from Berkeley. "My sister's life did not turn out well. I lost my mother in my mid-twenties and I'm the only one that made it out," he told National Public Radio in 2012.

The difference between the FII and public assistance could not be starker. Families that come in seeking help are in charge, not the bureaucracy.

Here's how it works. A family that comes in seeking help from FII is asked to look for similar families in its community with which it can start projects. "Go find six or eight other families that are friends of yours, and if you organize those families and come in, we'll talk to you as a group," says Lim Miller. FII then will pay for the families' time but not for their schemes to get out of poverty. FII, in other words, acts only as a facilitator; FII staff act as the catalysts and then just observe the progress. "They start buying houses, starting businesses, kids start doing better in schools, and a lot of it had to do with kind of this recognition, this validation that they were the solvers of the problem, that they were the ones that had to take the initiative and they could actually get access to re-sources through us because we were credible at that time." As Lim Miller ruefully put it, "it's been a forty-seven-year war on poverty and, you know, it's your turn."

"If you are going to try to change your life in the next two years, then we'll pay you for the time you spend showing us what the progress is that you're making," he told NPR.

FII rightly realizes that there's a role for government in catch-ing people about to fall into the abyss. "The 'safety net' approach is critical for those in crisis," FII's mission statement reads. The problem is that the welfare state of the last half century "is not a springboard out of poverty. Programs and services targeting low-income families and communities are set up with case managers and social workers charged with directing, leading, and helping their clients. This prevents families from setting their own priori-ties and goals; it keeps people from owning their own solutions. It places the program—instead of friends and family—in the position of supporter."

FII is one of several organizations undertaking the serious work of helping families build the social capital network in their com-munities. It is kind of like putting grains of sands in an oyster to encourage the growth of a pearl. Without those artificially intro-duced grains, the oyster may never get to work on its own.

Albuquerque, New Mexico–based Circles is another grain in-troducer. It helps run so-called Circle Groups, each made up of

twenty-five low-income families called Circle Leaders. They co-
alesce around plans to build financial and emotional support and
social resources as well as an Economic Stability Plan that corre-
sponds to that community's need. In other words, it is family-run,
and these families decide what the needs are, not a faceless bureaucracy.

Circles' founder, Scott Miller, breaks down social capital into
three components: bonding capital, bridging capital, and linking
capital. The first component consists of people and networks within
your socioeconomic group, who become allies and share your
stories; the second includes people and networks with a higher income, who pass on their habits ("If you want to make more money
you have to know people who make more money," as he put it to
me); the third is knowledge about how to access the system—how
to get scholarships or access good health care. ("Everyone assumes
that these programs are there and people know how to use them.
That's not true," said Miller.)

The reason you need civil society groups such as FII and Circles
to rebuild families' and communities' social capital is that in the
government "nobody gets paid to get people out of poverty," says
Miller. The problem is that the system is set up in a way that keeps
people dependent on government forever. "If people were getting
paid to get people out of poverty, the cliff effect would be gone by
Friday," he said, referring to the phenomenon by which people lose
all their welfare benefits once they get a job or earn above a certain
threshold. In many cases this means that their real income drops
dramatically (off a cliff) and they become trapped in a situation in
which they cannot get a job or are deterred from striving for a raise.
When this happens, welfare actually discourages people from moving out of poverty.

Why don't conservative politicians make the compassionate
case over and over to Hispanics for building communities' social
capital? Part of it is that they have bought into the caricature the
Left has painted of them as Randian individualists, a stance that
is more applicable to libertarians than to conservatives, who believe in organic community. All that some conservative politicians

carry in a nearly empty rhetorical quiver is that welfare programs are too expensive and fiscally unsustainable. As true as that is, telling Hispanics (or any Americans) that there's no money to take care of them or that soon there won't be any has all the warmth of presenting a profit and loss statement. It leaves out the fact that we care about the destruction of entire neighborhoods, that we desire to see Hispanics become part and parcel of the American family, and that there are ways to introduce the grain of sand into the oyster.

Another part is that they've been told by far too many conservative pundits that Hispanics are a lost cause. Just "reform welfare, grow the economy, get the free market working, and everything else will fall into place; trying to save the country by gaining the Hispanic vote is a wasted effort," some conservative pundits on talk radio and TV have said. Let's call this the Huntington effect.

The Huntington effect has taken a toll. It is the contention of this book that the downward assimilation suffered by some Hispanics is highly correlated with (and probably the result of) leftist policies such as the rise of the welfare state, but the story doesn't end there: conservatives must share part of the blame. If the Left, at its worst, has for political profit plunged too many Hispanics into government dependence, the Right has all too often abandoned them by not explaining its version of the American Dream. Rather than impelling them to act, harboring the same fears Huntington does has made some conservatives retrench.

Conservatives simply making the case for economic growth and reforming the welfare system and thinking that things will simply fall into place after that may find that these messages are not enough to win majorities against liberals offering goodies. The result is that the policies that reform the welfare system and get the economy going again will never be implemented. People who have entered into a Faustian bargain with government by accepting welfare—because they faced a moment of crisis in their lives or because they were persuaded by a Food and Drug Administration advert that it was their "right" to apply for welfare because they met some bureaucratic requirement—find it very hard to suddenly walk away from the benefits. They may not be ready audiences for a message of freedom that simply tells them that the benefit will be yanked away from them.

In some of the communities that have been decimated we simply must help get the people there to form networks again. You can't just take out the knife and let the wound heal by itself—you must apply coagulants. You must follow the harder path of working with community institutions to rebuild social capital.

Even without the deleterious cliff effects and marriage penalties or the crowding out that results when government programs come in and push out community-based solutions provided by churches and small and large private charities, which grow slowly and organically but once they are gone are difficult to replace, and even without the fact that the welfare system often enables or even promotes bad choices, massive immigration by itself ends up putting strains on communities.

We now have research that shows that diversity can be divisive, more so at the community level than nationally. This is not a reason to close the borders and clamp down on immigration. Ethnic groups have been displacing other ethnic groups since the Scots-Irish showed up in Pennsylvania before the Revolutionary War and pushed out the Germans. It is just a statement of fact and a reason why immigration has its critics in every country in the world.

Common sense tells us that the more a neighborhood is taken over by a sudden influx of "the other," the bigger is the strain on the original residents. But we also now have research from Harvard's Robert Putnam that confirms that a rapid growth in immigrants may itself lower a community's trust quotient.

In a much-cited 2007 paper, Putnam explained that although there were indeed long-term benefits to immigration, "in the short to medium run, however, immigration and ethnic diversity challenge social solidarity and inhibit social capital." Putnam's research showed that diversity dissolves trust in a community. This insight has troubling implications, as trust is the DNA of the interlacing social relations that are so important for the well-being of a community. If I don't trust you not to abscond with the church funds or to set up the swim team's snack bar, we're not going to work very well together, and the community and the individuals in it will suffer as a result. And if diversity erodes trust, which is the very bond of social capital, which is at the heart of little platoons conservatism, our community institutions and political leaders are going to have to take this challenge seriously.

This is why Putnam's discovery that social capital is lower in communities that become ethnically diverse is so important as we look at growing numbers of Hispanic Americans. In a comprehensive study of forty-one localities ranging from racially heterogeneous San Francisco to homogeneous Bismarck, South Dakota, what Putnam found was that the greater the diversity of a neighborhood,

- The lower the confidence in local government, local leaders, and local news media

- The lower the political efficacy—that is, confidence in their own influence

- The lower the frequency of registering to vote but more interest and knowledge about politics and more participation in protest marches and social reform groups

- The lower the expectation that others will cooperate to solve dilemmas through collective action

- The less likelihood of working on a community project

- The lower the likelihood of giving to charity and volunteering

- The fewer close friends and confidants

- The less there is happiness and the lower is the perceived quality of life

- The more time spent watching TV

These are all issues conservatives should be able to tackle head-on. If we don't, if we allow the government sector to provide the only solutions, we will have only ourselves to blame for losing elections (which after all lead to policy making). Thus, the worst thing we can do is allow noise over illegal immigration to prevent us from discussing the more important, deeper issues of how to manage demographic change, how to address the breakdown of the family, and how to stop the erosion of community.

Our political leaders must unsparingly speak to audiences about the need to save families and the neighborhoods they inhabit. They must be ready to support programs and institutions that are working to save communities. "The way liberals talk about government agencies and government programs, that's how conservatives need to talk about these civil society institutions. It needs to be part of the agenda. Otherwise it's just liberals saying, 'We want government to do this,' and us responding, 'We don't want government to do this,'" Mike Connolly, one of Senator Mike Lee's young bright staffers, said to me.

Political leaders can also help by activating the donor base, alerting it to the importance of supporting the types of family- and neighborhood-support efforts described in this chapter. "Donors can develop and support strategies that are effectively helping people transition off welfare supports and into gainful employment in the free enterprise economy. Politicians can promote policies that support people in the transition to work by minimizing regulatory barriers to employment and entrepreneurship," said Jo Kwong of the Philanthropy Round Table. Eventually the culture will have to be brought in as well. Getting a Selena Gomez or a Jennifer Lopez to participate in public service announcements on marriage would do wonders for the institution. For my money, the best politician on this issue is Senator Mike Lee of Utah, but as enamored as I am of his impassioned speeches on the issues of marriage, the family, and the welfare state, even I recognize that Lee is no J-Lo.

Chapter 11

HUMAN CAPITAL: EDUCATION

Education, then, beyond all other devices of human origin,
is the great equalizer of the conditions of men.

– HORACE MANN

I N MAY 2010, THE AMERICAN PSYCHOLOGICAL ASSOCIATION (APA)
published a handful of studies conducted on Latino students,
and they had their share of good news and bad news. The good
news was that overall, Hispanic immigrant parents care a great deal
about their children's academic future and provide the tough love
necessary for success. The bad news was that the longer their children were in the US public school system, the more they slipped
away from their parents' grasp and got involved with bad peers and
the worse they performed academically.

The researchers reached a conclusion that is dissonant with
everything we thought we knew about America: the reason these
students' academic work was deteriorating was that they were assimilating into American culture. The worst thing about this finding is that it is probably right.

"Immigrant kids begin school with surprisingly good social
skills, eager to engage teachers and classroom tasks, even though
many are raised in poor households," said one of the authors of the
studies, Bruce Fuller, a University of California at Berkeley professor. "This stems from tight families and tough-headed parenting."

Another of the study's editors, Cynthia García Coll of Brown
University, said, "These children benefit from a strong foundation
against outside negative forces, which contributes to their early

school achievement but fades over time, especially during adolescence."

So what is the problem? "Assimilation places many children at risk of losing tight bonds to family and [experiencing] school failure," García Coll was quoted as saying by the APA. She and other social scientists have taken to calling this phenomenon the immigrant paradox.

Fuller and García Coll have it right, of course, except that what they mean by assimilation is not the meaning we are used to. It isn't assimilation to virtues but assimilation to the pathologies we have come to expect in America's often dangerous and underperforming inner-city public schools.

What Milton Friedman said decades ago still holds true: "There is no respect in which inhabitants of a low-income neighborhood are so disadvantaged as in the kind of schooling they can get for their children."

This is a political scandal that politicians must speak about often to Hispanic audiences. Research demonstrates that the marker of the type of human capital most predictive of and useful in explaining whether someone moves up the income ladder is not raw intelligence but the level of education a person acquires. Our political leaders must thus offer solutions to the problems besetting Hispanic communities in this regard. Education is one issue in which all Hispanic groups will act as one. Puerto Rican and Mexican-American families are as eager to have their children educated as Cuban-Americans are. Talk to a Dominican in New York about what education means to her and the future generation and you'll get an earful. Everybody gets it. Not only do they want their children to be educated so that they can be successful; they want them out of dangerous schools.

The huge and growing gap between the educational achievement of non-Hispanic white kids and the children of Latin American immigrants is one of the most important problems we need to fix if we are ever going to break Hispanics free of the maws of government dependence. Unlike, say, perseverance and honesty, education is a type of human capital that society has a significant role in inculcating. One of the reasons the first waves of Cuban refugees had a measure of success in America is that they carried their education into this country, inside their heads and in their hearts, not on their backs; when Castro dispossessed them of their material goods, he couldn't take their education. More recent Cuban arrivals as well as Mexicans, Salvadorans, Puerto Ricans, and others who have immigrated in the last few decades do not always arrive with this asset. We need to encourage its creation here.

There are several reasons for the educational achievement gap between Hispanics and non-Hispanic whites. One obvious one we've seen already: Hispanics have a much higher rate of illegitimacy than do non-Hispanic whites: 53 percent to 29 percent. The education gap increases and falls with this rate. Puerto Ricans, with an out-of-wedlock rate of 65 percent, are the least educated group; Cubans, at the low end with a 48 percent rate (which until recently was much, much lower), are among the best educated. Hispanic children who don't have a father around and whose mother's behavior is not worth emulating need to find role models elsewhere.

"Their parents made poor choices, and this is what they have observed," says Tom Tillapaugh, who runs the Street School in Denver, a private institution for troubled children that is practically free and is more than 50 percent Hispanic, nearly all Mexican-Americans. "These children are not in rebellion when they smoke marijuana; they are doing what their parents do."

This is why one of the main things the Street School does is model to students what good behavior looks like. "We need to have quality modeling from quality adults. We need to show the children, 'This is how a quality single woman is supposed to behave; this is how a quality single man is supposed to behave; this is how a quality couple is supposed to behave.'"

Another reason for the existence of the gap is poor schools. There are many very good public schools in this country and many more that are adequate and functional. The problem is that Hispanic children are not in them in great numbers. In most school districts in our country, students are assigned to the school in the area where the family lives. Most immigrants cannot afford to live in neighborhoods and towns where the public schools are good, so often their children are essentially dumped into underperforming schools that are dangerous to boot. In no other service for which government helps defray the cost are people limited to the area where they live; it doesn't happen with medicine or with food stamps.

I had my own experiences in public schools in inner-city New York and suburban Miami in the 1970s. These two systems were poles apart in all aspects, from the academic achievement level to the safety of the schools and the demographics of the students.

In middle school (junior high to us back then) I attended I.S. 145 on Northern Boulevard, Queens, a fenced-in compound that a foreign visitor might have mistaken for a minimum-security prison, which in some ways it kind of was.

At lunch the students played boom boxes in the cafeteria and danced on the tables. Van McCoy's "The Hustle" had just come out, and platform shoes were flying. The classroom wasn't much better. One time a kid named Darryl occupied the teacher's desk. He just sat there and wouldn't budge. The teacher, Ms. Klein, evidently felt unable to do anything to dislodge Darryl and didn't even try. She attempted to teach from the back of the classroom, but that only made the situation more chaotic. That was not atypical. I also remember the one white girl in that eighth-grade class, a sweet Irish girl who was constantly picked on sadistically by the others. She often burst into tears, but the teachers did nothing to help her. I was newly arrived in this country and watched these events in shock but never lifted a finger to help her. Had I done so, I certainly would have ended up with a mouthful of blood but wouldn't feel so rotten about it today.

My mother knew that the odds of my doing well in this environment were not high, so by tenth grade we had moved to Miami and I was attending Coral Gables High. It wasn't the school assigned to our neighborhood, but we successfully argued that I deserved to go there in our personal resort to school choice. The experience couldn't have been more different. Gables was *Leave It to Beaver.*

So much so, in fact, that at first I was incredulous. A recently arrived immigrant with only three years in this country, I had never heard of a pep rally or a boosters' club in my life, nor had I ever seen so many blond Protestants. The school was an organic part of the town of Coral Gables, a leafy Spanish-style community with a beautiful pool that has a grotto in it and a chic shopping street downtown known as the Miracle Mile, down which the school paraded during something called Homecoming Week. Students left Coral Gables High to go to the University of Miami, the University of Florida, Florida State, or the Ivies, not juvie.

These are not experiences from a faraway past. If anything, this division between public schools that work and are majority-white and public schools that are basically dumping grounds for Hispanics and African-Americans is even more entrenched today because the white flight to the suburbs has accelerated over the past three decades.

My children today benefit from equally advanced classrooms in equally prosperous suburban Bethesda, where the school is public only nominally; in reality it is a public-private partnership in which the parents help run the classrooms and after-school clubs.

Not an hour away in inner-city Washington, DC; Prince George's County, Maryland; or other parts of Virginia, other students named Gonzalez enter schools through metal detectors. Parents can be so uninvolved that Washington, DC, is considering fining the parents of children who are truant too many times.

A Heritage Foundation research study conducted in 2009 in Washington showed that for some students, dropping out is a survival mechanism. The schools are so dangerous that it is safer to be outside on the streets than walking the halls inside the school.

The Heritage study pointed to statistics that showed that the DC public school system "is one of the most dangerous in the country. In 2009, the US Department of Education reported that 11.3 percent of DC high school students reported being 'threatened or injured' with a weapon on school property during the previous year—a rate well above the national average and higher than most states." Reports from nongovernmental sources also confirmed that "many students in D.C. schools are exposed to violence and crime on a regular basis." For example, the *Washington Post* reported in 2007 that nine violent school incidents are reported on a typical day in Washington, DC.

Heritage found out that many DC children are also exposed to violence outside of school: "A 2001 analysis by the Urban Institute found that most assaults and robberies against juveniles in the District occur between 3 p.m. and 4 p.m., at the end of the traditional school day. The weekday after-school commute had the highest frequency of crimes against District juveniles."

Sure enough, on the National Assessment of Educational Progress, the Hispanic–white gap for Washington, DC, students is twice the national average, by far the largest in the country. As Heritage noted, "An education gap between white students and their black and Hispanic peers is something to which most Americans have become accustomed. But this racial division of education—and hence prospects for the future—is nothing less than tragic."

One of the American Psychological Association study, which was led by Carola Suarez-Orozco, stated that "many immigrant youth also find themselves in racially and ethnically segregated schools, a factor that has been closely linked with reduced access to educational resources and negative school outcomes." Such schools "undermine students' capacity to concentrate, sense of security, and ability to learn."

The sad paradox is that despite these problems, Hispanics have shown that they understand that a college education is the ticket to success. According to the Pew Hispanic Center, 89 percent of Latinos age sixteen to twenty-five say that a college degree is essential to success, compared with 82 percent among all groups. Immigrant Latinos have the highest belief in higher education. Nearly all, 94 percent, said education was necessary; among second-generation Hispanics, 86 percent answered that way, and among third-generation Latinos—the native-born children of native-born parents—it dropped to 84 percent.

Their parents, too, put a premium on higher education. More than three-quarters of Latino youths told Pew that their parents "think going to college is the most important thing for them to do after high school." They try to act as buffers against the elements and help their children, using what Claudia Galindo at the University of Maryland calls "steady discipline that reinforces family solidarity."

As we saw in Chapter 8, the aspirations of Latinos do not correspond to the rates at which they graduate from college or even their stated expectations of getting a college degree. Only 48 percent of Hispanics age sixteen to twenty-five told Pew they expect to get a college degree, compared with 60 percent of the overall population.

Clearly there is a disconnect between the aspirations of Latinos and what the establishment has offered them. Many of them are not succeeding to the degree they would like.

The breakdown is so glaring that it gives hope something will be done soon. Social scientists such as Galindo and Suarez-Orozco have a liberal academic perspective. What is interesting is that when it comes to schools they reach some of the same conclusions as those on the right: there's a worrying dearth of social capital available to immigrant families in the cities into which they move. In California's Pico-Union, where ten different gangs operate in a community of 40,000 people, or in the South Bronx or Chicago's dangerous 13th Ward, there are few positive networks that can help individuals break out of poverty.

Many of the civil society organizations taking up educational activities that do exist in Hispanic neighborhoods throughout the country have been captured by the Left and have ceased to be true self-help groups; they are now little more than gateways to dependence on government social programs. In late 2013 that meant being faithful foot soldiers in the effort to promote the Affordable Care Act while the rest of the country was ridiculing Obamacare.

Consider Alianza Hispana in Boston's Roxbury or Casa de Maryland in Silver Spring and Hyattsville, Maryland, the first catering mostly to Puerto Ricans and Dominicans and the second mainly to Salvadorans and other Central Americans in the Washington, DC, suburbs. Casa de Maryland's "educational" material, or Casa Curricula, as the effort to sell illustrated books and pamphlets is called, does little to address the educational gap between the schools attended by Latinos and those attended by suburban kids. Casa does spend a lot of effort, however, turning these Central American kids into good community organizers. The problem with community organizers, however, is that they try to fit the community into the large national network—the system of unions, federal benefits, and so forth—not organize it to be an autonomous part of civil society. One of the books Casa offers in Spanish is *Historia Laboral Sindical de los EE.UU.* (Labor and Union History of the United States), which recounts "the history of the working class and the labor organizing movement in the United States that are often left out of traditional history books." Another is *Crossing Borders*, a book on the right to cross borders that Casa says can be used for cultural awareness training on such issues as "the history of domination and the pursuit of opportunity." Another book for sale, *English for Organizing,* does at least address the problem of non-English proficiency, but as its title suggests, the emphasis is on turning the new immigrants into cogs in the Left's wheel. Given the fact that the Hispanic community that Casa de Maryland caters to is the already left-of-center Salvadoran community, one has to wonder if stressing reading and math might not do more for the success of its members.

The leftward slant is nationwide and encompasses organizations that cater to nearly all communities, in fact, all areas except those where there is a strong concentration of Cuban-Americans who came in the first stages. Many of these organizations have a hard-edge, stick-it-to-the-man look to them that breeds antagonism to the system.

Contrast this with the example of the Knights of Columbus, a fraternal Catholic organization that since being set up in Connecticut in 1882 has helped bridge cleavages between Catholics of different backgrounds, especially Irish, Italians, and Germans. Or compare the in-your-face approach of some of the Hispanic institutions that have been taken over by the Left with the Educational Alliance, an organization founded in 1889 to help the masses of Eastern European Jews arriving every year. The Alliance strived to do the opposite—it tried to integrate immigrants into the system.

Whereas the organizations that have been taken over by liberals in different Hispanic communities seem intent on causing friction, the Alliance and other social capital groups that worked with previous immigrants sought to minimize the reasons for discrimination against members of their group. According to Paula Hyman of the Jewish Women's Archive, the Alliance devised programs to inculcate appropriately American behavior in youth.

A century ago, when the United States faced a similarly large influx of immigrants, all of civil society—the churches, the bonding and bridging institutions, private companies—were involved in the effort to teach immigrants the language and, overall, how to be Americans. That effort has now stopped. As Robert Putnam and former Florida governor Jeb Bush put it in a 2010 *Washington Post* op-ed:

> One important difference, however, that separates immigration then and now: We native-born Americans are doing less than our great-grandparents did to welcome immigrants. A century ago, religious, civic and business groups and government provided classes in English and citizenship. Historian Thomas P. Vadasz found that in Bethlehem, Pa., a thriving town of about 20,000, roughly two-thirds of whom were immigrants, the biggest employer, Bethlehem Steel, and the local YMCA offered free English instruction to thousands of immigrants in the early 20th century, even paying them to take classes. Today, immigrants face long waiting lists for English classes, even ones they pay for.

The big failure, of course, is happening in the public schools. There is a growing consensus that we are no longer integrating immigrants as we should. After the bombing at the Boston Marathon in April 2013, Suarez-Orozco and her husband, Marcelo, wrote an op-ed for the *New York Times* in which they observed that "many newcomer students attend tough urban schools that lack solidarity and cohesion. In too many we found no sense of shared purpose, but rather a student body divided by race and ethnicity, between

immigrants and the native born, between newcomers and more ac-
culturated immigrants."

A few days later Stanley Kurtz noted in *National Review* that
"the breakthrough here is that even the *New York Times* and liberal
immigration researchers are confirming the basic analysis of conservative scholars like [John] Fonte and [Althea] Nagai. Our assimilation system is broken."

Even *Mother Jones* magazine—*Mother Jones!*—seems to accept
this reality, writing in December 2013, "If you compare American
white kids to, say, Finnish or Polish or German white kids, we do
just as well. The problem is that we do an execrable job of teaching
our black and Hispanic kids."

Obviously, one of the reasons for the academic cleavage between
Hispanics and the mainstream and also for the failure of students
to assimilate is the failed social experiment that goes under the
label of bilingual education. The natural diversity that results from
a large and sudden immigrant influx would be difficult enough to
manage without our government going out of its way to make problems worse. Diversity in language takes a backseat to nothing else
as a divisive agent, and it is to the growth of bilingualism that we
turn next.

As negatively as the Irish were seen by native-born Americans
during the great Irish influx, they at least spoke English, having
almost completely lost their melodic Celtic language after centuries
of English occupation. German immigrants, of well-known probity
and work ethic, were by contrast feared at least partly because they
cleaved tenaciously to their language for generations. (This linguistic allegiance carries on to this day. My family and I have heard
German spoken in restaurants in Lancaster, Pennsylvania, whose
"German" and "Swiss" inhabitants have been there since the early
1800s.)

It's not hard to see why. A distinction that intellectuals all too
often fail to make is that polyglotism is an enviable quality in an
individual but a curse to a society. "The bond of language is perhaps the strongest and most lasting that can unite men," wrote the

most eminent observer of what made early America exceptional, the French nobleman Alexis de Tocqueville. Or, as Hillsdale College's Matt Spalding writes, "Republican and ordered liberty—not to mention the articulation of common political principles—requires clear communication, mutual deliberation and civic education, and that demands that citizens share one common language." Politicians from Ben Franklin to Teddy Roosevelt saw disloyalty in daily public use of non-English languages. It has hurt national cohesion in Canada, Belgium, and Switzerland, to stick with industrialized Organization of Economic Cooperation and Development societies and to say nothing of the horrors that can be visited on Third World societies "blessed" with polyglotism. Multiculturalism in the hands of the lesser minds who make up a proportion of all societies is tribalism.

This makes it all the more startling that at one point in the mid-twentieth century, the United States decided as a country—or rather our elites decided for everyone in the absence of a popular groundswell—to give Spanish-speaking children instruction only in their native tongue rather than have them slowly meld in the national melting pot. Nothing could have been done to create a wider gap between Hispanic students and their Anglo counterparts than to keep them apart right at the age when they are building identities and lifelong memories.

The nation got its Bilingual Education Act of 1968, the first federal law to say that children with limited English abilities had special challenges that needed to be met in this novel way, not as the country had handled immigrant children from the beginning. The act dangled before school districts grants for which they had to compete by designing educational programs that bureaucrats would define as innovative. Things got a lot worse from there. Nixon was not much better than Johnson and in some ways much worse. The law was amended in 1974 to make it mandatory for school districts to participate. Funding went from $7.5 million at the program's inception to $68 million, a lot of money back then.

I was one of those immigrant schoolchildren who arrived

precisely in 1974, and sure enough, I was immediately thrown into a bilingual eighth-grade class at my school in Queens. It was monolingual, really; I received all instruction in Spanish.

It was only six months into my bilingual ed class that I realized what damage it was doing. It was I who had to convince the assistant principal, in very broken English, that I needed to be immersed (my mother, having just arrived in this country, couldn't take time off from work to accompany me to school to argue my case with the assistant principal).

This middle-aged "educator" was anything but sympathetic, taking me into an empty classroom where he proceeded to warn me that I would not learn to swim but drown. I distinctly remember that he said, "You're quite ambitious," though not in praise but more as a warning that I had a disturbing level of hubris. I remember it well because it was the very first time I had heard the word *quite*. I instantly recognized what it meant within the context of the sentence.

This is one of the oddest features of bilingual education supporters: they ignore how children learn languages and insist that without a bilingual program, children will fall behind.

Conservative leaders must use to their advantage the growing consensus that public schools are failing to teach many Hispanic students what they need to know in the twenty-first century, to acculturate them, and even to keep them safe. Progressives argue for more government spending and reforming the school system from within, by which they mean acquiescing to the demands of the teachers' unions for more resources, which will then disappear down the rabbit hole of administrative services and political lobbying. The trouble is, we have been spending more and more and getting these results. The teachers' unions—the allies of progressives—also block any reform. Increasingly, it looks like the only thing that will get public schools to change—if they can at all—is to apply outside pressure. The only thing that will work is what always works: competition.

American public school education is not mediocre because we fail to spend money on it. Spending per pupil has been increasing steadily in this country for the last half century. In constant dollars, public schools spent $2,835 per pupil in 1962 and $12,500 in 2012, a more than fourfold rise. This makes us one of the highest-spending countries in the world. Only Luxembourg, Switzerland, and Norway spend more per pupil. Moreover, when total per-pupil spending is examined, from elementary school through college, the United States spends more than any other developed nation.

Yet the Organization for Economic Cooperation and Development (which brings together industrialized nations and is therefore referred to as "the rich man's club") doesn't rate our results very high. As *Business Insider* wrote, "The three-yearly OECD Programme for International Student Assessment (PISA) report, which compares the knowledge and skills of 15-year-olds in 70 countries around the world, ranked the United States 14th out of 34 OECD countries for reading skills, 17th for science and a below-average 25th for mathematics." Out of the thirty-four OECD members a mere eight have a lower graduation rate than the United States. And *Mother Jones* is right: the high failure rate comes from one section of our system: the schools where Hispanics and African-Americans go.

Compare spending among states. One of the highest spenders per pupil in this country is the District of Columbia, which according to the Census Bureau spends an astonishing $29,409 per pupil. This would put Washington, DC, at the top of the OECD, way ahead of Luxembourg's $15,198.

And what do DC students get for this? A graduation rate that hovers around 60 percent, one of the lowest in the country, with math and reading scores that are also at the bottom in the nation.

As Cato Institute analyst Dan Mitchell puts it, "Simply stated, it's increasingly difficult for defenders of the status quo to rationalize pouring more money into the failed government education monopoly. To paraphrase Winston Churchill, never has so much been spent so recklessly with such meager results."

So what gives? One big part is the teachers' unions and the monopoly they hold on our school system. They have consistently opposed any and all reforms that would make public schools safer and better at giving students the knowledge they need to succeed in life.

Teachers' unions have fought against reforming the tenure system, so bad teachers who have been at their jobs for decades cannot be fired. They've also fought against merit pay, and so good teachers cannot be rewarded. They've also fought against school choice, and so families stuck in bad schools cannot flee to better school systems.

Teachers' unions have ensured that more and more staff gets hired by public schools even though we keep hiring and the results keep getting worse. Enrollment at US public schools went up by just 7.8 percent from 1970 to 2010; educational staff increased by 84 percent during the same four decades. And yes, although the number of teachers as a percentage of that staff has decreased because the support staff is getting bloated, the student:teacher ratio has actually decreased in the last forty years, from 22:1 in 1970 to 16:1 today. You never hear this bit of good news from the mouths of a union organizer, however.

The unions need staff because staff members pay dues. During the 2009–2010 school year the largest union, the National Education Association, got $162 per teacher and $93 per nonteaching staff member. The unions take this money and make important political contributions to progressive politicians (though one would have to ask what's progressive about aiding the forces of the status quo in a failed educational system).

According to the Federal Election Commission, teachers' unions accounted for 39 percent of campaign contributions in 2010. The NEA alone, according to researcher Mike Antonucci, spends more on campaign contributions than do ExxonMobil, Microsoft, Walmart, and the AFL-CIO combined. Though 50 percent of NEA members identify themselves as being more conservative than liberal, 91 percent of NEA political contributions go to Democrats or liberal causes. Employees in twenty-eight states can lose their jobs if they refuse to join a union or pay dues to it.

The circular relation, which *Reason* magazine calls the "political perpetual motion machine," goes like this: taxpayers send their money to the government, which pays public education employees, who are forced to send part of their paychecks to the unions, which give lots of money to friendly liberal politicians, who keep taxes high once they get into office.

And the students? When a TV reporter asked Vincent Giordano, the executive director of the New Jersey Education Association, why poor parents shouldn't "have the same option to get those kids out of a failing school and into one that works," the union honcho, who makes $550,000 a year, shrugged his shoulders and answered: "Well, life is not fair and I'm sorry about that."

New Jersey public schools, in which one of every five students is Hispanic, have NAEP Hispanic–white achievement gaps that are larger than the national average.

According to Tom Tillapaugh at the Street School, the unions also make it more difficult for teachers to do the behavior modeling he thinks is so important. The unions, he told me, have "worked hard to make sure that their members spend less time with kids! No hall duty, lunch room duty, fewer expectations for after-school events." Public school teachers, he said, "are actively discouraged from interacting with the students after hours, such as when a Street School teacher takes a group of kids bowling, or to watch the Nuggets, or to his house to play video games and eat pizza (always in groups, of course)."

For all these reasons, this is an issue that is ripe for conservative politicians to discuss with Hispanic audiences. From a purely utilitarian, even cynical perspective, this is what political practitioners call a wedge issue, an issue that drives a wedge between two liberal constituencies: Hispanics and the teachers' unions. But our political leaders must act because this is a scandal that is laying a trap for the entire nation. There is no bigger warning that we are going to become a nation of hardened castes that are difficult to move out of, with Hispanic-surnamed Americans overrepresented in the bottom one, than our educational gap. Such a dystopian future would be un-American. Conservative politicians can be reassured that Hispanic audiences will be receptive to this issue.

Fixing schools should be the first thing we attempt, mainly because it comes under the heading of low-hanging fruit. Our public school system has deteriorated to the point that even politically correct Hollywood has started to make documentaries and movies about the basic inequities of what is fundamentally a two-tiered (or multitiered) system in which suburban public school students get on average a decent education and inner-city kids learn to survive. The teachers' unions, those long-term supporters of a corrupt status quo, increasingly have no place to hide. Latino parents are catching on and support school choice.

Many different types of schooling alternatives come under the category of school choice. At bottom, the phrase means just what it says: any combination of educational choices that gives families the ability to escape the cul-de-sac they find themselves in at the moment.

SCHOLARSHIP PROGRAMS

Scholarship programs give parents a voucher that they can use to place their children in a private school of their choice. The idea is that students will gravitate toward the good schools, providing competition for the worse schools, which will have to improve or close. The money for the voucher would be equal to what the local government would have spent on the public school per child.

In the nation's capital, for example, the D.C. Opportunity Scholarship Program gives Hispanic families opportunities they would not otherwise have. The OSP is a federally funded voucher program that awards grants of up to $8,500 for K–8 and $12,000 for 8–12 to low-income children so that they can go to private schools.

The program has a higher graduation rate than do public schools and is cheaper to boot. Because the unions hate voucher programs, however, the OSP was nearly eliminated by President Obama, who refused to fund it while his party held the White House and both houses of Congress in 2009–2011. Speaker John Boehner, a Republican, and Senator Joe Lieberman, a Democrat, restored the funding in 2011.

Eliminating OSP would have been a hard blow for people like Patricia Hernandez, a Salvadoran-born mother I met in that city's

Columbia Heights neighborhood who told me that the conditions at her son's public school had become intolerable.

"The situation was really bad. I would go to the school every day and had to stay with him because there was no supervision," Hernandez told me over coffee. "I was never notified when my son was not doing well."

Hernandez told me she was nearing the breaking point, when "one day I saw this huge sign on a bus for the D.C. Opportunity Scholarship Program, and the tagline was 'if you want something better for your child.' I started to cry, thinking, this could be my way out. I have everything to gain and nothing to lose."

Her son, she said, "became a completely different person after he started going to Sacred Heart," the private school she was able to afford with the voucher scholarship. "He became very motivated. He suddenly got different interests, like he was into dinosaurs. I saw a completely different side of him. His grades got better, his behavior, his self-esteem. He became more sociable."

Sacred Heart not only worked on Patricia's son; it worked on Patricia as well. "The school also gave the parents the resources to know how to get involved and stay involved. They told me about workshops on parenting, for example. Before, I hadn't understood how important it was to stay involved with your child's education, how important it is for the child to succeed."

"At Sacred Heart if they see that a parent is struggling, they will help. They know that I want to do better for my son," said Patricia. "Teachers would send me rewarding notes for being involved with him in the class. I cherish them like I would a boyfriend's letter."

My experiences with Patricia Hernandez were confirmed by a 2006 study by the Georgetown University School Choice Demonstration Project. The study found that Spanish-speaking families felt no buyer's remorse.

"The majority of Spanish-speaking parents stated their children are more motivated, focused on what they want, and striving for improved grades," the report said. "The Spanish-speaking parents were particularly pleased with the way the schools their children are attending provide incentives for good behavior and academic improvement."

These results are being replicated across the country. In Texas, 80 percent of Hispanics support vouchers, according to the Texas Public Policy Foundation.

CHARTER AND MAGNET SCHOOLS

Other types of school choice include charter schools, which are autonomous public schools that have fewer regulations so that they can get around union rules that make it all but impossible to improve the classroom experience. In exchange for the enhanced autonomy, charter schools have higher accountability than regular schools and receive less money from the government.

They are very popular with Hispanics, too. According to the California Charter Schools Association, in the 2011–2012 school year, 46 percent of state charter students were Hispanics, 32 percent were white, 10 percent were African-American, and 12 percent were Asian, Indian, Pacific Islander, Filipino, or multiracial.

New York, too, reports good numbers for its charter school students. The New York City Charter School Center reported that 72 percent of students at charter schools were at or above standards for math and 51 percent for English, compared with 60 percent and 47 percent, respectively, for regular public schools. One-third of the charter school students in New York's five boroughs were Hispanic.

In Chicago, where some of the highest-paid teachers in the country go on strike when the mayor wants them to lengthen the shortest work year in the country, the United Neighborhood Organization (UNO) grew from one charter school in 2005 to eleven in 2013. Almost all of its 6,500 students are Hispanic, 93 percent are from low-income backgrounds, and 38 percent are new to the English language. Yet its schools outperform Chicago public schools.

Another type is magnet schools. These schools often specialize in a specific field such as science or math, and kids must take a test to get in, as opposed to charter schools, which are open to all students. A study conducted at Georgia State University in 2013 showed that at the classroom level magnet schools improve white–Hispanic diversity, especially in honors classes.

SPECIAL INTEREST BARRICADES

Programs that come under the label of school choice have a couple of things in common. First, they outperform regular public schools, which admittedly is a very low bar. Second, they are so popular that they tend to be oversubscribed, which means that there are waiting lists to get into them or in some cases lotteries.

Not surprisingly, school choice is intensely popular with Hispanics who know about it.

A poll conducted in 2012 by Beck Research for the Hispanic Council for Reform and Educational Options found that Latinos prized education reform far more than did non-Latinos (and it is a higher priority for them than immigration) and also support school choice.

Hispanics were more likely to give a high priority to improving K–12 education than non-Hispanics, giving the effort an 8.8 average on a scale of 1 to 10 in which 10 was the highest priority (immigration reform, in contrast, averaged 7.7). Hispanics in the survey were also more likely than non-Hispanics to say that "giving parents more choice will improve the education system."

Hispanics also were strong supporters of opportunity scholarships, with 69 percent backing them, as opposed to 57 percent support among non-Hispanics. Finally, 65 percent of Hispanic responders agreed with the statement "Choice and competition among schools improves education" compared with 26 percent who said it hurts education. The same levels of support were seen when the questions specifically involved school vouchers, opportunity scholarships, or tax credits.

It's no coincidence that Michelle Fields, the journalist with whom Matt Damon tangled on camera in 2011 in a discussion over the inability to fire inept teachers—during which the liberal actor cursed while accusing Fields of "MBA-style thinking" and failure to grasp "complex" issues—is of Honduran descent.

The Cuban-American rapper Pitbull, whose real name is Armando Christian Pérez, evangelizes on the subject constantly. He remembers how his mother had to lie constantly to Miami school authorities to place him in better schools than those in his neighborhood and doesn't want future mothers to have to go through that indignity.

Hispanics are the first to benefit from strong school choice programs, as the example of Florida makes clear. That state in 1999, under then-governor Jeb Bush, enacted a very aggressive K–12 education reform that included public and private school choice, charter schools, virtual education, and, very important, performance pay for teachers and an accountability plan that required students to be tested annually so that the performance of their teachers could be measured.

One often used measurement is fourth-grade reading levels, because after fourth grade it becomes progressively harder to acquire literacy skills. Children learn how to read well in K–3 so that they can spend the rest of their school years reading to learn about other subjects. Using this yardstick, the results of the Florida reforms are in, and they are nothing short of stellar.

In 1998, average fourth-grade reading levels among Florida Hispanics were an appalling 25 points below the national average for white students. In a decade, the gap has gone down to just 6 points. Even more impressive, Florida Hispanics outscore or match the statewide reading average of all students in thirty-one states.

The success of the reform has meant that Florida Hispanics are now far ahead of other Hispanics in the country. On average, the state's average Hispanic student is almost two grades ahead of the average Hispanic student in the rest of the country.

In an op-ed written in 2011, Governor Bush observed, "Since 1999, Florida's graduation rate has increased by 21 percentage points, from 60 to 81 percent, and Hispanic students have made the greatest improvement, jumping 23 percentage points. Not only are more Hispanic students graduating, more are taking and passing Advanced Placement courses and leaving better prepared for college."

Florida's success proves several things. One is that states are better than the federal government at driving reform. The cumbersome Department of Education in Washington often turns to throwing money at problems, which doesn't work. The states are becoming the battleground for this type of reform, with Indiana, Louisiana, Wisconsin, Colorado, Arizona, and several others trying to emulate Florida's success with their own programs.

The second thing the Florida reforms demonstrate is that we do not have to live with an embarrassing education gap in this country. If we face up to the teachers' unions and institute school reform, we can give Hispanic students the same opportunity that other students enjoy.

Florida also demonstrates that school choice is good politics. Nearly two-thirds of all voters, Latino or not, support charter schools. In the Beck Research study cited earlier, 58 percent of Hispanics agreed with the statement "We need to hear more from the presidential candidates on how they will improve education," and just 37 percent agreed that "we need to hear more from the presidential candidates on other issues before we talk about education."

Conservatives will have only themselves to blame if they allow liberals to continue to take this issue from them. They should reach out to Hispanics, go to their communities, speak to parents about how schools are failing them, and explain to them that no, the answer is not to throw good money after bad; some schools you just can't fix. The solution they need to sell is to actually upend the whole structure. If conservatives did that, they would find a ready audience.

Many Hispanic mothers and fathers live in fear of losing their children to the streets. They work long hours, sometimes in two jobs, as they strive to make ends meet. Even when they have the best intentions, they often don't have time to keep an eye on not only their children's homework but also bad influences. They don't want to surrender, and when they do, it is with pain and resignation.

These are the people on whose side conservatives ought to be. They must not do it for political gain. Unless it is addressed soon, the education gap will ensure that Hispanics will remain an underclass permanently. But conservatives also must act because it is the right thing to do for our country.

Andrew Rotherham, a regular *Time* magazine columnist who cofounded Bellwether Education, a nonprofit working on educational outcomes for low-income students, wrote in 2011 in *Time:* "These two tectonic issues—our rocketing Hispanic population and the inadequate education of Hispanic students—are on a collision course that could either end in disaster or in another story of successful assimilation in America. The stakes are clear: how we meet this challenge will impact our politics, economy and our society."

The path will not be easy. There will be entrenched powers, such as the teachers' unions, that will fight to maintain the status quo. But there will be middle-class interests that also will resist change. Parents in the suburbs, especially those who have fled city blight, feel they have made sacrifices to buy a home and are not thrilled with the idea that those who haven't will also benefit from good schools.

These are all real obstacles, but conservatives should not flinch. They should take heart from the fact that the failure of our public school system is now all too clear and the nation is ready for action.

Chapter 12

GROWING FINANCIAL CAPITAL: SAVINGS AND BUSINESS FORMATION

A penny saved is a penny earned.

—BENJAMIN FRANKLIN

GETTING MARRIAGE, THE FAMILY, COMMUNITY, AND EDUCATION right is key to the success of Hispanics in this country; this is why we have devoted so much attention to those issues. They are issues that stand upstream from many other problems: lack of education and marriage breakup lead to many other dysfunctions, from deep and long-lasting poverty to high incarceration rates. These are the priorities in discussing human capital and social capital, respectively.

We also must stress, however, financial capital formation (greenbacks in the bank), which is so important to the welfare of individuals, families, and communities. Aside from the salutary effects of saving, individual and family savings are the main source of start-up capital for small business formation, which is so important for Hispanic success in this country. In an era when globalization and information technology put a premium on capital but discount labor and when employers have switched wholesale from defined benefits pension plans to defined contribution, familiarity with financial issues will make the difference between poverty and affluence.

Let's start with personal savings. Much research indicates that putting money aside is intricately linked to upward mobility, starting with educational attainment.

"There are three purposes of savings," says my Heritage

Foundation colleague Stuart Butler. "First, a certain level of liquid savings is for an emergency. Experts say about three months of earnings. So if you lose your job, or your car breaks down, or your child gets sick, you are not wiped out or get evicted because you can't pay the rent. Second, that emergency fund is also available to take advantage of an immediate opportunity—a new and better job opens up but you would have to move to the next town, or your uncle is opening a café and wants you to be his partner. Savings like that enable people to move up the ladder, and not fall down a rung. And third, building long-term equity."

The last point is common sense. If you feel you have some equity, you feel stable enough to take such risks as sending your daughter to college. It's called the wealth effect. But there's more.

It turns out that the act of saving *by itself* has an impact on other parts of people's lives, including whether they will settle down and marry and avoid sliding into bad relationships. Saving—no matter how much one actually saves—has positive knock-on effects. The Corporation for Enterprise Development, one of the leading non-profits helping low-income Americans build their assets, concurs, saying, "Since its founding more than three decades ago, CFED has consistently witnessed the power of even minimal savings to transform lives." This is important to bear in mind and to teach, especially to people who have little surplus cash and find it hard to stretch their meager wages.

The relationship between saving and upward mobility is worth exploring. Any leader or group working on issues that affect Hispanics should have a policy position addressing how to help raise their savings rate.

Though rags-to-riches stories used to be an American trademark, today we are beginning to resemble Europe or Latin America. Almost 70 percent of those born in the lower half of the income scale will stay there all their lives.

One thing that radically changes this picture is the habit of saving. According to the Panel Study of Income Dynamics (PSID) reported by Pew's Economic Mobility Project, half of all children born into the lowest income quintile will stay there as adults if their parents had low savings levels. That 50 percent drops to 29 percent, however, for lowest-quintile children who were lucky enough to have parents who, though poor, had high saving rates.

The numbers are even starker within an individual's lifetime. According to the PSID, 66 percent of adults who were in the lowest income quartile in the 1980s were still stuck there in 2005 if they had a low savings rate. Only a measly 2 percent had risen to the top quartile and 9 percent to the top half. However, among bottom-quartile adults with high saving rates, only 45 percent remained there in 2005 and 20 percent had made it to the top half (remember, they were just as poor as those with low saving rates, but they had the saving habit). Some may see a self-fulfilling prophecy at work here, but social scientists see more.

As Diane Calmus wrote for Heritage in December 2012:

> A propensity to save is also associated with character traits like grit, determination, perseverance and the ability to delay gratification that are necessary for consistent saving and generally helpful in other aspects of economic mobility such as completing college. The problem for many individuals, especially in low-income communities, is that weaknesses in traits like perseverance and delaying gratification make regular savings a major challenge, and this challenge is made worse by the societal pressures of American consumerism.

"People who tend to save are more likely to go to college and complete college," says Stuart Butler. "If you save, you're thinking about the future; that is what saving is: you stop thinking about the present and save to buy better things in the future. That can affect your behavior. Even knowing that other people in your community are saving will spur you to save. You don't want to think that you're below par."

The bad news is that Latinos are simply not saving enough. Between 32 percent and 40 percent of Hispanics do not even report having a bank account, compared with 18 percent of non-Hispanic whites. For other types of saving vehicles, the numbers are even worse. Only 24 percent of Latinos had 401(k)s and similar accounts in 2009, compared with 45 percent of non-Hispanic whites, according to Pew Research. Just 10 percent had IRAs or Keogh accounts, and around 5 percent owned stocks or mutual funds. In fact, 24 percent of all Hispanics had only one major asset, their vehicle, compared with 6 percent of non-Hispanic whites.

Not surprisingly, the headline fact when discussing Hispanic wealth is that the average household wealth of non-Hispanic whites is around *eighteen times* that of Hispanics—$113,000 to $6,000 in 2009, according to Pew Research.

Yes, that is partly a result of the deep economic recession that started in 2008. The origins of that economic problem were in real estate, and Hispanics derived a disproportionate ratio, nearly two-thirds, of their net worth from home equity. No other asset accounted for more than 10 percent of Hispanics' net worth, according to Pew. Thus, once real estate prices plummeted, much of Hispanic wealth was wiped out.

It didn't help, too, that real estate prices dropped disproportionately more in the marginal neighborhoods where many Hispanics live and in the states where they are concentrated: Arizona, California, Florida, and Nevada. In 2005, when house prices were rising, white households' wealth was only around seven times that of Hispanic households. But it is inescapable that one of the reasons home equity was so important to Hispanic households' net worth is that Hispanics on average don't have as much salted away in savings as do other groups.

Compared with family breakup and the education achievement gap, the links between Hispanic weaknesses in the area of capital formation and the entitlements mentality are less direct. But conservatives are well positioned to offer solutions that would help Hispanics. Assimilation into a culture of saving, as outlined above, would be one way.

To be sure, part of the reason for Hispanics' relative paltriness of saving is that their incomes are not as high. Hispanics with higher incomes who do save are weathering the recession better, and this may explain why the wealth gap *among* Hispanics has ballooned in recent years.

The percentage of the total Hispanic wealth owned by the top 10 percent of Hispanic households went up to 72 percent in 2009 from 56 percent in 2005, the highest concentration and sharpest rise among all groups. By comparison, the top 10 percent of non-Hispanic whites owned 51 percent of total white wealth in 2009, slightly up from 46 percent in 2005.

However, according to the Ariel Education Initiative, even Hispanics with higher incomes don't save as much as do their counterparts in other groups. The absence of a habit of saving among many Hispanics must account for some of this wealth gap between Hispanics and non-Hispanic whites.

Part of it has to do with immigration itself, and part with culture. Alicia La Hoz commented to me, for example, about how many adult Hispanics endured hardships as children and find it hard to deny their own children the clothes and creature comforts they want. This rings true for me because I see a version of it in my own household.

There are also the remittances discussed in earlier chapters, which are so important among Central Americans, Dominicans, and Mexicans. Every dollar sent overseas to support an extended family member—and there are billions of such dollars sent overseas every year—is a dollar not saved here for emergencies, college, or retirement.

There's also the fact that many Latin American immigrants arrive on these shores with a dim view of financial institutions. As Brenda Muñiz, a policy analyst at the National Council of La Raza, observed in a 2004 paper, "many new Latino immigrants may distrust financial institutions because, in their experience, banks were unreliable havens for savings in Latin America during economic downturns." This has been confirmed in interviews with many Hispanics, especially those from Mexico and Central America, who come here with bad memories of scams in their countries and don't trust schemes from 401(k)s to savings accounts.

In fact, many Hispanics have no relations with banks as savers or as borrowers. According to Muñiz, some 22 percent of Hispanic would-be borrowers had *no* credit score, compared with 4 percent of whites and 3 percent of African-Americans. Among Hispanics who do have a credit score, the majority are below 620, according to the National Resource Center for Healthy Marriage and Families. Many simply do not understand how important credit is in all sorts of capital formation in this country, from buying a home to acquiring an education.

This lack of credit history, according to Muñiz, "not only affects their access to affordable credit but, given the ubiquitous and ever increasing role credit plays in the U.S., seemingly unrelated issues such as insurance premiums and employment opportunities may also be adversely affected."

Hispanics' negative view of debt might be a good thing if it meant that Latinos do not borrow; they do borrow, however, just not formally. According to the Center for Financial Services Innovation, "42 percent of Latino consumers had used the grocery store for a financial transaction at least once in the last 30 days." They're also more likely to borrow money from a relative or friend than from a bank. Says Muñiz:

> Despite the fact that it is easier for immigrants to open bank accounts in some markets where financial institutions accept foreign identification, such as the Mexican matrícula consular, and have conducted extensive outreach in the Latino community, fringe banking providers have proliferated in communities where Latinos work and reside. For example, the check cashing industry has doubled in size over the last decade with 11,000 outlets across the nation. Despite their unscrupulous practices, these entities are often very accessible, are located in the community, and commit substantial marketing resources—activities not always observed in mainstream financial institutions.

The CFSI estimates that 47 percent of the Hispanic population either has no bank account or is "underbanked," a description that is applied to people who have only a current account and have made one or more nonbank financial transactions in the previous thirty days.

It would be wrong to assume, however, that the relative lack of savings is all due to the immigrant experience or to culture or to the fact that Hispanics are just plain irresponsible. Experts agree that lower-income Americans in general, not just Hispanics, have the same hurdles to retirement saving.

For many, saving is at best a tertiary goal. There are difficulties enough just making a dollar stretch to cover daily necessities. As Muñiz puts it, "many low to moderate income Latino families live paycheck to paycheck." When people get around to saving, it is usually for emergencies or, at the very best, for something more middle-term, such as college.

A second hurdle is informational. According to the EARN Research Institute, the vast majority of Americans do not understand concepts such as compound interest, inflation, and risk diversification, and this lack of financial knowledge is "widespread and especially prevalent among the lower-paid, the less educated, [and] minorities." Lower-income people are also risk-averse and therefore reluctant to invest either because they're not emotionally comfortable with risk or because they're not financially equipped to absorb losses in the principal.

These two hurdles are common sense. A third hurdle bears deeper analysis, though: retirement accounts have features that exclude lower-income Americans. As usual, the rich and the well connected get the benefits, and as usual, this is the fault of government.

The federal government spends an enormous amount—$130 billion in 2010—on programs that incentivize saving for college, health, and retirement, with the latter accounting for the lion's share, around $126 billion.

But just 0.2 percent of these federal tax benefits for retirement plans go to people in the lowest income quintile; a whopping 70 percent of the benefits go to folks in the highest quintile, according to a 2004 study conducted by Pew.

This regressive distribution of tax benefits for savers may betray doubts by policy makers that poor people will save at all even if they are encouraged. Research demonstrates, however, that lower-income people will indeed respond positively to saving incentives.

The federal government should approach the savings crisis among Hispanics and all lower-income groups by first taking a page out of the Hippocratic oath: First do no harm.

Along those lines, the government can revisit the asset limits in means-tested public assistance programs. Just as the marriage penalty (some estimates put the loss of welfare benefits after marriage at well over 50 percent of total income: quite a hefty marriage tax) creates perverse incentives for people to remain unmarried and have children out of wedlock, limits on assets for certain forms of assistance prevent lower-income folks from learning the saving habit.

In many instances, the asset limit forces people who worked hard and did the right thing to pay out all their savings when they hit a health emergency. That said, it *is* important to make sure assistance goes only to the needy. The balance now is often skewed against the hard worker in an emergency. Policy makers should work to get a better balance.

Another policy approach is to listen to former Obama regulatory czar Cass Sunstein, who advocates a method known as soft (or libertarian, though I would reject that adjective) paternalism, or, to use the title of a book he wrote on the subject, the nudge. It holds that when given a default option, people will take it even when they have other choices.

The approach here would be for companies to make saving part of the paycheck in a 401(k) or IRA the default option. The vast majority, or so goes the notion, will stick to the saving plan.

Taxing savings is also egregious, as all taxes discourage activity, and what we want to do as a society is to encourage saving. It's also double taxation, since we already have paid taxes on the income that we save. Nobody should pay taxes on saved income.

Other programs would waive the penalty for withdrawing money from certificates of deposit, since many Hispanics feel uncomfortable putting money away that they cannot access without a penalty. Another approach that caters to Hispanics' lower appetite for risk would be riskless or nearly riskless 401(k)s.

We need to keep in mind that the general problem is actually not the capacity to save but the lack of a culture of saving. Many low-income people use about 5 percent of their income to buy lottery tickets. "As we know from China or during the Depression, dirt-poor people can and do save if there is a culture," says Stuart Butler.

The goal here is not just to get Hispanics to save but to get them to be used to saving, especially since many of them have not developed this habit.

The issue of culture is central. Several studies have found that Hispanics have much lower risk tolerance—the ability to accept uncertainty about an investment—than not just non-Hispanic whites but also non-Hispanic blacks. This is important for those who worry about the emergence of a division in our society in which Hispanics are overrepresented in a less-well-off stratum. As one study put it, a young worker at age twenty-five who manages to put $3,000 a year in constant dollars in the stock market may end up with over $1 million at age sixty-five, whereas a more risk-averse equivalent worker saving the same amount in a government bond fund will end up with $210,000.

By contrast, a 2005 study for the Association for Financial Counseling and Planning Education found that Hispanics were considerably more likely than the other two groups to take "substantial risk." The study said that "one reason may be related to the cultural role of machismo." Sound investing, however, is not based on gambling for a quick payoff but on having the patience to save steadily decade after decade, putting delayed gratification ahead of immediate gratification. Moreover, a tolerance for substantial risk may leave a population vulnerable to get-rich-quick investment scams.

Attaining financial literacy is an important goal that often is overlooked by those who discuss Hispanics. Indeed, policy makers in this area have conducted very few studies focusing on the saving habit and Latino communities. Saving, however, is one of the key parts of the capital formation strategy that would help Hispanics thrive in this country.

The personal savings of a business owner and his or her family account for 62 percent of the start-up capital of Hispanic entrepreneurs, a proportion that goes up to 75 percent when one includes other nonsaving assets such as home equity loans. According to the Small Business Administration, these ratios are much higher for other immigrants, especially Asians, showing that the low saving rate of Hispanics is hurting their business formation.

Hispanics are great starters of small businesses in this country, anything from the corner stands where Miamians have their Cuban *pastelitos* and *cafecitos* to the Robledo Winery in Napa Valley, started by an immigrant from Michoacán. The number of Hispanic-owned businesses nearly doubled between 2002 and 2012. According to a 2013 study by the Kauffman Foundation, "the Latino share of all new entrepreneurs rose from 10.5 percent in 1996 to 19.5 percent in 2012." This means that Latinos are now overrepresented in new small business formation.

Here again, however, we see the same generational puzzle we've seen with other indicators. First-generation Hispanics are much more likely to own businesses than are the subsequent generations. A Bureau of Business Research study conducted in Texas in 2012 discovered "a clear negative correlation between the percentage of Hispanic business owners and the time they have been in the United States. For instance, first- generation Hispanics account for 32 percent of the BBR survey, while fourth-generation Hispanics account for only 14 percent of business owners in the survey."

The study was conducted only in the Lone Star State, and not surprisingly, 85 percent of the businesses in the survey were Mexican-American-owned. But other nationwide studies in the 1980s, 1990s, and 2000s also found much higher levels of business ownership among immigrants than among the generations born here. Though the study does not discuss this in terms of cause and effect, it may boil down to the fact that first generations— immigrants, in other words—are by definition risk takers who had the gumption to leave Cardenas (where Ted Cruz's father, Rafael, hails from) or Michoacán. Their children and grandchildren, however, will be all over the spectrum. We know at least one thing, according to another study by Kauffman: Hispanic Millennials say they would like to start their own businesses at a higher rate than is the case for African-Americans or non-Hispanic whites.

Again, lower levels of personal saving (especially compared with Asians) have an important knock-on effect. "Hispanic immigrant firms have lower levels of startup capital than the immigrant total and Asian immigrant firms have higher levels of startup capital," said a 2012 study for the SBA. "Among Hispanic immigrant firms, only 10.3% have startup capitals of $50,000 or more. Among Asian immigrant firms, 29% have startup capitals of $50,000 or more." The impact is felt directly on average sales—$257,416 average annual sales for Hispanic businesses versus $465,296 for Asians—and the percentage of businesses hiring employees—20 percent versus 36 percent.

Institutions such as CFSI and the Ariel Education Initiative, discussed above, and others such as the Corporation for Enterprise Development, which also emphasizes home ownership as a way to aid asset formation among low-income populations, have many good policy proposals for political leaders looking to appeal to Hispanic audiences. These are good policies for Hispanics in and of themselves. They also make good politics. Politicians or parties seeking to make headway with Hispanics could do much worse than to propose upward mobility schemes such as the ones outlined in the last three chapters.

Many of you who have noticed an antistatist bent in the thinking in this book so far will be asking yourselves, But aren't many of these solutions just more government programs? Yes, but they are not transfer payments. They do not have perverse incentives, in other words, but represent money spent on building the right kinds of incentives; they are aimed at building up human, social, and financial capital. This is how we get our country back.

Chapter 13

A CALL TO ACTION

*People don't care how much you know until they know how much
you care.*

—THEODORE ROOSEVELT

T HERE ARE TWO BROAD VISIONS OF AMERICA COMPETING FOR
the public imagination and ultimately political power. Because
Americans who originated at one point in Spanish colonies are
a rapidly growing group, we can assume that the political philosophy that captures their dreams and aspirations could be politically
ascendant for decades.

Thus the two sides in our great philosophical-political debate—
known as the Left and the Right or liberals and conservatives and
roughly represented by the Democrats and the Republicans—have
a lot at stake. But winning Hispanics' hearts and minds at the ballot
box is just one reason it is imperative to appeal to them. Our political leaders must also convince enough Hispanics that the course
the country is on is dangerous and that unless we change, America
will face a future that is very different from our past, one of a bifur-
cated society with an underclass where Hispanic surnames abound,
no matter which party is in power. In other words, it is just as important, if not more, to win Hispanics over with the right policies,
a program that will safeguard for future generations the promise of
American freedom and upward mobility.

The spellbinding growth of the Hispanic demographic in the
last five decades has coincided with an unprecedented growth in
the role government plays in our lives as well as a breakdown of

the marriage culture, the public school system, and the tradition of assimilating immigrants. At the same time, breakthroughs in technology and the lower cost of transacting in ideas and goods globally have increased return on capital (human and social as well as financial) and put downward pressure on low-skilled labor wages. A group that the government separates from the mainstream population by affixing to it a minority label can become a lower caste if its members are overrepresented in lower-income quintiles with diminished chances of upward mobility. The government, by relentlessly telling Hispanics that they are socially and economically disadvantaged because they suffer racial, social, and political discrimination, has promoted a victimhood mentality that is corrosive both for the way Hispanics view themselves and for the way they're viewed by others. By suggesting government solutions to problems, the government has made it harder for them to be upwardly mobile. It should surprise nobody, then, if the accumulation of human, social, and financial capital—the types that earn a premium in our new technology-driven, globalized society—has been slower among Hispanics than among the mainstream population and there is now the threat of an emerging Hispanic underclass.

In an important essay in 1995, almost two decades before the puerile Occupy Wall Street movement, Milton Friedman tried to put us on notice about the political implications of rising returns for capital and diminished expectations for unskilled labor. He left us with this warning:

> If the widening of the wage differential is allowed to proceed unchecked, it threatens to create within our own country a social problem of major proportions. We shall not be willing to see a group of our population move into Third World conditions at the same time that another group of our population becomes increasingly well off. Such stratification is a recipe for social disaster.

These are political issues that beg for political answers. Liberals, in charge of the bureaucracy for the last half century, have been very successful at selling Hispanics on their version of society and ramming that vision through Congress, the courts, and federal agencies. Conservatives must now join the battle and inspire Hispanics with their dreams. Once they get into office, conservatives must not let Washington's left-leaning bureaucratic stasis stifle reform. The forces I have described above need to be addressed now if we are to start turning things around over the long term.

ILLEGAL IMMIGRATION

This book has studiously avoided the question of what to do with the nation's illegal immigrants, but not because it isn't important. Rather, the conversation about illegal immigration takes up all the oxygen in the room, and we shouldn't let it. This book is an attempt to balance the debate and focus instead on what are the best policies for Hispanic Americans' future.

Is illegal immigration a gateway issue, the issue on which politicians must declare themselves before Hispanics will listen to them on other matters? I'm not sure, but there are smart people in Washington who say it is, among them Al Cardenas, the head of the American Conservative Union, and the pollster Whit Ayres. Univisión is intent on making it a gateway issue. Whoever emerges as the Republican Party's presidential candidate in 2016 will not be able to duck questions on the matter whether Congress passes a bill before then or not. This debate will be with us for some time, and what a candidate says about it will give voters an indication of what kind of person he or she is.

A conservative candidate should be ready at the very least to support a true temporary worker program that addresses the employment needs of our companies and people, which act as a magnet for Mexico's surplus labor. Preventing the problem of illegal immigration from becoming a recurring, permanent problem we will be dealing with beyond 2016 is something on which we all can agree. Businesswoman Helen Krieble of the Vernon K. Krieble Foundation says that such a program would even solve the current illegal population problem by allowing some to apply for nonimmigrant temporary worker status and drying up the reasons for those who don't pass the background check and don't qualify to stay here. A solid temporary worker program would also make securing the border an easier task. The bill the Senate passed in 2013 lacked such a true, circular guest program because the AFL-CIO opposed it and Senator Schumer blocked it on their behalf.

But the GOP's presidential candidate had better also be ready to address the real gateway issues with which this book has dealt. Poll after poll confirms that illegal immigration rarely makes it into the top five issues that most concern Hispanics. It is education, the economy, and the family—the issues we have taken up here—that trouble them most. A frank discussion with Hispanics is thus required on whether they are content with their minority status, their dependency on "entitlements based on their status as 'victims'" in the wise words of Linda Chavez, the consequent breakup of the family, the educational achievement gap, and the threat of a Latino underclass. These are also the issues on which our political class should concentrate. Hispanic voting patterns will not change if all we do is throw open the gateway and do not adopt a plan for the future.

MAKING A PRO-HISPANIC CASE

In making this case, conservatives must make clear that they are "for" Hispanics. Their reluctance to spend money on government programs is not only a question of cost but is based on the fact that this money comes at a very heavy price for its intended beneficiaries, often bringing breakdown and failure for their families and communities. Conservatives must always explain why we need to reform welfare—because in its present state it is a system that keeps you down. Authenticity will matter. Conservatives must say to them, "*Yo los comprendo*"—I understand you; I get your aspirations. Conservatives whose hearts are closed to the Hispanic element in our society should face reproach when they speak in terms whose purpose is to hurt people.

Because the liberal academic/Hollywood/media complex has unstintingly instilled in Hispanics the view that conservatives are heartless individualists who believe in an "every man for himself, devil take the hindmost" ideology, conservatives must use every opportunity to share with Hispanics their view of community and understand that their audiences may be hearing it for the first time. They must explain that we believe community is an organic entity organized in concentric circles that start with the family and extend to the neighborhood, the town, the state, and the country.

Conservatives must explain conservatism; it will strike a chord in the Hispanic heart. The conservative approach puts great stock in tradition, elements of which can be disregarded or even eliminated only after careful consideration. At its best, conservatism sees the current generation as a stage in the continuum that links those who have passed and those yet to come. Conservatives believe that government can play a role in offering temporary relief to the needy but that that help should come from the lowest governmental level possible—the principle of subsidiarity. More important, conservatives believe that when devoid of requirements for behavioral change, social assistance becomes at best an enabler of bad behavior and at worst a promoter of it. For conservatives, American exceptionalism is rooted especially in the historically unique view of community being voluntary in nature, the place where we come together by our own volition to pitch in and give one another mutual aid. Suspicious of government, conservatism is rooted in patriotism and God.

These are ideals that will spark the imagination of Americans of Cuban, Mexican, and Puerto Rican background just as much as they did Americans of Italian, Jewish, and Irish background, perhaps even more. Hispanics are respectful of tradition and of the good judgment of their ancestors (the phrase *nuestros mayores*, "our elders," carries with it special sentimental connotations). They are wary of remote authority, and they have reverence for the family; conservatives making a case for saving the family will get people nodding in assent. Hispanics may be less acquainted with the

American tradition of volunteerism because it is unique to America, but conservatives can help implant in them the idea of the little platoon.

EXPLAINING LIBERALS

Conservatives should lay out the true liberal agenda; it will be the first time Hispanics have heard it. To be sure, we should try when possible to assume good intentions on the part of liberals if we expect to convince at least a few Hispanics that what liberals are doing is wrong. As the philosopher Isaiah Berlin once put it, "I am interested in the views of the opposition because I think that understanding it can sharpen one's own vision." Progressives haven't built a government dependency culture because they're evil. Government in their view is the best agent for solving problems, not civil society. A fair presentation of liberal views to Hispanics will go further than hyperbole.

Liberals have noticed all the same things we have. For the last few years the subject of inequality has had much press discussion (in fact, conservatives have let liberals own the issue, though the balance was being redressed in 2014).

Liberals also fear the rise of a Hispanic lower caste. Princeton's Douglass Massey argued in a 2012 paper aptly named "The New Latino Underclass" that "as Latinos grew in number and visibility in the United States after 1965 they were subject to a systematic process of racialization—a dedicated campaign of psychological framing and social boundary construction intended to position them as a stigmatized out-group in American social cognition." Like the vast majority of progressives, Massey, however, absolves the government of playing a role in any of this.

On the contrary, liberals see government as the only force capable of dealing with the big issues. Government, its proponents say, is better at giving aid because it is impartial and, most important, nonjudgmental; it comforts the afflicted without wagging fingers. Government can prevent the two-caste society by redistributing money from one caste to the other. Some liberals don't even like to discuss social capital, intuiting (rightly, incidentally) that some assimilation will be required from families trying to tap into neighborly support mechanisms, and assimilation is something that always sends liberals running for the hills. They also (again, rightly) see in talk of social capital a rebuke of central planning. As for the family, as we saw in earlier chapters, many progressives believe it to be a patriarchal institution that too often demands the observation of norms, and progressivism is about breaking down norms.

Finally, liberals don't believe that many Americans can make good decisions or that government at least needs to protect individuals from their own choices. Government, then, is the only organizing agent of society, the nodal point at which the various parts of the country come together to solve problems.

There was perhaps no better exposition of this view than President Barack Obama's second inaugural, when he said, "No single person can train all the math and science teachers we'll need to equip our children for the future, or build the roads and networks and research labs that will bring new jobs and businesses to our shores. Now, more than ever, we must do these things together, as one nation, and one people."

Obama's "we" was government, not society. But unless conservatives relentlessly point out the difference, liberals will get away with blurring the distinction between the two.

Conservatives must be candid with Hispanic audiences about why liberals have an easier time selling their vision to them. Superficially, it's easier to convince people you are compassionate if you're handing out money—even if you're promising to free people from responsibility for one another and entrapping those you ostensibly want to help in a cycle of dependency on government.

Liberal internationalism also appeals to Hispanics on a superficial basis. Telling Salvadorans that their country of birth has nothing to learn from ours and may indeed be superior may flatter them in the short term, though it begs the question of why they had to immigrate here in the first place and may delay the onset of pride in being American.

Because they believe that government is a better agent than civil society, liberals embrace immigrants as a force that will accelerate a fundamental transformation to a country in which government plays a larger role, as it does in France or Germany. Their intuition tells them that their relationship with the immigrant and his or her son or daughter becomes symbiotic once they've gotten immigrants to see themselves as victimized minorities who need government help. Conservatives should not spare their Hispanic audiences from seeing the quid pro quo that liberals are really proposing, however. Ross Douthat of the *New York Times*, one of a raft of young and very insightful conservative thinkers, put it best when he said in 2012:

> Are Democrats winning Hispanics because they put forward a more welcoming face than Republicans do—one more in keeping with America's tradition of assimilating migrants yearning to breathe free? Yes, up to a point. But they're also winning recent immigrants because those immigrants often aren't assimilating successfully—or worse, are assimilating downward, thanks to rising out-of-wedlock birthrates and high dropout rates. The Democratic edge among Hispanics depends heavily on these darker trends: the weaker that families and communities are, the more necessary government support inevitably seems.

It's important for conservative political leaders speaking to Hispanic audiences to expose them to what progressives really think about civil society, communities, families, and country and to the connection that exists between weak families and communities and government. Conservatives also must explain the problems inherent in the vision and platforms of the Left and draw comparisons. Poverty programs that rely on the central government have to be means-tested or they become a free-for-all, but means testing can lead to cliff effects that prevent users from making the right choices in life. Local communities can fail too, but because the failure is by definition localized, it is never as catastrophic. Family members can disappoint, too, but anyone who has participated in a family that however imperfect it may be still works knows there's no substitute for it as an organizing principle. The data on that are pretty strong.

As for the country, it too has many imperfections, but the nation-state is the best unit for self-government, and we have only to look at the democratic deficit of the current European experiment to see how valuable a strong nation is. Having God in our lives not just on Sunday but during the week may not be for everyone, but religiosity is universally shared for a reason, and many studies show that the communities with the highest rate of upward mobility are filled with religious people. Is there anything on the left that compares with community, family, God, and country?

Conservatives must explain progressive policies to Hispanics because progressives themselves won't do it. They often dress their policies in our language, portraying their views as favoring family, community, and the country and, even better, as being based on the precepts of Judeo-Christian charity. Then they turn around and ascribe to conservatives the worst intentions and motives, especially when it comes to Hispanics.

CONSERVATISM AND CHANGE?

There were signs after the 2012 election that conservatives were finally getting the need to appeal to Hispanics across all these fronts and not just adopt a defensive crouch. If the impact of the 2012 election is to create urgency about the need to reach out to Hispanics and share with them the conservative vision, the effect will be salutary. It's important to this end to understand the roots of the circumspection that some conservatives harbor about Hispanics. To fix a problem, you must first accept that you have one and then try to understand it.

The right of center in America can be a very large tent that stretches on some issues from the Christian Right all the way to atheist libertarians. The media devote all their attention to the small minority that exhibit nativist attitudes toward Hispanics, ignoring conservatives who welcome immigrants not just for business reasons but because they replenish America's vitality at regular intervals. Completely overlooked is the indispensable guardianship that conservatives exercise over civilization. Any society with a living, organic culture shared by both elites and common folks alike will have opinion leaders with a basic conservative mind-set to thank for it.

Axiomatically, conservatives like to conserve and tend to regard change with a certain wariness. The problem is compounded if conservatives come to see immigrants as a threat to the republic they know and love.

Edmund Burke, the Anglo-Irish parliamentarian said to have founded modern conservatism in the eighteenth century, wrote insightfully of conservatives' attachment to the wisdom of their ancestors, which people could call upon when they had neither the time nor the sufficient experience to confront a problem. The frequently used analogy is a man confronted with a wolf; he has no previous experience with wolves and doesn't know this wolf's intentions, but he has the benefit of folk wisdom prescribing wariness in encounters with wolves.

This sentiment, cherished by all conservatives, Burke called by its proper name: *prejudice*. In one of his most famous defenses of the term he wrote, "Prejudice is of ready application in the emergency; it previously engages the mind in a steady course of wisdom and virtue and does not leave the man hesitating in a moment of decision, skeptical, puzzled and unresolved. Prejudice renders a man's virtue his habit; and not just a series of unconnected acts."

Burke did not mean ignorance or narrow-mindedness. More than 150 years later, another paragon of conservatism, the American Russell Kirk, explained to twentieth-century audiences Burke's use of the word: "Prejudice is not bigotry or superstition, although prejudice may sometimes degenerate into these. Prejudice is prejudgment, the answer with which intuition and ancestral consensus of opinion supply a man when he lacks either time or knowledge to arrive at a decision predicated upon pure reason."

Conservatives, then, two of conservatism's main thinkers are telling us, have a healthy respect for this "kind of collective wisdom, the sum of the slow accretions of a thousand generations," as Kirk put it. Prejudice can, however, decline into bigotry. It is a distinction worth remembering.

One way to attenuate or remove prejudicial feelings toward Hispanics is to ensure that they are seen as part and parcel of the American nation, a group whose contribution to forging the American spirit was essential, not as a minority element isolated from the majority of society.

There are differences we should not overlook. Some Hispanics will not be acquainted with America's conservative tradition of volunteerism, which is a direct descendant of Edmund Burke's "little platoons." Remember, America has this tradition exceptionally—no other country has it, not even Burke's homeland. The history of Latin America is very different. At its dawn you don't find settlers willing to work the land for religious or commercial reasons, as in New England or Jamestown, building along the way traditions of cooperation born of mutual interest. Hernán Cortés spoke for many of my ancestors who conquered Cuba when he snapped at a colonial official offering him land, "But I came to get gold! I didn't come to till the land like a peasant." Former Mexican foreign minister and current eminent scholar Jorge Castañeda's masterpiece *Mañana Forever* contains this important observation:

> In the United States, there are approximately two million civil society organizations, or one for every 150 inhabitants; in Chile there are 35,000, or one for every 428 Chileans; in Mexico there are only 8,500, or one for every 12,000, according to Mexican public intellectual Federico Reyes Heroles. Eighty-five percent of all Americans belong to five or more organizations; in Mexico 85 percent belong to no organization and, according to Reyes Heroles, the largest type, by far, is religious. In the United States, one out of every ten jobs is located in the so-called third sector (or civil society); in Mexico the equivalent figure is one out of every 210 jobs.

The result is that high-trust societies such as the United States are comfortable with impersonal networks such as capital markets and social clubs, whereas low-trust societies such as those in Latin America don't trust nonkinship relationships. This helps explain, incidentally, why so many Hispanic Americans are unbanked and exhibit such risk aversion in finances.

But these are learned patterns. No one says that Hispanics, with no national tradition of volunteer association, cannot develop a taste or even love for it. It only means that if we want Hispanics to understand why volunteerism is superior to government fiat, we conservatives must explain it to them.

The real tragedy, in fact, may be that Hispanics are familiar with the liberal view of the world not just because progressives have been very good at promoting it but also because conservatives have been laggards in making their case to Hispanics. If all you have ever been told is that government will take care of you, send you to school, make sure you get admitted into college, feed you, look after your health, and protect you from the ravages of a racist population (and that conservatives hate you), who can blame you for supporting Obama and buying into the skewed liberal view of government-led society? If nobody on the right has made the effort to tell you this is a Faustian bargain that might let you get by but will prevent you from getting ahead, you may not think of it. If no conservative has ever driven home the point that a better guarantee of getting financial capital is to save as much as you can and diligently build over time social and human capital in yourself, your family, and your local community, will you develop these habits on your own?

Though some voices on the right counsel not reaching out to Hispanics because they fear pandering, it is imperative to do one and not the other. This book is not intended as a counsel of despair; on the contrary, it is a warning that a big undertaking lies ahead for conservatives. The task is not Sisyphean, but it will require strategy and effort. Most of the best conservatives I know are the ones who relish a big challenge. This is sure to be one.

DON'T PANDER; OFFER MOBILITY

It is important that conservatives avoid getting into a contest over who can offer more benefits to Hispanics. As Representative Raúl Labrador of Idaho put it in the House of Representatives in June 2013, "If what we start doing is we start pandering and we start giving goodies out to people, then we're going to get into a bidding war with the Democratic Party. And if we get into a bidding war, we always lose, because the Democrats are always more willing to give goodies to a certain group than we are. So what we have to do is do things based on principle."

History proves that Labrador is right. Time and time again officials in the Nixon administration supported radical leftist positions that were bad for the country in a shortsighted and explicit push to win the Hispanic vote. These strategies very rarely work in the short term and never in the long run. However, it is important not to get into a pandering competition not just because conservatives would lose it but because the reason to win Hispanics is to save the country from being transformed into something different.

The trick is to offer Hispanics an alternative, not more of the same, to show them that though superficially the liberal version of community may appear more attractive, it is the conservative one that leads to the good life.

To do this, conservatives will have to make a mobility argument to Hispanics. Conservatives will need to go out into Hispanic neighborhoods and explain that liberal policies have held Hispanics back. They came to this country to thrive and join the community at large, not to be balkanized into pockets of poverty. Whatever the appeal of its siren song, what government has offered has had the opposite result.

The case we need to make is the case that Heritage's Stuart Butler, the American Enterprise Institute's Charles Murray, and Harvard's Robert Putnam have been making for decades: households at the bottom of the income scale, where most Hispanics are, are becoming trapped and are finding it harder and harder to experience upward mobility. Instead, lower-income families are becoming something never really seen in America before, though this is common in Europe and especially in Latin America: a distinct class that it is nearly impossible to break out of.

Conservatives need to be forthright with Hispanics and sometimes even pose uncomfortable questions such as, Is this what you want for your children and your progeny? Is your present situation what you or your mother and father sacrificed for in coming here? Do you really want a legacy of broken families, broken schools, and broken dreams? Do you want your son or daughter to be a gang member or a doctor? In terms of the future, what do you want the name Pérez, Garcia, or Fernández to be associated with 150 years from now, when untold numbers of your descendants will be bearing it in the streets of New York, Houston, and Chicago?

But as we do this we must remember to be of good cheer and carry a positive message. It is not good to point out problems if we don't offer solutions. Arthur Brooks, president of the American Enterprise Institute, thinks it can be done. In a May 2013 op-ed for the *Wall Street Journal* he called for pitching to Hispanics many of the policies we have discussed in Part III of this book:

> Put education reform in poor communities front and center. Today, students from low-income families are five times as likely to drop out of school as students from high-income families, according to data from the Department of Education. It is a civil-rights scandal that we effectively accept this opportunity-denying status quo. Conservatives must be the warriors for pro-child, pro-parent, pro-innovation and pro-choice education reforms.

Brooks had an added insight: Hispanics famously vote at a lower frequency than do other groups in America. In 2008, only 52 percent of eligible Hispanics voted for president, compared with 78 percent of non-Hispanic whites and 79 percent of blacks, according to the National Opinion Research Center's General Social Survey.

What do we know about these nonvoters? According to the

General Social Survey, says Brooks, 52 percent of them say they are more likely to vote conservative! By contrast, non-Hispanic whites who don't vote are 40 percent less likely than white voters to be conservative.

These nonvoting Hispanics may be the sweet spot. They are more likely to say that hard work is important to moving upward. As Brooks has shown elsewhere, only earned success truly fulfills men and women and makes them happy. Government benefits (or inheriting money or winning the lottery) make zero difference to a person's level of happiness. This is an important point to get across.

Remember the Resurgent Republic poll from Chapter 1, in which majorities or pluralities of mostly Mexican-American voters agreed with conservative positions but by large margins rejected Republicans, who they said almost never reached out to them. A later survey of 800 Hispanic adults nationwide by John McLaughlin and Carlos Rodriguez in July 2013 confirmed that Republicans had image problems with Hispanics, yet 56 percent of Hispanics said they would consider voting for a Republican member of the US Congress.

It is hard to come away from these independent polls without concluding that conservatives are failing to reach many would-be Hispanic voters who may be eager to hear their message.

DEPENDING ON EACH OTHER, NOT ON WASHINGTON

Conservatives can make the moral case to Hispanics on several fronts rather than cede this ground to the Left and allow it to paint us as selfish or uncaring. Appealing to Hispanics' inner pride and their Spanish sense of a moral code is a trump card that should not go unused. The Left has gotten away for far too long with the assertion that the welfare state makes us all stewards of one another. We need to challenge that claim because it is baseless.

Conservatives must explain how the welfare stare actually does the opposite. We need to blow a hole through President Obama's false binary choice between savage individualism and caring government. Hispanics will be open to the argument that we're all dependent on one another, and conservative leaders must remind them at every turn that the question is whether we should rely on people we know and love who at some point will rely on us or on some distant functionary. I depend on my wife and she depends on me, and our children depend on both of us. That is the normal arrangement, one Hispanics should recognize.

We should ask, then, who is the best decider for your children: you, who know them best and love them unconditionally, or some faceless bureaucrat who's never met them and can't even pronounce the name Gutierrez? Hispanics will respond well to the question.

The centerfold for the liberal view of society is Julia, the character in the infographic that captures the heart and soul of the 2012 Obama campaign (or rather the lack of them). In "Life of Julia" the woman in question went from cradle to grave unaided by anyone else in life, unmarried and free of any relationship except for her dependence on Big Brother to supply her with the comforts of life. Julia didn't come out of nowhere. As Yuval Levin reminds us, the goal of liberalism from the Progressive Era to the present is to liberate us from "unchosen relational obligations."

Nothing, absolutely nothing, could be more alien to the soul of a true Latin in America today than this dystopian and abstract view of life. These unchosen relational obligations are Mom and Dad, and *Abuela*, and *Tío Manolo*—the people who make life brighter and give us warmth and cheer. Hispanics will intuit the view of life that sees the living generation simply as present-day custodians of ancestral and progenitive pride. This is who we are.

Hispanics, who do care that the poor and needy get the support they need and who understand social cohesion, will get that it is the welfare state that stands for raw individualism, because it attempts to free us from mutual obligations and encourages failures of responsibility. This happens not just through such inanities as the marriage penalty but because of *the very nature of the welfare state itself.*

The primacy of sacrificing for one's family will ring true to working Hispanic moms and dads who head out into the cold and snowy New England morning, disregarding their weary bones, to wash dishes at a restaurant in Boston or Providence because their children depend on them to do so. Hispanics have an incredible work ethic, as anyone who drives through any American city at dawn and sees Hispanic hard hats on their way to work can attest.

Conservatives should take great care not to insult or in any way disparage those who have fallen through the cracks and need public assistance but reveal to Hispanics for the first time the toll that such programs can take on the individual, the family, and the community that surrounds them if they become permanent. Just as liberals often remind Hispanics that they need to claim the state benefits for which they qualify, conservatives must work twice as hard to put a warning label on those programs.

WHY REPEAT HERE WHAT FAILED THERE?

It is also important to ask Hispanics why they would want to repeat here the policies that made them flee their countries in the first place. One of the greatest ironies is that Latin American immigrants vote in large numbers for policies they should recognize and reject. But this case has never been put to Hispanics. Republicans have the opportunity to do so.

The case of Cuba is pretty straightforward. Cuba had many problems in the 1950s, not the least of which was a corrupt dictator named Fulgencio Batista (against whose rule both my father and his father battled, my dad briefly going to prison for it and my grandfather having to take refuge in the countryside several times). But economically, Cuba was a success in the 1950s, as United Nations statistics from that time will attest. In terms of GDP per capita, cars and TV sets per inhabitant, life expectancy, and the like, Cuba was not just ahead of most of Latin America but also ahead of several European countries. Half a century of communism has ended all that and left Cuba pauperized economically, culturally, spiritually, and politically. Why would a Cuban fleeing that mess today want to replicate big government here? Michael Moore may sing the praises of the Cuban health system, but Cubans, especially ones who suffered under it, know better.

In the case of Puerto Rico, a New Deal–influenced settlement failed to produce enough jobs for the people. Planning failed, and the likes of Adolfo Carrión, whom we met in Chapter 2, had to find themselves in Manhattan fighting Irish-Americans.

In El Salvador, leftist guerrillas armed by Moscow ravaged the countryside while an anti–free market right-wing oligarchy perpetuated itself in power economically through its connections with governments all too eager to grant official privileges.

For Venezuelans and Colombians, growing groups we have not had time to discuss, the issue is also clear. In Venezuela, the clownish populist Hugo Chavez nationalized industries at will and wasted petrodollars. In Colombia, leftist guerrillas allied with drug traffickers created dangerous conditions that made living in that country difficult.

But it is the case of Mexico that is the most telling, because its failed leftist policies throughout most of the twentieth century are seldom discussed in this context and also because Mexicans form the majority of Hispanics in this country.

Mexico could potentially be as rich as Texas, a state with which it shares a large border, topography, and oil, lots of oil. Mexico, however, insists that its oil must be owned by Mexicans—read the Mexican government, not actual Mexican shareholders. Thus Mexico has wasted this gift from God through mismanagement, cronyism, and lack of foresight—all traits we associate with large bureaucracies.

Understanding the need to reach out to Hispanics with these messages and policy proposals would be the positive result of the 2012 debacle and important to the continuation of the American experiment of free people. If conservatives come to understand that ignoring Hispanics is no longer a sound strategy even in the short term, the defeat of the last election will not have been for naught.

A BIGGER THREAT

But an even bigger mistake would be for conservatives to sue for peace and accept the notion that demography is destiny and that we must change from being a liberal democracy in which everyone has equal rights under the law and become one in which the state itself is expected to mete out different treatment according to people's race or ethnic background (or sexual orientation and so forth). In fact, that future may already be here.

The Pentagon in 2012 published a report that is pretty open about its agenda of moving away from assimilation toward something new. Called "From Representation to Inclusion: Diversity Leadership in the 21st-Century Military," the report offers ample evidence that we are entering new unchartered ground.

The Pentagon report states, for example, that in this new age, "diversity means something broader. It goes beyond differences among demographic groups and requires more than affirmative action." Ominously, the report affirms that we must embrace "a definition of diversity that goes beyond the concept of equal opportunity for all." The report goes on:

> It is not about treating everyone the same. This can be a difficult concept to grasp, especially for leaders that grew up with the EO-[equal opportunity] inspired mandate to be both color and gender blind. *Blindness to differences, however, can lead to a culture of assimilation in which differences are suppressed rather than leveraged* [my italics].
>
> ˌ Cultural assimilation, a key to military effectiveness in the past, will be challenged as inclusion becomes, and needs to become, the norm. Traditional basic training, for example, is focused on assimilating individuals into a fighting force tied together by adoption of similar terminology, custom, and attitude. However, current military operations are executed within more complex, uncertain and rapidly changing operational environments that defy the warfighting standards of the past and that need to be met with an adaptive and agile leadership that is ready to respond more flexibly and with greater propensity for inventive strategizing.

It's hard to imagine anything more inimical to the principle of equality before the law, which has been the guiding star of

America's destiny from its inception. This principle has attracted millions of immigrants to our shores, and it is the most tragic of ironies that today this principle would be violated in their name. A perhaps greater irony here is that the military, which is supposed to defend our system of equality, is buying into this dangerous nonsense.

The Pentagon, to be sure, is hardly alone in telling Americans that we are now in a multicultural environment where equality is no longer the goal. In late July 2013, the Secret Service announced that it planned to observe "Unity Day" to "pay homage to the contributions and accomplishments that various ethnic groups, other cultures, and people with disabilities have made to American culture."

The private sector is not much better. Chief diversity officers now dot the landscape of the Fortune 500, ensuring not that hiring practices be color-blind but its opposite, color-conscious.

Conservatives should be wary of accepting these trends as immutable. In fact they must work hard to reverse them. The fact that all our levers of power are being used to instill a new vision of a balkanized nation in which differences are celebrated and adherence to common values is discouraged should trouble us. The price we pay, which is already high, may become exorbitant in a national emergency that sows chaos in our society.

A large patriotic gap already exists between native-born Americans and immigrants who have become citizens, with foreign-born Americans showing considerably less ardor for their new country compared with the natives, a reversal of the earlier stereotype of the naturalized citizen wearing his patriotism on his sleeve. This patriotic deficit should prompt conservatives into action.

How we got here is no secret. America's leaders decided to change from what had worked for two hundred years—Americanization—and astonishingly opted for a federation of ethnolinguistic groups—what I will call Ottomanization. In short, said the researchers of the Hudson Institute, "we have sent immigrants the wrong message on assimilation. *It is our fault, not theirs, that this gap exists*" [emphasis in the original].

America knew how to do immigration and assimilation, and it worked so well that millions were knocking at our doors constantly. And then for some reason some of our leaders decided to throw away this great model and stopped treating newcomers as individuals but instead herded them into discrete groups that will be accorded different treatment.

A minuscule example from a charter school backed by the National Council of La Raza would be amusing if it weren't so troubling. *Academia Semillas del Pueblo* (Seeds of the People Academy) is "dedicated to providing urban children of immigrant families an excellent education founded upon native and maternal languages, global values and cultural realities." The school tries to replicate pre-Columbian practices and "the Aztec numeric system," which is based on 20, as well as follow the "indigenous Mexican political form," the *calpulli*.

Our government's actions in abetting these trends—not to mention *calpulli* practices—would astonish the Founders, to whom assimilation was near and dear. They worried that as a nation of immigrants—which we have been from the start—America needed to assimilate newcomers into the values needed to maintain the republic. Assimilation was the compromise. As conservatives make the case for assimilation, they should, however, be aware that its enemies have tarnished the term over the years in the eyes of Hispanics.

Assimilation does not mean abandoning your past any more than loving your wife means ceasing to love your mother or your grandmother. In fact, it is often the case that the man who is a good son will also be a good husband. Some research suggests that the balanced family that celebrates its Irish, Italian, Cuban, or Mexican background will also love Old Glory and fight for her on foreign fields.

Assimilation never meant abandoning love of pasta or Saint Patrick's Day parades. On the contrary, these customs, foods, and styles of dress became part of the American fabric. Nor did it mean that people of the same origin didn't concentrate in the same neighborhoods, as witnessed by Boston's Southie or New York's Little Italy or Astoria. What it meant was the acquisition of values.

I love wearing a Cuban guayabera shirt as much as I love eat-ing Spanish delicacies such as *serrano* ham and Christmas *turrón*. But I know that when on Memorial Day weekend the church choir leads off with "America the Beautiful," it is impossible for me to sing out the words without a quiver in my voice as my son puts his arm around me and says, "Cry it out, Dad."

Conservatives must figure out how to take up the challenge that Putnam's research raises—that diversity is divisive at the commu-nity level on a short- and medium-term basis even if benefits ac-crue over time nationally. "We must remind ourselves how to be a successful immigrant nation. . . . Most immigrants want to ac-culturate," Putnam writes. Conservatives need to do it not just to help Hispanics become upwardly mobile but to save the country. Without equality and individual citizenship you don't have liberal democracy.

There is a historical background with which we all should be acquainted. The United States already had this debate during the last huge immigrant wave in the 1910s and 1920s. The nation then came down decisively on the side of integration and assimilation and firmly rejected the multicultural approach.

Then called transnationalism, it was advocated by intellectuals such as Randolph Bourne and Horace Kallen and later by Herbert Marcuse. America's lot, wrote Bourne, was "to be a federation of cultures . . . a novel union of men" deprived of a unifying philoso-phy. These progressives then spoke on behalf of Bohemian, Scan-dinavian, German, and Silesian peasants who lived in tenements in New York, Chicago, and Cleveland. Today's multiculturalists have taken up this fight on behalf of Colombians, Salvadorans, Mexi-cans, and Cubans, but it is the same fight over the same issue: dis-solving the America we know.

Would we continue to be free under this transnationalism or multiculturalism? Not really. We wouldn't be individual citizens with equal rights under the law. Even as groups we would not have the same rights and privileges. Marcuse's theory of repressive tol-erance withdraws tolerance of speech that liberals don't like (sound familiar?). This is still the plan. The American principle, in contrast, has always been that it is especially the speech of those whom society finds noxious that must be protected.

It is not too late to reverse course. Conservatives must battle multiculturalism not just because it might condemn the immigrant and her descendant to separation and locks them in the lower economic strata but also because it leads to tyranny for the country at large.

Our government therefore must stop making it hard for Hispanics to assimilate. As the Hudson research paper warns, over the last four decades "American elites have created a structure of laws and administrative procedures that discourage immigrants from forming a strong American identity." This nonsense must end, and our leaders must dismantle these barriers. The money saved by ending multicultural programs, which are not in our national interest, can be used to do the opposite: help immigrants and their descendants—that means all Americans, not just Hispanic ones— forge a strong, unified identity that would help see us through an emergency and save the republic.

Which brings us to the term *Hispanic* itself. Because throwing such disparate groups into one catchall artificial ethnicity has prevented the integration that Hamilton and Jefferson understood was necessary, conservatives should work at moving away from this label.

Hispanics lack any of the attributes of ethnicity, from a unified race to a unified culture. And if it is the Spanish language that constitutes ethnicity, then Julián and Joaquín Castro are not Hispanic, because they don't speak Spanish.

The government and all its institutions must therefore start treating Hispanics the way it should treat everyone, as individuals equal under the law. Let the private sector do what it wants to do if it needs the collection of statistics as long as it, too, respects the constitutional right to privacy of individuals. Let private companies, whether in the media or in the automobile sector, market their products to "Hispanics" or "Latinos" if that is what they want to do. But the government doesn't need to be in the business of herding people into groups.

So stop collecting census information on who is Hispanic. We collected data on "Mulattoes" in the censuses of 1850, 1860, 1870, 1890, 1910, and 1920 and rightly stopped thereafter.

Conservatives have silently gone along during the whole creation of Hispanics as a minority group, which has been very shortsighted. They would have done better if they had taken the approach that Hispanics are the newest immigrant group. Allowing the bureaucracy and the liberal institutions to create a minority and then endow it with government protection in no way helps the promotion of conservative policies and has in fact hindered it. One of the reasons Hispanics who convert to evangelical Protestantism become conservatives is that they shed some of their Hispanic identity as their main identity marker and don that of evangelicals, fitting into this community on an equal basis as fervent believers. How we see ourselves determines how we fit in.

As Putnam once put it, identity itself is a social construct "and can be socially de-constructed and re-constructed."

Our policy makers also should consider eliminating Hispanics from the category of people who receive affirmative action. There is no moral justification for keeping them in as the overwhelming majority of Hispanics in this country today came here or are descended from people who immigrated here of their own volition and can show no pattern of past official discrimination that should be remedied. As Nathan Glazer put it, "ideally, we should aim at a society in which individuals are treated without regards to race and ethnicity for purposes of employment, promotion, or admission in selective institutions."

Affirmative action does nothing to address the real problems besetting Hispanics. Let's by all means stop this nonsense that only calls into question the achievements and successes of our children. Our political class must instead use every opportunity to decry what affirmative action, family breakdown, bad schools, and dependence on welfare have done for Hispanics. This is a case, if put in this manner, that would appeal to any proud American of Latin descent.

THE CULTURE

Hispanics are already an integral part of the culture. This is particularly true of the Mexican-American or Tex-Mex culture; it is deeply woven into the fabric of America. It is the cradle of Southwestern traditions especially. Nothing in the Italian, German, or Silesian who made up the immigrant stock in the nineteenth and early twentieth centuries can compare with the Southwestern Tex-Mex cultural contribution.

Conservatives ought to care about these traditions and need to start seeing Hispanics and Mexican-Americans in the national context as two conservative icons, John Wayne and Bill Buckley, did. With 50 million Hispanics, a number that's growing, the oppositional relationship Mexico and the United States have had has become an unaffordable luxury. It should be put in the context of the antagonism that once held between Britain and the Union. In other words, it should be removed.

Giving Mexican-Americans a reason to be proud of our country's past would only increase their stake in our country's future and increase their devotion to the common interest, something else our schools should be teaching children of any background. This new understanding of our country's history, one that celebrates the Hispanic component in the nation's makeup, is not the same as multiculturalism; it is its opposite. This is the difference between Texas traditionalists and California radicals. One celebrates America's unity, the other its divisions.

Conservatives, who care as deeply about the future of their progeny as they do about the habits of their ancestors, have no choice.

They also have a clean slate if only they understand that. The reason far too many Hispanics are becoming trapped in an economic underclass with little chance of mobility is that liberal policies have been put in place: the welfare state, the continuation of counterculture, the creation of a minority ethos, the end of assimilation, the start of multiculturalism. Conservatives can point the way to prosperity.

Again, and this is a point worth reemphasizing, conservatives must do this or they risk seeing all they love—all I love—be lost.

WHY CONSERVATIVES NEED TO ACT

In this book I have made the case repeatedly that demography need not be destiny, that America has absorbed many, many previous waves of immigrants and its promise of freedom and opportunity not only has come through unscathed but has been improved on. From the Germans in the 1600s to the Italians in the 1900s, with Chinese, Japanese, Mexicans, Irish, Ethiopians, and many others in between, America has remained the place where people come to realize the American Dream. We have remained a nation rooted in the values of the Founders, not a confederation of different groups.

Sometime during the middle of the last century we gave up on what had worked, and I have at length explained how and why. Unless conservatives act to reverse many of the changes that took place, including the way immigrants are seen and are absorbed, we most assuredly run the risk of ceasing to be the land of opportunity. This would be a tragedy not just for us but for the world as well, as it will have lost its escape valve from tyranny and economic idiocy.

We invented this demographic change first by changing laws that opened the country again to high immigration (from which I benefited and with which I have no problem) and then by changing the meaning of demography itself. A February 6, 2014, mass e-mail to conservatives explained how, though partly unwittingly.

It came from the indefatigable and thoughtful Pete Wehner, a White House advisor for George W. Bush, and was titled "Demographics and the GOP." It was at heart a plea to conservatives to be inclusive or lose any chance of winning the White House again. It included a throwaway line that caught my eye not just because it elucidated the problem but because it is always a throwaway line and as such never includes a solution.

Pete first laid out the chilling stats we all know: of the last six presidential elections (1992 to 2012), four of them have been won by the Democrat with an average of 327 electoral votes to 210 for the Republican. However, in the prior six presidential elections (between 1968 and 1988) Republicans won five of the six contests.

Mitt Romney carried the white vote by an unheard of 20 points in 2012 and still lost. Why? Pete tells us: "White voters, who traditionally and reliably favor the GOP, have gone from 89 percent of the electorate in 1976 to 72 percent in 2012." That is eye-opening, but what always gets lost is what Pete wrote immediately afterward about this change in demographics, which he tellingly put in parentheses: "(This decline is partially an artifact of a change in the way the Census Bureau classifies Hispanics, who used to be counted among whites before being placed in a separate category.)"

This is not a parenthetical observation. It explains a lot. The country—or rather our almost always liberal elites—pushed the new Hispanic incomers and the ones who already were here away from the majority mainstream—exactly the opposite of the evolution that had taken place with every group before. Conservatives went along with this phenomenon, blind to it, not realizing what it would do to their chances of being elected and enacting conservative policy. The Rockefeller wing of conservatism that never wants to stir the pot but seeks to manage change happily accepted this new disposition, and the bigot wing was happy that newcomers could be fitted tidily into a discrete group that could be disliked. The pro-community, pro-values, pro-tradition wing—the heart of conservatism—was too busy raising families to notice.

But now we need to notice and act. Conservatives need to reverse course and invite the newcomers to the great American feast. These are (we are) but the latest group of immigrants to this country. We came to this country to benefit from its sweet freedom and golden opportunity, to pitch in and contribute to it. I hope this book has been one contribution to that if it succeeds at making conservatives understand that to take our country back, we need to take Hispanics back.

ACKNOWLEDGMENTS

This book would not have been possible without the loving support of my wife, Siobhan, who read and helped me edit all the chapters and, along with my children Jack, Saskia, and Rafe, stoically put up with lost weekends and evenings for well over a year. My friend and former colleague Georgianna Nutt was instrumental as well, also reading all the chapters and offering me sound advice. And of course, the book wouldn't have happened had Dana Perino not brought the idea to the attention of the publishers, for which I am forever indebted to her. My editor, Mary Choteborsky, was patient and thorough and helped steer the book in the right direction. Heritage's President, Jim DeMint, gave this project unstinting support and important feedback, for which I am grateful. Stuart Butler was an inspiration for many parts of this book and also edited parts of it. Daniel Woltornist, also at Heritage, provided me with invaluable editing. Other Heritage colleagues who helped me with editing or with guidance are Ryan Anderson, David Azerrad, Keesha Bullock, Lindsey Burke, Wesley Denton, Lee Edwards, Beverly Hallberg, Jennifer Marshall, Derrick Morgan, Izzy Ortega, Donald Schneider, Joshua Shepherd, and Genevieve Wood. I am also indebted to the following for reading and/or editing parts of the book or providing me with useful advice on whom to interview or what subjects to explore: Alfonso Aguilar, Professor Jonathan Bean, Mauricio

Claver-Carone, Javier Cuevas, A. J. Delgado, Ben Domenech, Chuck DeVore, M. Stanton Evans, Adam Gimbel, Lucy Gonzalez, Jennifer Sevilla-Korn, Joan Kwong, Tania Mastrapa, Ken Oliver-Méndez, Emily Parker, Steve Rasin, Matt Spalding, Scott Thomson, Joshua Treviño, and Juan Williams. Obviously, the inclusion of these names here in no way implies that they endorse my opinions.

INDEX